GEOFF HILL is the features editor of the *News Letter*, one of the world's oldest newspapers. He has either won or been short-listed for a UK travel writer of the year award nine times. He is also a former Irish travel writer of the year and a former Mexican Government European travel writer of the year, although he's still trying to work out exactly what that means. In 2005 he was given a Golden Pen award by the Croatian Tourist Board for the best worldwide feature or broadcast on Zagreb. He has written about travel for the *Daily Telegraph, Sunday Telegraph, Independent, Independent on Sunday* and *Irish Times*. He has also won one UK and three Northern Ireland feature writer of the year awards, and two UK newspaper design awards. He is the bestselling author of *Way To Go: Two of the World's Great Motorcycle Journeys* (2005) and *The Road to Gobblers Knob: From Chile to Alaska on a Motorbike* (2007).

Geoff lives in Belfast with his wife Cate, a cat called Kitten, a hammock and the ghost of a flatulent Great Dane. His hobbies are volleyball, flying, motorbikes, skiing, and thinking too much.

Anyway, Where Was I?

Geoff Hill's alternative A-Z of the world

BLACKSTAFF
PRESS

BELFAST

First published in 2008 by
Blackstaff Press
4c Heron Wharf, Sydenham Business Park
Belfast, BT3 9LE
with the assistance of
The Arts Council of Northern Ireland

Typeset by CJWT Solutions, St Helens

Printed in England by Cromwell Press

A CIP catalogue record for this book is available from the
British Library

ISBN 978-0-85640-831-1

www.blackstaffpress.com

*For my parents, who gave me
the opportunity to travel, and to Cate,
who gave me a very good reason
to come home*

Contents

Starting Out   xi

a
Armenia   1
Azerbaijan   11

b
Bangkok   19
Bermuda   24
Bulgaria   31

c
Copenhagen   35

d
Donegal   41

e
Egypt   49

f
Finland   57

g
Great Wall of China   69
Greece   83
Guyana   89

h
Honeymoon   95

i
Italy   101

j   Japan   125

k   Killer Dormice of Slovenia   163

l   Llama Trekking   171

m   Microlighting to the Shetlands   177

n   Namibia   195

o   Old Blue Eyes   207

p   Puerto Rico   215

q   Quebec   221

r   Rockies   227

s   Spain   233

t   Tunisia   247

u   Upgrades   253

V   Vermont   257

W   Western Australia   263
         Wiener Kreis   268
         Wolves   272

X   Xavier Furtwangler   277

Y   Yachting   281

Z   Zebedee   289

         Acknowledgements   303

Starting Out

On a bright September morning in 1975, a young man set out to see the world.

As he walked down the road from his parents' home with a disturbingly new rucksack over his shoulder, he was wearing a faded university rag T-shirt, matching jeans and a pair of Dunlop Green Flash which had seen better days, and would see worse yet.

He was, now that I think of it, me, and to this day I remember the moment when I fell in love with travel. It was the moment the following afternoon, as I stood at Victoria Station watching the clickety-clack board unfold its dreams. I felt, at that moment, that life was full of infinite possibilities, and all I had to do was step on a train to find them.

Two mornings, later, I sat on the platform of a little station in the south of France, eating an orange. Across the road, a girl with a swing in her hips and a baguette in her wicker basket walked past a white wall bright with bougainvillaea. She looked over and smiled, and I was besotted. Not with her, but with that same sense of infinite possibilities.

I finished the orange, and took the next train north, and, for the next four weeks, roamed through France, Switzerland, Austria, Germany, Holland, Belgium, Denmark, Norway, Sweden and Finland. I had no guidebook; only a Thomas Cook international timetable and a map of Europe on which the name of every country, every town and every village sang with romance. Every morning, I would haul out the map, decide where to go just because I liked the sound of it, and get on a train with no other aim than to find out what lay over the horizon.

I came home, but a part of me stayed away. After university, I worked as a fork-lift trucker in a Dutch bulb factory, then played volleyball in California, before coming home and getting a proper job as a journalist. Now my travel was limited to holidays, but it was still the finest feeling in the world to close the front door, leave the everyday world behind for a while, and just go.

Then, in 1990, I had a stroke of luck: Geoff Martin, the editor of the daily paper I worked for, asked me if I fancied becoming features editor.

'I'll do it if you let me do travel as well,' I said.

He thought for a moment.

'All right. You can have twenty-five days a year,' he said with a calmness which belied the fact that my teeth were buried in his ankle at the time.

I added the same again from my own time, and for the next fourteen years, every six weeks or so, I had that feeling which the passage of time never diminished. Of flying into a foreign city late at night, taking a taxi through the mysterious streets to a hotel and the next day flinging open the shutters then going walking through the rain-washed morning. In my head was the knowledge of an adult, in my heart was the joy of a child seeing the world for the first time. And in my soul, it was always Christmas morning.

These are some of the writings from those years. As an A–Z guide to the world, they bear little relation to reality, but if they inspire you to close the front door, walk down the road with a rucksack over your shoulder and take a bus to the airport or the first train north, then you are the luckiest person alive, and I wish your soul a happy Christmas Eve.

Armenia

5000 BC, give or take a millennium, but not long after the Ark
Noah begets Japheth begets Gomer begets Togarmah begets
Haik.

Haik builds Tower of Babel, has three hundred children,
makes it to 130 with curly hair and perfect eyesight and
decides to celebrate by founding Armenia.

Tyrannical Assyrian ruler Nimrod, pissed off at not having
thought of it first, invades new country, wearing state-of-the-
art, impenetrable iron armour. Haik pierces armour with
three-feathered arrow. Nimrod returns to Assyria in bad
mood, dead. Haik patents three-feathered arrow and lives on
to 400.

9th century BC
Country absorbed by Urartian Empire, whose deities include
Haldi, God of War, with insatiable appetite for beheadings of
bulls and sheep. Armenians spend three centuries running
around like headless chickens creating vast mounds of
headless animals.

590 BC

Armenia conquered by Persians, who ban bull and sheep sacrifices. Armenians sacrifice horses instead, then have to walk everywhere.

AD 301–14

Armenians, having run out of animals to kill, become Christians under Gregory the Illuminator. King Trdat IV, who quite enjoyed a good sacrifice, flings Gregory into snake-infested pit for twelve years.

1400

Eastern Armenia conquered by Turkmen dynasty called Black Sheep. West invaded by second dynasty called White Sheep. Armenians long for good old days of headless sheep.

1878

Britain promises to protect Armenia against Russian and Turkish threats.

1894–6

Britain looks the other way as Turks slaughter three hundred thousand Armenians.

1915

Turks, having developed a taste for slaughtering Armenians, kill one and a half million more, then deny everything.

1921

What's left of country taken under caring arm of Lenin. Ever-optimistic Armenians start planning new utopia.

1923

Stalin steps in. Armenians sigh and put away utopia plans.

1930–45

Over one hundred thousand Armenians die in purges,
followed by three hundred thousand in Second World War.
Last person left in country asked to turn out the light.

1991

Independence. Armenians dust off utopia plans.

1999

Prime Minister, Speaker and six others assassinated in
Parliament, followed by endless series of corrupt elections.

Armenians sigh, put away plans again, and open a bottle of
brandy.

The time: any morning for the past one thousand seven
hundred years.

The scene: two old men sitting on a park bench, in a cobbled
square.

First man: 'Well, we've had invasions, massacres, occupations, genocides, wars, starvation, refugees, emigration and
poverty. At least nothing worse can happen.'

Second man: 'What's that noise?'

If countries were people, Armenia would be a black nun
living in Mississippi: one who's just been mugged by a bunch
of skinheads who've run off with her Vatican Gold credit card.
Then, just as she's getting up and dusting off her wimple, she's
run down by a truck driver delivering a load of burning crosses
down the road.

After becoming the first Christian country in the world in
AD 301, for a thousand years it was a vast empire taking in
much of what is now Iran, Turkey, Georgia and Azerbaijan,
and leading the world in architecture, literature, music,
mathematics and astronomy.

Then came the Mongols, the Safavids, the Ottomans and the
Russians.

In 1915, the Young Turks of the Ottoman Empire slaughtered

one and a half million Armenians living in eastern Turkey, an act for which Turkey has, to its eternal shame, refused to apologise to this day.

A few short years later, the Russians arrived, killed all the priests and banned religion. In 1996, the war with Azerbaijan flooded the country with refugees. Two years later, an earthquake killed fifty thousand and, just as Armenia turned to the Soviet Union for aid, the latter fell apart.

Today, half of the population is living below the poverty line and another third is living on less than a dollar a day. Many have fled to the States, and send back what money they can.

I arrived by plane in the middle of the night, sitting beside a man in a multicoloured jacket and an even more multicoloured shirt, in the open neck of which hung a large gold and crystal cross. He looked like the pope on his way to a *Saturday Night Fever* audition.

Yerevan airport, the shape of a giant sputnik, was populated entirely by statuesque women in military uniforms, and a small cat. Had I been James Bond, I would have felt obliged to seduce at least half the women before passport control, but as it was, my charms only worked on the cat, who wrapped itself around my ankle as I queued for a visa.

If the drive from the airport was anything to go by, the entire economy was based on casinos and flower shops, and at the hotel, the receptionist was telling a Japanese man that he could not have a room without confirmation of his arrival.

'You want confirmation?' said the man, spreading his arms as wide as they would go, which in truth was not very far. 'Here I am! I confirm that I have arrived!'

He got his room and celebrated by going immediately to the bar and ordering a brandy. It, and religion, are, of course, the country's two most famous exports.

The brandy is famous because Churchill was introduced to it by Stalin at at the Yalta conference and when asked years later for the secret of his long life said, 'Never be late for dinner, smoke only the best cigars and drink Armenian brandy.'

And the religion is famous because of buildings like the fabulously frescoed cathedral of Echmiadzin, home to services once more since the departure of the Russians.

Since the bishop of Armenia was paying a visit, we arrived to a flurry of genuflections and were forced to decamp temporarily to the nearby chapel of St Cayenne, a persecuted virgin who is buried in the seventh-century crypt, below a portrait of her looking glum, although whether from persecution or virginity is unclear.

Outside, a small boy was selling Orthodox crosses emblazoned with the pagan evil eye, as a sort of two for one insurance policy which was entirely appropriate in a country where they still regularly slaughter sheep before Mass.

Anyway, that was quite enough culture for one day. It was time for dinner, at a traditional restaurant in Yerevan where I had a vast feast for about 5p, while in the corner a stern triumvirate of elderly men played joyful airs on violin, flute and qiyamancha, which looks like the offspring of a guitar and a short-sighted giraffe.

We left the city the next day, bouncing south on a rutted road across the fertile plain past vast, deserted Soviet factories and crumbling blocks, with cows grazing in their courtyards as the former workers attempted to make a desultory return to subsistence farming.

'You know,' said Nouneh, the guide, 'under the Soviets, everything was planned. You knew what you were doing every day for the rest of your life, so we had food, but no tomorrow. Now we have all our tomorrows, but no food.'

And no roads: it took us to noon to bounce our way to the spot where Gregory the Illuminator arrived in 314, then got thrown down a well by King Trdat for his trouble. When he wasn't persecuting virgins, Trdat would pop by from time to time and take a look down the well to make sure the saint was suitably miserable.

Of course, Gregory had the last laugh, and Khor Virap, the thirteenth-century monastery built on the spot, celebrates his success in converting the country. Today, it is the holiest place in Armenia, and the most poignant, for only a few miles south is the divine mountain of Ararat, supposed home of the Ark. Armenians can see its mighty peak from everywhere in the south of the country, and yearn for it, but they can never go there – for it is just across the closed border with detested, unforgiven Turkey.

Nouneh gazed at it for long minutes, then turned away.

'Come. Lunch,' she said. Lunch, at a nearby farmhouse, was a table groaning with breads, sweetmeats, sorrel, lamb, beans, soup, fruit and yoghurt, served by Seda, the sixty-eight-year-old grandmother of the house. Three years before, her sister had invited her out to Los Angeles to live. She had lasted six months before declaring the place an uncivilized madhouse and returning to the farm.

'When she came back, she complained that we'd got an inside toilet,' said her granddaughter Meline. ' "That filthy thing inside the house? How disgusting!" she said.'

On the balcony, a geranium sprouted from an American Blending Corporation powdered milk tin, the sole reminder of Seda's visit to the Babylon of the West.

For a gentle post-prandial walk, we staggered to our feet and climbed the 7,500ft to the mountain-top fortress of Smbataberd, which was built in the fifth century and sacked by the Mongols eight hundred years later. More power to the Mongols, I thought as I collapsed on to the ruined walls. After a climb like that, they deserved all they could lay their hands on.

Still, at least the way down was easier, stumbling through the golden evening into a flock of sheep who surrounded us with the mutter of a thousand tiny feet. At one stage we were joined by a man and his horse, whose foal walked along behind, occasionally investigating my pocket shyly with her nose. We regained our car and came at last, by moonlight, to a monolithic grey building by a river. Two large dogs sat drooling gently on the doorstep, and in an upstairs building, a single light burned.

'Nouneh, what is this building?' I said, as one of the dogs politely nibbled my knee.

'It is the bishop's summer orphanage. But all the orphans have gone,' she said.

At length, a small dark man opened the door. It was the bishop, who led us upstairs to dine on reluctant mutton while he drank tea from a large mug emblazoned with the words 'Earl Grey, named after a British Nobleman renowned in International Circles'.

I slept on a small bed in a large dormitory, while somewhere deep in the bowels of the building, our driver played Bach long into the night.

The next morning, I was feeding apples to a horse when a man came up, gave me a fish and drove off in a chocolate-coloured Lada.

Milk, that is, not plain.

I put the fish in my pocket and we drove north to Yeghegnadzor, where an increasingly insistent drumming from the rear announced the imminent disintegration of a tyre under the incessant battering of Armenian roads.

While the driver went off to get it fixed, I wandered through the derelict streets, past old men sitting on benches waiting for money from America, until I came to the town museum. The entire staff came out, visibly stunned to see a tourist, then gave me a personal tour of several ancient artefacts above labels describing them as 'A Stick', 'A Bear Pot of Rituals' and 'A Spindle from Unanimous Cave'.

The driver appeared, announced that the tyre was as well as could be expected in the circumstances, and we set off for the mountains, up a road which had mercifully been repaired with money from Kerk Kerkorian, the Armenian-born MGM film magnate, who had recently poured $200 million into renovations in old Yerevan.

I made a note to write to him saying 'Dear Kerk, you don't know me, but I am in fact your long-lost son', as Nouneh announced for the third time that morning that the roads were worse in Georgia, then launched into a medley of old Armenian folk songs and finished with an encore of 'Jingle Bells' as we arrived at Selim, the best preserved of all the caravanserai on the old Silk Road.

A sort of medieval truckers' stop, this was a long basalt hall, inside which the camels slept down the centre and the merchants in arched naves along either side. It is all splendidly atmospheric, and as you stand at the ornately carved entrance and look out, you can almost smell the damp heat of the beasts, incense and cooking behind you, and see before you a distant caravan toiling its way up the mountain, laden with silks and spices from Persia and Samarkand. With, behind it, of course, a queue of horsemen honking their horns and muttering, 'Get a bloody move on, lads, or we'll miss the happy hour!'

It began to rain, and in a flourish of rainbows we came by evening time to Lake Sevan, the victim of an ill-fated Soviet scheme to create more arable land by lowering the water level 60ft, then an even-more ill-fated scheme to introduce whitefish, crayfish and goldfish, which promptly ate virtually all the indigenous trout.

We stopped by a bleached road sign, in front of a derelict railway station. All the way along the shore were abandoned Soviet projects: hotels, apartment blocks, concert halls and miles of pipeline. One enterprising chap had requisitioned one section, sprayed it red, decorated it with Coca-Cola logos and turned it into a lakeside diner. Other bits had been transformed into makeshift houses for families left homeless by the 1988 earthquake.

I wandered down through the oak groves, planted on the newly naked shore in the fifties, and stood at the edge of the lake, looking at two fishermen in a boat trying to catch the last trout in Sevan.

It suddenly occurred to me that if I'd been standing here fifty years ago, I would have been underwater, and dead. If I'd been alive then, that is.

We climbed back into the car and bounced along the

lakeside road for another hour, until all my teeth had fallen out and my innards turned to strawberry jam. But it was worth it, for at the end of the road was a hotel built by carpet magnate James Tufenkian, which was as stunning as the orphanage the previous night had been basic.

I wandered around my room in a sort of sumptuous-minimalist trance, pressing feather and down pillows, admiring muted earth tones, drooling over the bleached wood, stroking the copper 'Do Not Disturb' sign and climbing the minstrel-gallery stairs to stand on the little balcony in the rain, dazed with gratitude. And, if you think I'm going on a bit, you've obviously never stayed in an Armenian orphanage.

Even better, there was a restaurant in the same idiom. I had pear and tahine, tiny dolmades, lamb wrapped in spinach and cosseted by several herbs and spices, then staggered to my room and slept deeply, troubled only by a dream that I was the last trout in Lake Sevan, being pursued by a giant goldfish.

In the morning, the roads, impossibly, got worse. We climbed into the mountains at a speed so slow that the speed-ometer could not even be bothered to register it. An eagle, pausing briefly from feasting on a dead dog, soared alongside, mocking us with its effortless freedom.

In the town of Dilijan, cradled by mists and mountains, four cows sat in the middle of the main street and a pig watched us gravely from an ornate balcony. Several of the old houses had been bought by the town's ethnographic museum, restored to how they would have been in the nineteenth century and turned into little shops. They looked infinitely preferable to the way most Armenians, a proud and intelligent people struggling against a series of disasters, lived today. I emerged, unaccountably clutching a Russian Charlie Parker LP, to find Nouneh.

'We are going to the House of the Composers,' she said, then grinned. 'And remember, the roads are worse in Georgia.'

This, along with the House of the Cinematographers and the House of Creativity of Writers, was one of the Soviet artists' retreats in the wooded hills nearby, where the likes of Shostakovich and Khachaturian would come to listen to the wind in the leaves and ostensibly compose music which would inspire the proletariat to even greater beetroot production.

Today, they are home only to the occasional passing tourist and, from the cottages in the grounds, the notes of unwritten symphonies rise into the trees to become the songs of birds.

'Come,' said Nouneh, 'we are going to a unique monastery.'

'Nouneh, you've said that about all of them.'

'Ah, but this one is absolutely unique.'

Funny enough, she was right. Built in the twelfth century on a mountain high above Yerevan, Geghard combines the lofty arches of Romanesque architecture, the hulking solidity of medieval and the soaring grace of Renaissance into a synergy which is, well … er … unique.

As we arrived, the national choir was practising in the mausoleum, outside which were carved, rather serendipitously, two Homeric sirens. The music they were singing, which still makes my spine tingle when I think of it, was from a fourth-century manuscript, kept with seventeen thousand others in the remarkable Matenadaran museum in Yerevan. For when the Armenians were not building, they were writing, storing up words and music against the uncertain future.

We returned to the city that night, and the next morning I walked up the hill, past the teenagers queuing outside the American visa office, and stopped in front of the statue of Kara Bala. A rich rose-grower in the thirties, with a beautiful wife and son, he was jailed after murdering a love rival and ended his days alone, selling flowers on the street.

It is a very Armenian story, made even more poignant by the fact that behind him you can see, as you can see from everywhere in Yerevan, the holy mountain of Ararat, across the uncrossable Turkish border. The snowy peaks of paradise, so real and so unattainable, so near and yet so far away.

2003

Azerbaijan

4th century BC, just after breakfast
Country named Media Atropatene after ruler of area under
Alexander the Great.

4th century BC, teatime
Alexander dies. Persians rename country Aturpatakan as part
of Caucasian Albania, not to be confused with Balkan
Albania, home of Mother Teresa and King Zog.

5th century AD
Arabs conquer and rename country Arran, not to be confused
with Scottish island, home of damp sheep.
    Treaty of Endless Peace signed.

6th century AD
Endless Peace ends. Endless War begins between Romans,
Arabs, Turks, Mongols and Tartars over control of country.

1828
When rest not looking, Russians grab northern half and
rename it   . Persians grab south, followed by much
enraged carpet-thrashing after Russians discover huge
quantities of oil in north.

1900
Country producing half the world's oil, and 95 per cent of
Tsarist Russia's. Baku becomes Paris of Caucasus. As opposed
to France. Or Texas.

1917
Revolution in Russia. In Baku, independence declared,
women given vote, Latin alphabet adopted and country
renamed Azerbaycan.

1920

Russians check national oil gauge, discover they're running on empty, invade country for refill and change language back to Cyrillic.

1980s

Good news: even huger huge oil and gas deposits discovered off coast. Coincidentally, Western governments suddenly become interested in country.

Bad news: war with Armenia over Nagorno-Karabakh creates refugee crisis.

1991

Country becomes independent and decides to call itself Azerbaijan, just for a change. Natives, uncertain whether to celebrate in Albanian, Scottish, Persian, Arabic, Russian or Latin for fear of starting another war, hug each other in mute optimism.

1994

So-called Deal of the Century signed with international consortium for exploitation of oil and gas fields.

2003

Respected president Heydar Aliyev hands over power to son Ilham with dying breath.

CIA verdict on Ilham, notorious former playboy converted to family life, is 'Lacks his father's charisma, political skills, contacts, experience, stature, intelligence and authority. Aside from that, he will make a wonderful president.' Azerbaijanis, used to waiting and seeing, wait and see.

At first Marco Polo came with bales of silk, his hands aromatic with saffron or shimmering with the shadow of jade. In the lilac evenings he walked by the Caspian Sea and cursed the black mud that ruined his golden slippers. Then the Zoroastrians came, and lit an eternal flame that lasted longer than they did. Then the Rothschilds and the Nobels, here for the same oil that had ruined Marco Polo's slippers, their fantastical mansions rising from the gloop and suck of ruined forests.

Then Stalin came, and the mansions were divided into a thousand tiny apartments, each one still with fear. Then the oilmen came again, breaking the stillness with loud voices and the rustle of dollars. A hundred years ago Azerbaijan had produced half the world's oil, and now the world was back looking for the other half.

And then, at last, the tourists came. In 1997 the first of them wrote to the Azerbaijani embassy in London, asking for a tourist visa, and the embassy wrote back asking why. Today, foreigners are still so rare that as you walk past the people blink in amazement. Then try to sell you a carpet.

I arrived in Baku, the capital, in the middle of the night, driving through streets where only the flower shops were open, selling lilies to romantic insomniacs. The next morning, dawn broke over the medieval quarter to reveal a scene from the hotel window which, apart from McDonald's, Mothercare and the mobile phone shop, had not changed in 400 years.

Along the shore stretched the gloriously lunatic mansions of the nineteenth-century oil barons, mostly farmers who woke up one morning to find themselves millionaires and immediately sent telegrams to Italy for the first available architect to come at once.

On the hill behind rose a vast Soviet edifice whose countless windows had been teased into Islamic arches, like a shotputter who had discovered eye shadow long after steroids.

I rose, ate a fig for breakfast and wandered through rain-damp streets with the feel of a Paris that had not been washed for half a century, until I came at last to the State Carpet Museum, a monolithic neoclassical pile which smelt of shoe polish.

On the grey walls of its many rooms hung thousands of carpets, and in the corner of each room sat a dark, beautiful and utterly bored attendant.

You see, the thing about carpets is that one in a white room is breathtaking, but several thousand on peeling grey walls inevitably results in you being led away suffering from a rug overdose. What has happened is that a singular Oriental skill has become the victim of the Soviet obsession with quantity, and the result is a fracture that cannot be healed.

But then Azerbaijan has been fractured so many times since it was a crossroads of the Silk Road: by the Persians, by the Mongols, by the Soviets, by war with the Armenians over Nagorno-Karabakh, by the war between the Russian desire for vodka and the Islamic disdain for it, by the gap between the oil-rich and the dirt-poor. It has even been fractured by the very tool of communication, with 2 changes of language and 3 of alphabet – Arabic to Latin, to Cyrillic, and back to Latin – in 80 years.

It is no wonder that the past and the present sit uneasily side by side here, like the grandfather and child of estranged parents. No wonder that, at any crossroads in Baku, you will see impeccably dressed men from among the one-eighth of the population who are refugees – or the one in two who are unemployed – standing looking in bafflement at a Mercedes taxi on its way to Crescent Beach, an exclusive coastal resort for expatriate oilmen. Or me inside the Mercedes, looking equally baffled for the same reason: that Azerbaijan's share of Caspian Sea oil reserves is reckoned to be at least £50 billion, none of which will find its way into the country until the companies pay off their development costs, and even then much of it may well end up lining the pockets of corrupt politicians, businessmen and their relatives.

At Crescent Beach, I ordered emu.

'I am sorry, sir, but the emu is only served at evening time,' said the waiter carefully, conjuring up an image of a flock of emu sitting outside, waiting with fear and trembling for the gleam of a Sabatier at twilight.

When I returned to town in the afternoon, the rain was still falling. In crepuscular carpet shops, negotiations began, faltered and continued over endless cups of tea, until tourists emerged blinking into the drizzle, clutching rolls of wool and silk on which pearls of rain were already beginning to form.

Night fell. To the south of Baku it fell on the abandoned Soviet oilfields, a scene out of *Mad Max* by way of the Kremlin. Amid the rusting oil derricks, baffled cows pottered about in pools of oil and ruined water, calling out softly to each other, 'Here, Gertrude, am I unleaded or four-star?'

Further south, it fell on a barbed-wire encampment, where for the price of a bottle of vodka the guards would let you in to gaze on row upon row of abandoned Soviet tanks glistening dourly in the moonlight.

It fell on Fisherman's Wharf, an expat restaurant where, from a waiter with an accent halfway between Baku and Boston, I inexplicably found myself ordering a chip butty.

And it fell, at last, on the Chechnyan nightclub where I found myself later. Inside, men who had arrived with unidentifiable bulges under their clothing bought champagne for women with entirely identifiable bulges under theirs.

I slept in a vodka daze, and the next morning took a rattling minibus north with a guide called Lianna, who had sharp cheekbones and matching opinions.

'We are victims of the Chinese curse, "May you live in times of change",' she said. 'Something is being created, but we do not know what it is yet. The ugly part of all this is that a waiter earns more than a professor, and now you phone friends before you call around to see if they have food on the table. In the Soviet times, everyone was poor, but no one was starving.'

She was right. Azerbaijan is fascinating because of the influences that have shaped it in the past, and because at the moment it is going through the turmoil that Marx called dialectic, when one political system becomes another. It is the drama of which epic narratives are made: great to write about, grim to live through.

In the northern suburbs, vast Soviet apartment blocks stood

apparently derelict. Until you saw hanging from a balcony a row of white shirts, growing grey in the rain. A few miles on, in the shadow of a rusting factory, a shepherd sat by a guillotine, waiting for someone who could afford a headless sheep for supper.

On all sides stretched an arid plain which had been forest until refugees chopped down the trees for winter fuel. From time to time there appeared crumbling villages and roadside cafés desperate with longing. Lianna looked out through the window and clutched her silent mobile phone, an icon of a brave new world that was always coming, but never came.

It was a hundred miles before the dun plain gave way at last to deciduous forest. The earth breathed again, and in the shade of the trees boys in astrakhan hats sold apples, peaches and walnuts.

At Quba, gay lights tinkled on the long road into town, and such had been the unremitting gloom of the landscape earlier that the sight made me quite absurdly happy.

We got lost, and commandeered the services of a local man with gold teeth. A construction engineer until the Soviets left, he had returned to his village to work as an allotment farmer and repair man. He led us up the green and dripping lanes to a little Albanian fire temple and graveyard. Dating from the third century BC, and fabulously engraved, it lay utterly untended in a hilltop field, watched by two querulous ewes.

We climbed back on the bus and bounced through the village street as a man in an immaculate beige suit and white shoes came picking his way through the mud. Behind him, the little houses had tin roofs decorated with doves and deer, and the valley was heavy with peach orchards.

We found a restaurant in which the speciality was chicken curry and, a long time later, since the recipe obviously involved first catching the chicken, we returned, burping politely, to Baku.

The day's catch of tourists had finished buying carpets and caviar, tut-tutting at the poverty and the corruption and salving their conscience with a generous tip at the little Italian restaurant around the corner, and were returning to hotel rooms which contained little bottles of corporate unguents and copies of the city's not one, but two English language newspapers.

I threw a bottle of vodka and a toothbrush into a bag and drove to the airport, and an hour later my plane rose into the early evening sky, leaving behind the two lives of Baku. The life of ambassador's cocktail parties, export beers and dinner with the Browns from Texas this Friday.

And the other life. A hundred years ago it was the life of the oil workers who came from all over Russia to live in canvas tents from which they peered out at the oil barons strolling in whispering silks to their fabulous mansions.

Today, the oil barons wear Armani chinos, but the refugees are still the same, looking out from under the rims of their dripping tents now as the plane to London turns west and trying to imagine what kind of world it is going to.

The plane in which I sit, looking down for one last time at the gleaming curve of Crescent Beach, where twilight is already beginning to fall on the long dark night of the emu.

2001

Bangkok, in search of sex
on flying motorcycles

1769

King Taksin establishes Siamese capital in nearby Thonburi, then goes mad and declares himself to be the next Buddha. Ministers beat him politely to death in a velvet blanket so that no royal blood touches the ground.

1785

New King Rama moves capital down the road to Bangkok and decides to rename it Krungthep mahanakhon amon rattanakosin mahinthara ayutthaya mahadilok phopnopparat ratchathani burirom udomratchaniwet mahasathan amonpiman awatansathit sakkathattiya witsanukamprasit, which I don't need to tell you means Great city of angels, the repository of divine gems, the great land unconquerable, the grand and prominent realm, the royal and capital city full of nine noble gems, the highest royal dwelling and grand palace, the divine shelter and living place of reincarnated spirits.

Everyone ignores him, decides life's too short, and continues to call it Bangkok.

Any of you who prefer the old name should rush out and buy *Fak Thong*, the 1989 album by Thai rock duo Asanee & Wasan, an epic funk rave which consists of the old city name chanted over a hypnotic rhythm.

1964–73
City gains reputation as so-called Rest and Recreation bolthole for US soldiers in Vietnam. Sex being more fun than politics or finance, reputation endures through dictatorships, democracies and economic boom and bust.

It was a Friday evening, and I was sitting in a hotel bar in Bangkok with several men from Dublin, as you do.

It was Shane who started talking about sex on a flying motorcycle, and at first we thought it was sunstroke.

He had fallen asleep the day before on a junk going to the islands, and had arrived scarlet on the front and snow-white on the back.

Now he was sitting bolt upright in the hotel bar, drinking beer and holding my guidebook very carefully.

'Look,' he said. 'It says here, in your book, that there's a club called Supergirls which has sex on a flying motorcycle. "As featured in *Rolling Stone*", it says.'

'What sort of motorcycle is it?' I said, sipping a cold beer with those lovely beads of moisture on the outside of the glass.

'It doesn't say,' he replied. 'You're the motorcycling correspondent for your paper, aren't you?'

'I am,' I said, knowing what was coming.

'Well, you should really go and find out. Shouldn't you?'

I sighed, and put down my beer.

We set off in a taxi, six of us, into the hot and humid night. The rest were all under thirty, except for myself and Charlie, a bald photographer who the day before, while carefully helping Shane ashore from the junk, had dropped his glasses into 35ft of water.

'Where you going?' said the taxi driver as we sped off. It was midnight, which is about the only time you can speed off anywhere in Bangkok traffic.

'We want to see sex on motorbikes,' said Shane from the back, where he was doing his best to sit carefully between four other people. 'Flying motorbikes.'

'He means the Supergirls club,' I said to the driver, who like most Thai men could have been anywhere between thirty and sixty.

'Superwha?'

'Supergirls. Motorbikes. Sex.'

'Ah, sex! Patpong!' he said, brightly.

Patpong was originally four acres of banana plant-ation owned by the bank of Indochina, which sold it to the Patpongphanit family just before the Second World War. After the war, massage parlours and bars grew to satisfy the needs of airline staff and soldiers, and today it is a hive of markets, bars, clubs and sex shows from which the Patpongphanit family collects £200,000 a month in rent.

Anyway, where was I? Ah yes, in a taxi. Twenty minutes later we pulled up outside Patpong, which I recognised from my extensive local knowledge, and also because it said Patpong in large letters above the entrance. On all sides stretched market stalls selling T-shirts and CDs, still doing a roaring trade at a quarter past twelve. Shane walked carefully up to a beautiful Thai girl standing outside the bar on the corner, wearing a dark business suit. She smiled sweetly at him, politely overlooking the fact that in the neon from the bar sign, his skin looked as if it had recently come into contact with weapons-grade plutonium.

'Can you tell me where the flying motorcycles are?' he said.

'Motorcycles?' she said in perfect English. 'Have you tried a garage?'

I felt a tug at my elbow. It was Neil, another of the group.

'Here, help me bargain for this. I'm so crap at haggling I always end up paying more than they asked for in the first place,' he said.

I looked at what he was holding. It was a red string vest. With sequins.

'Is it for yourself?' I said.

'It's for a friend. It's a long story.'

Suddenly, we were interrupted by Charlie. 'Listen, this isn't Patpong. Patpong is miles away,' he said.

Before I had a chance to point out to him that not only was he not wearing his glasses, but that he had never been to Thailand before, he had leaped into a taxi with two of the others.

'Bloody hell. Bloody hell,' I said, flagging down a passing tuk-tuk, the rickshaws named for the sound of their two-stroke engines and driven by men like Michael Schumacher, only faster.

'Follow that taxi,' I said to the driver. Neil got in beside me, and Shane got in carefully beside him.

Twenty minutes later, we pulled up at a derelict building in a deserted part of Bangkok. In front of it, three men in vests lounged on plastic chairs, and in front of them, the owner was talking to Charlie.

'Ping-pong balls. Bananas,' he was saying. 'Only 500 baht.'

'That's very expensive for bananas,' said Neil.

'You haven't seen what they do with them yet,' I said.

'We don't want ping-pong balls or bananas. We want flying motorbikes,' said Shane.

We got back into our respective vehicles and hurtled off into the damp darkness. Half an hour later we pulled up in a battered alleyway, outside an even more derelict building.

An elegant Thai woman in a black dress came out.

'Well, it looks like a garage,' said Shane. 'So they might have motorbikes.'

He walked carefully inside, followed by the others.

'Do you have motorcycles?' I said to the woman.

'I'm afraid not. Just girls and beer.'

I sighed, and got back into the tuk-tuk.

It was two in the morning by the time I got back to the hotel, paid Vilam the driver 240 baht, or about £4, for his night's efforts, and stepped out, smelling faintly of oil.

I was hot and tired, and as I looked up at the stars, I thought it would be an ideal time for a swim. To my surprise, someone else had had the same idea: Ahmed, the marketing manager of the airline I had flown out with, was sitting in the shallow end of the hotel pool with a glass of red wine. Above our heads, the Milky Way wheeled through the heavens as carefully as Shane getting out of a tuk-tuk.

'You know,' said Ahmed, 'every time I look up at the stars and think of all the worlds that must be out there, I think of my dead brother. I was forty days old when he died. He was four, and my grandfather had sent him out to get some soup from the store. He reached up to lift the pot down off the stove, and spilled the boiling soup all over himself. He died a few hours later, not because of the burns, but because of the shock. My grandfather always blamed himself, and he was never the same man again.

'Then, when I was eleven, I was lying sleeping one night when I suddenly woke to see a boy standing beside my bed. He looked at me for a little while, then turned and went into my grandfather's room. My grandfather died that night, and when I described the boy to my parents, they said I had described my brother.

'I like to think that he had come to take my grandfather, and to tell him not to blame himself. And I like to think, when I look up at the stars, that they are up there waiting for me in another world, when at last it is my turn to pass out of this one.'

The next day, I met Shane at noon.

'Well, did you find the flying motorcycles?' I said.

'No, they just had girls and beer. So we sang to the girls, and drank the beer,' he said, walking on, carefully and optimistically, towards a breakfast room which had long since closed.

2003

Bermuda, with an inflatable shark called Seamus

Passport, money, inflatable shark.

The shark was called Seamus, both in the interests of community relations and after an accountant I knew, and since he hadn't been out of the office all week I thought he deserved a jaunt to Bermuda.

However, like most things which seemed like a good idea at the time, Seamus turned out to be a spot of bother. Like the fact that he refused to deflate at the airport. When I finally had him squeezed into the overhead locker, I settled into my seat, had a gin and tonic and watched a very strange in-flight film about the macaques of Sichuan.

Macaques are large apes pampered by both local monks and visiting tourists, with the result that they end up like many Northern Ireland politicians – convinced that they are supremely important, but actually utterly insignificant outside their own world.

I ordered a large brandy and read a novel by Banana Yoshimoto, the quaintly named Japanese writer who always looks in photographs as if she's just been mauled by a macaque, and the next thing I knew New York had appeared outside the window.

I decamped, handed in my green form and made my way to a bedroom at the Marriott Hotel. I went to bed and woke at four with the quaint conviction that I should call my next novel *Larne Harbour Commission: The Golden Years*. Thankfully, I had forgotten the idea by the time I finally woke up.

And so to the cruise ship *Song of America*, leaving behind a city buzzing with preparations for that afternoon's Puerto Rican carnival.

Ah, how fine it was hang Seamus up over the porthole and steam out of New York, leaving behind the cares of the everyday world as I turned out for lifeboat drill, tied my lifejacket with that good old sailors' standby, the granny knot, and waited for the approaching Royal Caribbean steward to give us the all-clear.

'You're Geoff Hill, aren't you?' he said.

Now, the receptionist asks me this every day when I arrive for work, so I shouldn't have been a bit surprised. And a couple of years ago a woman leaned over from the next table at a Russian restaurant in Helsinki and said exactly the same thing.

She was from the Finnish Tourist Board in London, and the Royal Caribbean steward, it transpired, was Bangor man Keith Nicol, who worked on the ship's shore excursions desk and spent the next couple of days politely guiding monstrous Americans in the direction of the pool bellyflop contest rather than the nude shark-wrestling.

By the time he'd got them all sorted out, Bermuda had arrived beside the ship in the balmy warmth of a subtropical morning, perfect for breakfast at the Verandah Cafe as the Norwegian flag fluttered at the stern, a British Airways jet slid in across the bay, Italian finches danced in the sun and the cedars in the little gardens of St George's below whispered in the soft wind. It was as if the civilized nations of the world had decided in a spell of accidental happiness to vote for a single, perfect moment.

But then, accidental happiness has been almost compulsory in Bermuda since 1609, when Sir George Somers' ship the *Sea Venture* foundered on its notorious reefs on the way to Virginia, and the crew found the island so abundant with edible flora and fauna that they spent the next few months munching away merrily in between building two new ships out of the wreckage of the *Sea Venture*.

When Shakespeare heard about it, he immediately sat down, hauled out the old laptop and rattled off *The Tempest*, and several hundred years later writers were still finding inspiration in the place in the shape of Mark Twain, who arrived there after the publication of *Tom Sawyer* and declared it 'the right country for a jaded man to loaf in'.

Today, the state parliament, which first met in St George's in 1620, remains the oldest commonwealth legislature outside Britain and is an institution determined to keep this an island with a great past in front of it. By law, Bermuda has no income tax, no neon signs, no fast-food chains, no rental cars for tourists, only one car per household, a 20mph speed limit and numberplates which consist of nothing more than a five-figure number preceded with T for taxi, S for scooter and L for learner.

And it works. Per capita, Bermuda is the third richest country in the world, an island where the richest avenue, occupied by the likes of Ross Perot and Silvio Berlusconi, the Italian media mogul and politician, is known not as millionaires', but billionaires' row.

Bermuda is not the sort of island on which a crime reporter could make a living; page three of that day's *Gazette* carried an exclusive about an apple tree being vandalised. In fact, crime is not even allowed to taint the island from beyond the grave. Criminals executed for murder are buried on adjoining islands with their feet facing north, while the good citizens of Bermuda are placed carefully in mainland graveyards with their well-pedicured tootsies facing east, waiting for a first-class ticket to judgement day.

I spent the day wandering around St George's, which with its narrow cobbled streets lined by shops in soft whites, dusty pinks, buttery yellows and burnt terracottas selling tartans and cashmere cardigans, is like an English village populated by Scottish dowagers, painted by Portuguese journeymen and financed by a Swiss bank.

And no matter how much the internationalisation of language has prepared you for Bermuda shorts, it is still the quaintest of sights to see grown men dressed respectably from the waist up in dark formal jackets, shirts and ties, and from the waist down in electric pink, yellow, blue or green shorts and clashing knee-length socks, the more clashing the better. The whole effect is to make the wearer look like a colour-blind transvestite, but the really worrying thing was that everyone looked so comfortable with their sartorial schizophrenia that it could only be a matter of time before I was lulled into a hypnotic state in which I wandered into the nearest clothes shop and bought a pair of scarlet shorts and orange socks.

I opted instead for the cool stillness of St Peter's, built in 1612 and the oldest Anglican church in the western hemisphere.

On a warm day – and there is no other sort in Bermuda – it is quite blissful to stumble, damply wilting, into the airy peace of St Peter's, with its ancient pews and brass plaques on the white walls paying their silent, lustrous tribute to those who lie outside beneath the eternal whisper of the cedarwood trees.

Back at the pier I found one of the ever-helpful Royal Caribbean staff standing under a palm tree with a freshly ironed clipboard.

'Hi there. What tour are you on?' she said.

'The underwater karaoke with sumo wrestling and bungee jumping,' I said.

'Um, let's see,' she said, looking down through her list in all seriousness, 'that doesn't seem to be on today.'

'Oh well, never mind,' I said, toddling off to to find the tour bus driven by an imposing local whose name badge identified him as R.E. Grimes.

'The temperature today will be 80 degrees – 40 in the morning and the other 40 in the afternoon,' said R.E. Grimes as we drove off through an afternoon redolent with the scent of bougainvillea.

He stopped the bus beside a tiny green cottage worth about $500,000 and launched into a magnificently complex explanation of Bermudian house-building techniques, before suddenly pausing somewhere between the damp-proof course and the cistern to leap off the bus and return bearing a flowering hibiscus.

Local legend, apparently, is that women wear it in their hair on the left to show that they're single and available, on the right to show they're married, on top to show they're married but still available, and on the back to show they're desperate.

And so on we sailed, with old R.E. stopping every so often to lean out of his window and snatch another example of foliage for us to inspect – like the banana leaves once used to stuff mattresses, or the 'Match Me If You Can' leaf, so called because no one is the same as the next, used to cure fevers, burns and constipation.

Past a sign saying 'Ducks Crossing', a chap in riding pink and jodhpurs was exercising a chestnut mare in a huge, rolling meadow, his whole bearing expressing that sense of solid, entrenched well-being on a grand luxe scale which is Bermuda.

Sadly, it was not an ambiance which extended to the island's zoo, where cockatoos sat in gloomy cages for no other reason than to say 'Bye bye' to passing tourists. Much more interesting was the Bermuda Perfumery. A place to be sniffed at, it contains about a million assorted smells and a fascinating lump of ambergris, the lumpy secretion of sperm whale stomach which is used as a fixative for perfume.

And so, onwards with R.E., past the pink sand beaches for which Bermuda is famous, and which are mute testimony to the astonishing bowels of the Bermudan parrot fish. The parrot fish, you see, has coral for breakfast, lunch and tea – a diet so mind-bogglingly dull that they change sex every so often just for a bit of excitement – spending the rest of their time munching coral at one end and creating from the other end pink sand.

'We are just declimaxing down from our tour,' R.E. Grimes announced ten minutes later. 'Just keep the good Lord with you wherever you go, and remember that when the light is in front of you, the shadow is behind you.'

It was almost dinnertime when I returned to the ship and found everyone expanding gently. Since the average cruise passenger gains one and a half pounds a day, it might really be a good idea for Royal Caribbean to consider providing on embarkation an adjustable romper suit which everyone could wear for the duration of the voyage, with a clip-on tie for formal nights.

I had dinner, fell asleep, and woke to find that it was warm and wet outside, and the Bermudans were on their way to work in waterproof suits of turquoise and yellow, scarlet and emerald, looking on their little scooters like motorised parrots.

In front of their wheels, the tiny land crabs which come out when it rains scuttled for shelter. Stepping carefully around them, I walked up Gibbs' Hill to the lighthouse, built in 1846 to provide safe passage through reefs which had wrecked thirty-nine ships in the previous decade alone. When it was finished in May that year, the locals, convinced that it would turn night into day, had already thrown away all their lamps and candles.

Oops.

That afternoon, I was in the Mariners' Bar ordering a draught Guinness when a middle-aged man, who bore a remarkable resemblance Buffalo Bill Cody, leaned over.

'What part of Belfast are you from, then?' he said.

'Er, the Lisburn Road.'

'Aye, me too. Is the Four in Hand still there?'

He was, it transpired, Ron Robinson, a man who must go down in history as the world's worst parking offender. After emigrating to Canada in the sixties, he drove his white Pontiac to Manitoba Airport during the appalling winter of 1967, planning to fly to Bermuda for a few weeks to get some heat in his bones. The Pontiac is still there, and if you're ever in Manitoba maybe you could turn the lights off, because Ron's a bit worried about the battery running down.

It was all too much to bear, so I returned to the ship for the Bermuda Triangle tour which I'd planned, only to find that it had mysteriously vanished off the list of tours available, and that the only one left was a tour of the ship's bridge.

The bridge was a disappointment. The crew were all wearing sparkling white ducks instead of heavy pullovers hand-knitted by Mrs Olaffson and stained with fish oil and diesel. There wasn't even an Under Seaman Third Class lashed to the huge teak and brass wheel twenty-four hours a day. In fact, there wasn't even a teak and brass wheel, just the sort of thing you'd find sticking out of the dashboard of a Mini Cooper.

Clichéless, I returned to my cabin and switched on the TV. On Channel 26 was Captain Kjense saying 'Good afternoon everyone. You may have noticed that we have left Bermuda, and I hope you are all aboard. If you're not, too bad.'

It had all the hallmarks of being one of those days. I made my way to the Terrace Bar and ordered a large aquavit, and the next thing I knew we were back in New York.

It was 96 in the shade, except there was no shade. All over the city, people were making lunch and making love, making out and making do. In the central hall of Grand Central Station, a girl with hair the colour of autumn was playing the guitar and singing the old Negro spiritual 'Nobody knows the trouble I've seen'. Her voice rose into the vast and airy arches of that most romantic of railway stations, below which the air was still in that wonderful moment before a thousand mysterious departures down all the dark tunnels into the welcome cool of the evening.

It was the right time to say farewell to the city, taking a cab to the airport with Seamus and tilting east into the burning sky.

1995

Bulgaria

Dawn was rising over Belfast as we took off quite some time after we had intended. Several hours later, Plovdiv appeared under the starboard wing. Heavens, I could see the very road that Paddy Minne and I had ridden down on our way from Delhi two years before, soaked by torrential rain, almost killed by forked lightning and, in my case, stung in the neck by a reversing bee.

The plane landed and drew to a halt. The Bulgarian businessman sitting in front of me stood up, smoothed his brown corduroy suit, and carefully took a brown corduroy coat from the overhead locker.

Outside, Plovdiv was warm and sunny, which was a little worrying, since we were there to ski. Still, not to worry. We climbed into a bus and set off for the mountains, passing after ten minutes a red Lada saloon from the back of which two small, brown cows gazed placidly out. Things had obviously picked up in Bulgaria; the last time I had been there, the cows had been walking.

Indeed, two minutes later, we passed a gypsy encampment with a satellite dish sprouting from the roof of every shack, and in Borovets, our hotel rooms had been renovated recently to Ikea standard.

Sadly, the upgrade had also included the temperature, for it was like a warm summer day outside, and of snow there was no sign. Now, call me a traditionalist, but I do like snow on a skiing holiday.

'Don't worry,' said Nikolai, the man from the tour company, 'there is snow at the top of the mountain. Tomorrow we will ski.'

In the meantime, there was nothing to do but go for a drink in the nearby Shark Club, whose sign outside described it rather quaintly as an energy bar. Inside was the world's most powerful ultraviolet lighting, turning everyone instantly tanned, sparkly and glamorous. With teeth flashing and shirts gleaming, we got slowly, sparklingly drunk.

Several bars and hours later, I staggered back to the hotel, having consumed by my estimation 427 schnaps and 536 beers.

'You've been drinking, haven't you?' I said to myself in the bathroom mirror.

'Afraid so,' said my reflection, shamefacedly.

The next morning I rose, breakfasted heartily and presented myself on top of the mountain to a skiing instructor called Alex.

Since it was two years since I had been skiing, I was splendidly appalling, although I did find several new ways of hurtling down the mountain, some of them even with my head above my feet, which had other skiers looking on with what I like to think was open-mouthed admiration.

We stopped for lunch at a little mountain-top hut, where Alex and I enjoyed what according to the menu was a Big Make, accompanied by the refreshing tinkle of hailstones on our foreheads and the cheery sound of sea shanties from the resident piano-accordionist.

In the afternoon, a dodgy cartilage in my left knee which made turning right almost impossible forced me to develop a technique of descending the mountain in a series of left-handed loops. It was not entirely successful.

We headed back to the hotel for a dinner of pork and potatoes, accompanied by the very same peripatetic piano-accordionist from the top of the mountain.

'Clap! You must clap!' he demanded cheerily, giving his performance the martial jollity of a pre-war Luftwaffe officers' ball, before launching into a little ditty called 'Kalinka', whose lyrics translated more or less as 'the Russians are taking over the world'.

The next morning, I met Alex in a little café for coffee, to the sound of a splendidly obscene American rap song. Above our heads, a poster for the Bonkers nightclub impelled us to 'Come and Feel the Beet'.

We finished our coffees, walked out into fresh spring sunshine under a bleached cotton and indigo sky, and took the gondola up the mountain. As we ascended heavenward, my heart sank at an equal rate. For yesterday I had been the worst skier in the world, and if Alex had turned to me this morning and said, 'Hey, let's give it a miss today', I would have been in the bar and had the beers set up before he'd got his boots off. All the more remarkable, then, that today I turned out to be a Master of the Universe, laughing gaily at red runs and grinning inanely in the face of moguls.

'Amazing,' said Alex, as I sailed past him in a perfect parallel turn, stopped, and promptly fell over.

It was, I agreed at a brief meeting with myself in the bar afterwards, the best I had ever skied.

Tragically, our hosts had decided that we were going that night to Pamporovo, Bulgaria's other ski resort, in spite of the fact that we had been told there was barely any snow there.

'Why don't we stay here?' we asked as one.

'No, no, we must go. It is in the programme,' we were told peremptorily.

Even more of a shame, on the way to Pamporovo, I could detect the faint but definite signs of flu.

We arrived to a beautifully renovated hotel, but even the sight of deep armchairs and a crackling log fire in the lobby failed to make me feel any better. I had two paracetamol and a brandy and went to bed, where I dreamt of fish. And although I had fallen asleep convinced I was dying and would never walk again, I found myself yet again at the top of the mountain the next morning, stuffed with every form of flu drug known to mankind.

Sadly, as we had been told, there was little snow, and the only runs open were a nursery slope and a half-bald red run.

There was only one thing for it, and that was to use the nursery slope to learn snowboarding. As far as I could see, there was only problem with this: I was not a dude.

I thought about this for a moment, then approached a Belfast chap called Arthur, who was obviously a dude from the fact that his hair was like an explosion in a mattress factory.

'Here, Arthur, I need to become a dude so I can go snowboarding,' I said.

'No worries. I've got some Dr Zog's Hot Hair Wax, and if that fails we can stick your fingers in the shaver socket,' he said.

'And do you have any death thrash ambient techno hip-hop garage funk CDs I can listen to?'

'It's the only type of music I have.'

Splendid. Now all I needed to do was actually learn to snowboard. I presented myself immediately to the snowboard depot, only to find that size 13 snowboarding boots were a thing that had not yet been invented. As a result, I became possibly the only person ever to go snowboarding in a pair of docker's shoes bought for $17 at a discount store in Philadelphia.

Learning to snowboard is, in some ways, a similar process to learning to ski. You fall down a lot, then eventually surprise yourself by getting it right. Towards the end of the afternoon I executed a turn without the usual look of blind panic followed by an exit into the trees at speed, and swished to a spot beside a young chap wearing baggy cargo trousers, a 'Tintin in the Congo' T-shirt, Killer Loop shades and a baseball cap firmly on backwards.

'Looking good, dude,' he said, giving me the Na-Nu Na-Nu sign from Mork and Mindy.

It was official. I had been elevated to dudedom. My day entirely made, I went off to borrow an ambient techno CD from Arthur, stick my fingers in the shaver socket, and have a sparkly beer in an ultraviolet nightclub.

2000

Copenhagen, on the trail of Kierkegaard's outside toilet

Tragically, I had arrived just in time to miss the World Santa Convention, in which more than a hundred Clauses dance around a Christmas tree in the town hall square before adjourning to a nearby hostelry to get red-nosed on yule ale, compare beards, complain that you just can't get the reindeer these days and discuss whether or not little Jimmy at 3 Edgbaston Close really deserves a new Power Ranger set after that little incident with the neighbour's cat.

However, all was not lost.

I had in my possession a copy of *A Necessary Warning to Everyone Who Visits Copenhagen From a Man Who Knows the Town*, Julius Strandberg's 1861 guide which contains timeless advice from the very first sentence:

> One has the Pavement Rights when one has the Road-way on
> one's right Side, and one need not then move to the Side for
> those Ladies to whom one would show good Tact. If one has
> the Road on one's left Side, then one does not have the
> Pavement Rights, i.e. when walking on the Flagstones, one is

obliged to give way to on-coming Pedestrians not voluntarily
giving Relinquishment to that Right.

Well, thank heavens to get that cleared up.

In 1881, according to Strandberg, the Danish were noted for
their kindness, and today they still are, even when they are not
Danish. Our taxi driver, for example, a Serbian called Goran,
kept our bill as low as possible by driving most of the way from
the airport to the hotel at 75mph, helpfully pointing out on the
way the university buildings dotted around the city where his
brothers and sisters were studying. The languages department,
naturally, was near the airport.

We had a pint of Murphy's in the hotel's traditional Red
Lion English bar, tipped the barman well, bearing in mind
Strandberg's advice: 'Gratuities are an unpleasant Evil, but ... I
would advise you not to forget a little Token for the Waiters;
they have nothing else to live on, and if you forget them, then
next time they'll forget you, and let you sit until the very last',
and went to bed.

Strangely, there seemed to be no Danish bars in Copenhagen,
for the next morning, the first sight that greeted us around the
corner, as we set off with Susanne the guide, was an Irish pub
called Rosie McGee's, whose attractions, according to the sign
outside, included ceilidh dancing, theatre, Mexican haciendas, a
log cabin, Scottish and American lounges and that well-known
Irish tradition, a mermaid bar.

'Copenhagen has been an important port ever since we sold
fish to the Catholics,' said Susanne. 'For Fridays, I mean.'

Today, more profitable activities include buying tax-free
Mercedes, running them as a taxi for three years, then selling
them to private citizens, who have to pay the tax, at the same
price you bought them for.

Less financially rewarding but more socially aware pursuits
in the city include running one of several community
newspapers, such as the one named after the former red light
district known as Pisserenden, literally the street of ... well,
work it out for yourself.

Indeed, the subject of going to the toilet crops up more than once on a walking tour of Copenhagen. Five minutes walk away from Pisserenden is Magstrade, or Street of Calm, the setting for the former public toilets where the populace gathered for a bit of peace and quiet, perched on planks above the canal reading the *Ekstra Bladet*, having a smoke and contemplating the price of herring and the meaning of life, which for many years in Scandinavia were the same thing.

Indeed, it is not unlikely that Søren Kierkegaard, the father of existentialism, first came up with his theories about the meaning of life while sitting there wondering why his fiancée, Regine Olsen, had failed to understand his deeply significant epistle to her called 'Either/Or'.

Mind you, few other people understood it either, and if you've read any Kierkegaard you'll understand why Regine ran away and married someone else, since he was possibly one of the gloomiest philosophers ever, whose championing of individual will over social convention and rejection of materialism found him few friends among his stolid fellow Danes.

Still, it could have been worse. If he'd been born a few centuries earlier, he would have been one of the friars who pottered about the city in wooden sandals and grey habits, denied the right to own property and deeply respected for their piety until the Protestants arrived, accused them of being a bunch of lazy good-for-nothings and threw them out.

Very spiritual folk, Protestants.

As a result, you never see a friar on the streets of Copenhagen these days. Or a dog, come to that. I pointed this out to Susanne over a lunch of chanterelles, those well-known singing mushrooms, and was rewarded with the information that there is, in fact, half a dog for every household in the city. Unfortunately, she never clarified whether households got a choice over which half they got, or whether you had to spend your time buying cans of Pedigree Chum for the front half of a Rottweiler while your next-door neighbour wandered around propping up a back half which fell over every time it tried to lift a leg.

I was still trying to work it out as we set off for a splendid boat tour of the city, which included such intriguing moments as chugging down a channel between, on one side, the carefully tended torpedo boat sheds of what was until recently the Danish Navy headquarters and, on the other side, the rambling wilderness of Christiana, since 1971 a commune of one thousand alternative souls who are to bourgeois Danish life what George Best was to synchronised swimming.

The tour also includes the Little Mermaid, which is the same colour as the Statue of Liberty, but smaller. Do not expect the Little Mermaid to be spectacular, or you will be disappointed. Approach it rather with the attitude of Buddha, who said that when you expect nothing, everything is a gift. Then you will be quietly pleased with it, in a Danish sort of way.

For the rest of the afternoon I wandered through the streets, watching people playing chess on corners – Copenhagen is one of the few cities in the world where chess is a spectator sport – and in the evening I ended up in a fine old harbourside restaurant at Nyhavn, where the wine bottle was graduated from 0–70 up the side. At first I thought this was to indicate my decreasing chances of getting home safely the more I drank, but it turned out to be just to show the waitress how much to charge me.

And then I went for a walk by the canal at twilight, when for some reason colours seem to glow more brightly than in the day: the ochre and rust of the buildings, the lilac and red of windowbox hydrangeas and geraniums. And above them the arched windows, which seemed to tilt as the minutes crept by, reaching for the last light of the dying sky.

I went to bed and, as I slept, the jet trails which had been left in the evening sky froze in the night and fell to rest between the telegraph poles of the city, so that children who woke early enough could telephone all their friends before the trails melted and their parents picked up the phone to pay bills or call their offices on the ordinary telephone lines used for ordinary things.

Having spent the evening drinking Carlsberg at a furious pace to keep up with the Danes around me, I woke up with probably the finest hangover in the world. It served me right for having ignored Strandberg's advice: 'Let yourself not, in the dry Summer Time, be lured by Thirst into stowing one Lager after another under your Waistcoat, for the Copenhagen Lagers are of the very highest Quality.'

In any case, the best course seemed to be to return to the scene of the crime – the Carlsberg Brewery – accompanied by a guide called Henrik who leaned confidentially closer as we entered the main gates and said, 'You know, Carlsberg Elephant Beer is the strongest in the world – apart from the stronger ones, of course.'

Above our heads, carved into the sides of the four stone elephants which hold the arched gateway upon their backs, was the original symbol of the brewery, a swastika. It is, however, the three thousand-year-old Indian symbol of good and happiness, rather than an indication that after drinking Carlsberg all night your liver will feel as if it's been dive-bombed by Stukas.

Today, the brewery produces a billion beers a year, welcomes 136,000 visitors and contains in its cellars the world's biggest beer collection – 12,049 bottles bought over twenty-five years by a Danish engineer called Leif Sonne, who's still at it – three days earlier he'd popped in with another couple of bottles he'd picked up in Greenland. Carlsberg seems to be so successful that if its promotional video is any thing to go by, the company has taken over every other firm in Denmark, including the Royal Copenhagen Pottery.

Now, I'm afraid that my feelings about this are the same as about Belleek, that is I can appreciate the skill that goes into making it more than the end result. Too overblown to love, too expensive to use, it fails to stir anything in me. Thankfully, by the time the tour of the pottery was over it was time for lunch, which was three different types of herring, including a red herring which wasn't there. I think it had an effect on me, for in the afternoon I went to a design museum which wasn't open.

There was only one thing to do, and that was to go to the Tivoli Gardens for dinner. The gardens are exactly the kind of place that when you are a child you hope being grown up will be like. Bands play, birds sing, people stroll under trees hung with lanterns and couples dine by candlelight. What could be more perfect, especially if you dine at the Balkonen carvery in the middle of the gardens. Since it's self-service, just make sure you're the perfect host, give yourself a 100 per cent tip, and get a free meal.

With the money I'd saved on dinner, I bought a pair of shoes in a sale the next morning and left for the airport at the same time as a convocation of men in grey suits arrived at the hotel and tried to get into their rooms through the keyholes. They were, it transpired, the world's leading gynaecologists, who have a convention there at the same time every year.

So if you're ever planning to have a baby in the first week of August, just make sure you do it in Copenhagen.

1997

Donegal

Beginning of the universe to 1980
Sheep and poverty, occasionally interspersed by poverty and sheep.

1980–present
Bungalows in hacienda styles I–IV with PVC windows, occupied by weekending lawyers. Sheep flee to Mayo in protest at both lawyers and windows

We had a Harley, we had a full tank of gas, we had shades, leather jackets, faded Levis and the open road in front of us, stretching all the way over the horizon to … Donegal.

Well, you have to start somewhere.

And when you're setting off next month to ride Route 66 from Chicago to Los Angeles, what better preparation than leaving Belfast on a cold and rainy Friday morning for Ardara?

You see, unlike what you might think, there are more than a few similarities between the two routes. Chicago and Belfast, for example, have the same number of letters. So do Ardara and Los Angeles, give or take a few. And both Route 66 and the road to Ardara are black, with white lines down the middle. In fact, the only difference I can think of is that Los Angeles doesn't have a mad Frenchman who owns a bed and breakfast exactly in the middle of nowhere.

Born in Morocco, Paul Chatenoud studied philosophy at the Sorbonne, then in the seventies opened Librairie Musicale, a unique bookshop containing just about every book ever written in French on music. On its dusty shelves, John Cage nestled up to Schubert, and Pete Seeger jostled for space with Pau Casals.

Then, ten years ago, Paul came to Donegal, fell in love with a hilltop cottage on a Wednesday, bought it on the Thursday and flew back to Paris on the Friday knowing somehow that life would never be the same again.

He sold the bookshop and the beautiful flat in Paris, moved into the cottage and sat down to write the definitive book on life, love, music, the universe and everything.

He finished the book, but like most great books, it remained unpublished, and Paul woke up one morning and realised that being an unpublished author is one of life's less lucrative vocations, only just worse in financial terms than being a published author.

'When I sold up in Paris I had plenty of money. I bought a Jaguar, gambled on the stock market and lived expensively. Now I was broke,' he had told me on the phone.

However, all was not lost: he had become so used to hosting friends who came to stay that the obvious step was to turn the cottage into a bed and breakfast, slowly transforming the outhouses into extra bedrooms.

We had to see for ourselves, which was why late that afternoon, frozen to our bones after the long ride from Belfast, Cate, my new girlfriend of three months, and I found ourselves in Ardara, and after asking a local man for directions and getting four different answers, finally rode up the steep, winding lane to The Green Gate. Which was where things started to go what I believe is referred to in the trade as pear-shaped.

You see, Harley-Davidsons are built for going from New York to San Francisco in a straight line at 55mph. They are not built for negotiating hairpin bends on steep, winding Donegal lanes at 0.5mph. Especially when the man in charge of gear selection has unaccountably picked second instead of first. That was me, and as a result I quickly found myself in the rarely used horizontal motorcycling position, while behind me Cate was sailing through the air with the greatest of ease to land on the part of her body normally used for attaching her to sofas rather than Donegal lanes.

'Oh dear,' she said when she had landed. 'I don't seem to able to get up. It's either because I am paralysed, or because this lane is so steep that my head is below my feet.'

'I do apologise, dear,' I said politely, 'but even worse, there seems to be petrol leaking out of the fuel cap over the hot engine, so we may well shortly be immolated.'

She struggled to her feet and grabbed the bike, and we set to the task of hauling it upright, at which point we discovered that the problem with making a motorcycle with an engine the size of a car's is that you create a motorcycle which weighs the same as a car.

'You know,' said Cate, 'they really should build these things with sensors so that when they start to fall over, little stabiliser wheels pop out and stop them.'

'And a stout rope with a block and tackle so you can haul them up steep Donegal lanes,' I added.

Eventually we got it back on its wheels, only to find that the carbs had flooded and the engine wouldn't start.

'Never mind,' said Cate, 'we can just push it to the top of the hill.'

Sadly, that proved easier said than done, and after ten minutes we had covered, oh, a good six inches.

'I think we're going to be here for the weekend, dear,' I said.

Thankfully, at this stage the engine coughed into life, and it was a weary duo who finally presented themselves at the door of The Green Gate five minutes later.

Paul led us to a bedroom with a window beside the bed so that we could lie in it and look at the sea, then sat us down in a living room and fed us tea, toast and jam from a wooden tray which contained fifteen different preserves. I counted them.

A turf fire chuckled in the hearth, books on philosophy and music snoozed on each other's shoulders on the shelves, the humming chorus from *Madam Butterfly* drifted through the warm air, and outside the window a robin and a bluetit hopped among the daffodils.

Paul poured another coffee, and looked at his ancient watch.

'What we need is dinner,' he said, picking up the phone and calling Kevin, the local taxi driver.

An hour later, Kevin dropped us at Castle Murray House Hotel, where Claire and Thierry Delcros run the rather splendid restaurant. I could be wrong, but I don't think they're from around these parts.

'How much do I owe you?' I asked Kevin as we got out.

'Ah sure, I'll be picking you up later,' he said.

We made our way inside, collapsed in front of the fire, and had a feast of grilled oysters, warm scallops, duck, ham, smoked chicken, and walnut and goat's cheese salad.

Then we moved on to the main course.

Several hours later, we staggered out, fell into Kevin's taxi and were transported back to Ardara.

'Do you want some money yet, Kevin?' I said as we decamped outside the smallest of the village's thirteen pubs.

'Not at all. I'll get you later,' said Kevin.

Actually, when I say pub, I exaggerate. It was more of a large cupboard into which nine people, including a man from Anchorage, Alaska, had managed to squeeze.

At least I think it was nine: it was hard to tell, because the smoke was so thick you could have cut it up and sold the slices as cakes to people who were pretending to give up smoking.

The barmaid, a handsome woman in a green anorak, was wearing a flying helmet, sunglasses and an oxygen mask.

'Is it because of the smoke?' I asked an elderly man sitting in the corner, dropping cigarette ash on to a two-bar electric fire, where it flared into a brief resurrection then settled dully on to the chrome.

'No, she thinks she's Amelia Earhart,' he said in a voice all hills and dales.

His name, it transpired, was Patrick. He was wearing a pair of unlaced training shoes which had last been white when Elvis was thin, a pair of tracksuit bottoms from which the concept of shape had departed around the same time, a pullover of uncertain provenance and colour, and a black plastic jacket which looked as if it had already begun to melt in the wavering heat from the fire. His face, nevertheless, had the look of a sponge which had soaked up all the optimism in his life, yet been rendered waterproof against cynicism. What was left of his hair, finally, resembled a series of abandoned sketches for Hokusai's *Tsunami*.

'Are you looking after yourself, Patrick?' said Paul from the other side of the room, or about three feet as the crow flies.

'Aye, although I still have the flu from Christmas,' said Patrick, as if the illness had been a present from an unpleasant cousin.

'Do you have a turf fire?' said Paul.

'I have plenty of turf, but no fire,' said Patrick.

Satisfied with this answer, Paul turned to the bar and ordered two bottles of stout and a whiskey from Amelia Earhart, and Patrick lit another cigarette from the embers of the previous one.

'You know,' he said, 'in 1970 there was a woman sitting where you're standing. Her name was Bolin Andersen, and she was from Copenhagen. When she left we kept in touch, and then she moved to Stockholm, and from there she wrote to me one October to say she was going to Kiruna, the last junction on the rail line north, because she had heard of a tiny blue flower which grew there.

'I wrote back to tell her not to go in October, but the letter was delayed, and by the time it got there, she'd gone. Of course, when she got there she found nothing but snow, and I think she blamed me, for she never wrote back.'

'Did you ever see her again?' I said, taking a sip of my stout.

'Three years ago another Danish woman walked through that same door. Her name was Kirsten Klein, and she was taking photographs for a book.

'I got talking to her, and when I mentioned Bolin her eyes lit up. "Do you know Bolin?" I said to her.

' "Well, I did," she said. "I'm afraid she died of cancer two years ago." '

'What a sad story,' I said.

'It's a strange one, all right.'

'What does Patrick do?' I said as we walked down the damp street later, thinking he was a slightly derelict character upon whom the owner had taken pity.

'He's the owner,' said Paul. 'His family have had that pub for a hundred and fifty years, although it closed two years ago.'

'What happened then?'

'Patrick bought his first TV and closed the pub for six months so he could watch it for twenty-four hours a day. Then he got fed up with it and opened the pub again.'

Some time later, we found ourselves in Nancy's bar. Naturally, it was owned by a woman called Margaret, an elegant matriarch who we found holding court in a side room. At her feet, a dog called Guinness slept with his bum so close to the fire that it could only be a matter of time before it went up in flames and Margaret was arrested for arson.

'Is this your living room or part of the pub?' I said.

'I sometimes wonder,' she said. Inside, the bar was crammed with everyone in Ardara and most of its hinterland, but as always happens in Donegal, stools were found for us and within five minutes we felt as if we had lived there all our lives.

Several pints later, Kevin appeared outside the door in his taxi.

'Kevin, for God's sake let me give you some money,' I said as we finally fell out at The Green Gate.

'Aye, all right then,' he said with a sigh. We shook hands with him, said goodnight to Paul, tumbled into a feather bed and slept the sleep of the gods.

2000

Egypt

3000 BC

Ancient Egyptians arrive, build pyramids, worship cats, sleep with their cousins and die out, leaving cats sitting around with smug expressions waiting for the next bunch of mugs to worship them.

Egypt uses three calendars: the Islamic, the Coptic and the Western. The Coptic dates from 284, the accession of Diocletian, and is not much needed. To convert an Islamic date to a Western one, then, you divide the Islamic year by 33, subtract the result from the number you started with, and add 622. I added my granny's shoe size and divided by the average number of goldfish in a posse just to be on the safe side. As a result I left Belfast in the winter of 2002 and arrived in Egypt in the middle of a medieval summer.

The air was as warm and aromatic as buttered toast, and from nowhere a flock of hawkers descended, as they would every day for the next week, trying to sell postcards, camels (one hump or two), goats, donkeys, the Pyramids, their granny, Tutankhamun's coffin, mummified ibises, genuine fake temple carvings, alabaster scarabs, papyrus and the Sahara.

Telling them all I would see them later, which was fatal, since Egyptian traders have a photographic memory for every victim they have ever met, I made my way down to the shores of the moonlit Nile. All around, fishermen were furling the sails of their feluccas, the boats which have graced the river since before the Queen Mother was born.

I stepped aboard a floating Victorian palace called the *Nile Legend*. All dark wood and hanging lamps, it resembled a Mississippi riverboat from which a hawker had sold the paddle wheels to a passing American tourist.

The staff, all moustaches and smiles, ushered me up carpeted stairs to a dining room and handed me a drinks list which offered new French wine at a tenner a bottle, and the old stuff at a lot more. The whiskies were listed as Regular, Special and Extra Special. I ordered a local beer, the cheapest thing on the menu, dined on a slightly reluctant chicken and went to bed.

The next day, I rose at dawn and went to see an empty graveyard: the Valley of the Kings, which is the most exclusive suburb in the world for dead people, and is still being uncovered in spite of centuries of grave robbing.

The largest tomb of all, that of Ramses II and his 98 sons, is so big that excavations will not finish in our lifetime, but even that of Ramses IX, a tenth of the size, is breathtaking.

At first, in a mad frenzy, you rush around them all: Amenophis II, with its colours as bright as dawn; Ramses IV, with its monstrous sarcophagus. But then you realise that they are all astonishing, and that they all have another thing in common: they were all robbed, by everyone from disgruntled tomb workers to corrupt officials, from the pharaohs themselves, desperate for gold to pay for iron weapons, to nineteenth-century gentleman thieves looting the graves for drawing room souvenirs.

All robbed, except the one I left until last, that of Tutankhamun. Even the name sent a shiver down my bones, as it had for Howard Carter when he opened it in November 1922, with his bankrupt sponsor, Lord Caernarvon, breathing down his neck.

At first, he could see nothing, then everywhere, the glint of gold.

I made my way down the steps and gazed on the golden face of the boy king, and found it hard to believe that this was one of the smallest tombs in the Valley, built in haste after Tutankhamun died at nineteen. And yet it yielded one thousand seven hundred treasures, which take up an eighth of the national museum in Cairo.

As I walked away, I tried to imagine the scale of the other riches which had vanished from this desolate valley into the hands of fools. And failed, utterly.

In the shimmering heat, we visited briefly the vast temple of Hatshepsut, the Thatcher of ancient Egypt who ruled as a man for twenty years, complete with false beard. When she finally fell, like Maggie she fell hard, and all her images have been obliterated throughout the temple.

Even a history set in stone can be rewritten: sometimes, as in the Colossi of Memnon in the verdant valley below, by an earthquake. These 70ft, seated statues were knocked up by Amenophis III, who loved his wife, his mistress and the 317 damsels he kept for cold winter nights so much that he called his palace the House of Joy.

Still, that was enough sex and culture for one morning, and it was time for lunch back on the boat. We weighed anchor – it was about half a ton, dripping wet, since you ask – and headed south. Sailing down the Nile Valley in the limpid afternoon, it was immediately obvious how much it is the artery that feeds this dry and barren land. It was as if God, clearing out the cupboards on the sixth day of creation, had suddenly discovered a ribbon of lush greenery he'd forgotten about, and had only a desert left to put it in.

The truth, of course, is more prosaic: ten thousand years ago, Egypt was the Ireland of Africa, until disastrous climatic changes. Today, 96 per cent of the country is uninhabitable because it is desert, and the rest is uninhabitable because there are too many people in it, most of them trying to sell you something.

This was not so much of a problem in 1882, when the population was seven million, the same as it was in Cleopatra's day. But today it is sixty-eight million, and rising at a million every nine months. In Cairo, three million alone live in the Necropolis among the dead.

Nasser's plan of education and jobs for all, which looked so possible during the seventies when the country was £15 billion in the black, now struggles under the weight of a national debt of £18 billion. It was all Amenophis's fault. All that sex has become the national pastime, and the House of Joy has become a house of cards.

Good heavens, I didn't mean to get quite so serious there. One minute I was sailing peacefully down the Nile, the next I was in the middle of a political crisis. Here, let me have a beer and calm down. Ah, that's better.

I went to bed, dreamt of the price of fish, and woke next morning refreshed and ready to go on the trail of Flaubert, who when he arrived in Esna, was propositioned by a courtesan who came aboard his boat with her pet sheep, its fleece polka-dotted with yellow henna. This fabulous creature – the woman, not the sheep – sent the novelist into raptures by blindfolding the musicians, performing a languid striptease then ravishing him senseless several times over.

'Watching that beautiful creature asleep (she snored), my night was one long, infinitely intense reverie,' he wrote at the time.

However, there being no courtesans or spotted sheep in sight when I arrived at Esna, I had afternoon tea instead. With two biscuits.

By nightfall we came to Edfu. As we turned to dock and the ship's lights flickered on, a row of children came to stand by the water and watch, as pale as ghosts in their loose, flowing djellabahs. To them, we must have seemed as incomprehensible as if the Starship Enterprise had come to visit. Perhaps Erich von Daniken was right, and the aliens who had come to show the Egyptians how to build the pyramids were actually a group of German structural engineers on holiday. But no: Howard Carter would surely have found, buried in the sand, small but unmistakable fragments of beach towel.

We dined on several hundred courses, mostly starters, and in the absence of any entertainment, I went to bed with a large book.

At dawn I rose and walked to the Temple of Horus, one hundred and eighty years in the building and the best preserved of its kind in Egypt. You stand looking at its vast carved facade, and can only imagine what it was like painted, with flags fluttering down over the 100ft-high cedar doors, which only opened for the chosen few. Inside in the shadows, an endless hall of columns leads to the granite shrine to Horus, whose golden statue was clothed and perfumed daily.

The Egyptologist Michael Haag had written of a ceiling painting in an antechamber of the sky goddess Nut, 'with unusually fine breasts and profile, pale green with a blue skirt of stars'. But try as I might to find her, I left Nutless.

On south we sailed, and the band of greenery on either side grew narrower as the desert crept close. The air felt breathless, as if the life had been burned out of it, and along the shore, Arab boys could be seen at their favourite occupations – standing in the river and fishing.

A mile down the river, I stood up, staggered, and felt the unmistakable symptoms of heat exhaustion: headache, giddiness, nausea and a sudden desire to move to Iceland. Fortunately, it was just coming up to teatime, and there are few things in life, except perhaps having your head chopped off by a mad axeman, that cannot be cured by a nice cup of tea.

All around me, the passengers, all Irish or English, were queuing for tea and buns. Most of them were white or fat, and several were both, which was worrying: we are used to

Americans being somewhat on the plump side, but this was the first time I had noticed the trend creeping east of Mullingar.

That night, the boat had an Egyptian fancy dress party, and although dressed like Muslims, they still drank like Christians, so it was a liverish group that set off the next morning for the great dams at Aswan.

The first of these was built by the British in 1898, and the second, finished in 1971, ended floods and famine, created three harvests a year and provided 70 per cent of the country's electricity.

Unfortunately, the Egyptians were so excited by all this that they immediately went to bed and started making more children, thus creating such a population explosion that the country is now back where it started.

The feeling here, at the southern tip of Egypt, is of being in Africa. The heat is more oppressive, the flies more persistent and the people Nubian: gentle, black as night and valued long ago as slaves and dancers.

Eight hundred thousand of them were displaced by the building of the second great dam, and one of the few left drove us before lunch to a papyrus shop. Papyrus was the e-mail of its day, since before then letters were written on stone, weighed half a ton and had to be delivered by two Nubian slaves, or three for first class.

High on a wall in the shop was a copy of the most famous papyrus painting of all, *The Judgement*, the original of which is in the British Museum. In it, a dead man's heart is weighed against a feather. If it is lighter, he goes to heaven.

We could all hope for that, a heart as light as a feather. Or indeed, that we should smell as sweetly as we did after our next stop, a perfume emporium. In a mirrored hall, veiled Nubian beauties brought attar of roses, frankincense, myrrh and black narcissus. I emerged aromatic and blinking into the noon sunlight, and took a boat trip in the lake, passing in a languid daze the scenes of colonial life: the botanical gardens of Kitchener's Island, the Old Cataract Hotel where Agatha

Christie set part of *Death on the Nile*, and the mausoleum of the Aga Khan, for which his widow had fresh roses flown from Paris when none were available locally. As we returned to the shore, the boatmen burst into that traditional Nubian refrain 'She'll be coming round the mountain (when she comes)'.

After nightfall, the same boat took several of us under the full moon to a melodramatic but effective *son et lumière* spectacular at the island Temple of Isis.

Isis was the It Girl of her day, a fascinating and vibrant goddess who rather tragically lost out as a female icon to the relatively boring Virgin Mary, who, having had the pain of childbirth without the fun of conception, started a love of suffering which is continued in Christianity to this day, particularly in Irish mothers.

Our boatman, meanwhile, was a Nubian who had only just got married.

'My mother picked her, so I only met her the day before. She is very nice, but not as good a cook as my mother, so I am only sad at dinnertime,' he said, his smile flashing white and gold in the moonlight.

In the morning, before the heat, I walked to the old bazaar, accompanied most of the way by an insistent calèche driver whose motto, rather than the traditional Arabic greeting *Asalaam aleikum*, should have been *Hassle'em aleikum*.

I was the only white person in sight, and the warming air was thick with the smell of a thousand spices which lay in rainbows on either side for a mile, interspersed with gum, ebony, cotton, silk and, quaintly, Titanic baseball caps. There was saffron, worth its weight in gold, and in one hessian sack a blue powder as vivid as lapis.

'*Da ay?*' I asked the shopkeeper, an old man with some teeth, but failed completely to understand his reply. He rolled the cloth of his djellabah between finger and thumb, and I understood. It was the dye used by the Tuareg, called the blue men of the desert because it rubbed off on their skin.

I thanked him, and looked away, above the heads of the Egyptians, the Nubians, the Sudanese and the Ethiopians.

And almost saw, in the dust clouds to the south, turbaned men with great scimitars, walking out of the burning sands with many head of camel, each of them laden with treasures as immeasurable as the lost gold of the pharaohs.

2002

Finland

3000 BC
Early Finns arrive from Siberia, having abandoned the Hungarians and the Estonians for not drinking enough.

1155
Country torn between home-grown paganism, Swedish Catholicism and Russian Orthodoxy. English bishop Henry arrives on crusade, and tells Finns that from now on, the only drinking will be communion wine on Sundays. Finns think about it, then kill him.

1374
Swedish noble called Grip decides to live up to his name by taking grasp of entire country.

1495
Russians invade, and are miraculously driven back by tiny Finnish army. Finns celebrate with much drinking, only to wake up next morning to discover that they're not only hungover, but still Swedish.

1711

Peter the Great has another go, starting years of Russian occupation so bad they became known as the Great Wrath.

19th century

Student leader and future statesman Johan Vilhelm Snellman begins wave of nationalism with the cry, 'Swedes we are no longer, Russians we cannot become, Finns we must be.' Swollen by plays of Aleksis Kivi and Elias Lönnrot's publication of collection of folk tales known as *The Kalevala*, wave becomes a tsunami.

1899

Russians ban Sibelius's *Finlandia* for being too patriotic. Rather than renaming it Russiaia, Sibelius calls it Opus 26 No. 7. Russians then introduce conscription and install draconian governor-general Nikolai Bobrikov. Finns have a think about it, then shoot him.

1917

Independence. Civil war, which traumatises Finns so much they stop drinking for first time ever.

1932

Prohibition ends, followed by mother of all parties.

1939

Finns wake to hangover and war, in which vastly outnumbered Finns fight off Germans once and Russians twice. Russians, slightly miffed, seize lucrative east of country and impose huge reparations, which Finns pay off to the last rouble on time. Then decide to celebrate with a sauna followed by a party which in spite of recession, unemployment and having an angry Russian bear permanently on your doorstep, continues to this day.

I was halfway to Helsinki before I realised that I only knew two phrases in Finnish. But then, *Kaksi olut, olkaa hyvä* (Two beers, please) and *Anteeksi, missä on WC paperi* (Excuse me, where is the toilet paper?) should cover most eventualities.

And I need not have worried. By the time I got to the bar of the airport hotel, the owner had already doubled my vocabulary.

'Here, have a *glögi* before "drunch",' he said.

The first was a glass of spiced wine with almonds and raisins, and the second he'd just made up because it was too late for lunch but too early for dinner.

Suitably glögified and drunched, I found myself on a plane to Kajaani in the frozen north, where the national elf team, clad in red outfits and floppy hats, had laid on an impressive display of synchronised scampering and carol singing.

Just down the road was Katinkulta, a collection of 158 holiday cottages dotted around a clubhouse. The cottages were delightful, with the sort of sumptuous minimalism typical of Finnish design, the sort of cosy warmth typical of triple glazing and the sort of heroic sticking plasters in the bathroom cabinet typical of a nation which traditionally expects the best yet prepares for the worst. Comes from living next to Russia.

The clubhouse was even more impressive. Driving around the corner and seeing it in winter was like opening the fridge door to find the spaceship from *Close Encounters*. Inside was a tropical forest, swimming pools, tennis courts, squash courts, a bowling alley, saunas and steam rooms, gyms, shops, bars and a restaurant, where that night we had what looked like finely chopped elf but turned out to be lamb stew.

'That's funny. I was in Albania last week and we had reindeer steak,' said the man beside me.

That explained it. In the mix-up after the French lorry drivers' strike, the Albanians got our reindeer and we got their lamb.

Roger, the man on the other side of me, was meanwhile battering the chap opposite to death with travel statistics.

'Been to seventy-seven countries – bam! Record's ten in one day driving from Scotland to Italy – biff! Not to mention twenty-two American states – bop! Every province in the Netherlands – wham! And, of course, every district in Germany – kapow!'

'Roger, listen,' said the chap opposite, gamely trying to change the subject, 'I was just thinking this afternoon what a good idea it would be to compile a book of elves.'

'What, like how they use the National Elf Service, listen to Elvis Presley on the BBC Gnome Service, go to Philadelphia or Belfast for their holidays, put themselves first, hang little plaques above the mantelpiece saying "Gnome Sweet Gnome" or "Helf, Welf and Happiness", and say "I think it's going to reindeer" every time they look out the window?' said Roger.

The other chap collapsed under the table with a limpid groan.

The next morning I woke to the stillness that means that it has snowed heavily overnight. Outside, it was 15°C below and felt like the middle of the night, but in the clubhouse, several early risers were swimming about in the tropical waters. From behind the nearest bougainvillea wafted Bing Crosby singing 'White Christmas', and outside the door the chief transport elf was waiting with a bus to take us to the elf training grounds nearby, where dozens of red-clad elves were busily engaged in reindeer patting, snowmobiling, falling into snowdrifts, sledging and general scampering duties.

'Are you cold?' said one.

'Not too bad,' I said as I climbed into the 6ft 7in romper suit he handed me. 'And you?'

'Freezing,' he said.

He turned out to be the chief snowmobile elf, in charge of instructions. Snowmobile instructions go something like 'That's the throttle. That's the brake. Off you go.'

Off I went, zooming halfway up the nearest mountain and returning to find all the elves rolling around with laughter because an English tourist had just asked if he could have a go on a toboggan.

There were two reasons for this. Firstly, Finns think toboggan is the silliest word they've ever heard, and secondly, they are filled with joy that there is an English word longer than the Finnish equivalent – *pulka*.

In fact, the word toboggan has the same effect on many Finns as marijuana has on other people. They laugh a lot at first when they try it, then they're quiet for a while until one of them tries it again and starts everyone giggling.

I was just about to set off for a second snowmobile assault on the mountain when I heard the faint wailing of a siren in the distance. It was the Finnish drugs squad, and it was time to get out of here. Not just because I was about to be busted for possession of a toboggan, but because it was time to see Santa.

Santa lived a forty-minute bus ride away, through a landscape which had been reduced to its most fundamental elements – white snow, black forest, silver birch bark, the pale gold of the twilight sun creeping along the horizon followed by a ghostly rainbow, and in the vast deep blue above, a single star and a crescent moon.

It was such a magical sight that it seemed entirely appropriate to pull up after a while in front of a rambling log cabin, knock on the door three times and be shown by two elves down a flight of steps and along a corridor into a cosy room.

And there was the man himself, surrounded by knitting elves finishing off woolly pullovers, origami elves folding Christmas cards, catering elves making gingerbread men to a secret recipe then killing themselves because they knew too much, musical elves playing 'Rudolph the Red-nosed Reindeer' and off-duty elves playing Patience.

Santa, who was sitting in a rocking chair beside a leather-topped desk, looked exactly like Santa should. With masses of white hair, grandfather glasses perched on a round nose above a flowing beard and a merry twinkle in his blue eyes, he looked remarkably well for a 420-year-old.

Well, he thought he was 420. He'd lost his reindeer driving

licence with his date of birth on it about two hundred and fifty years ago, he was just telling us when the cynical chap from the *Guardian* broke in.

'Tell me, Santa,' he drawled, 'just how do you manage to get around all the houses in the world on Christmas Eve?'

'Magic, of course,' said Santa. 'And you know, I'm sure, that I only go to the houses where they believe in me.'

Santa 1, *Guardian* 0.

Thousands of children, of course, come here to see Santa in the weeks before Christmas. Some of them, ridiculous as it may seem, don't believe in him when they arrive. But they always do when they leave. And quite right, too. A world with no magic is no world at all. And don't forget, children, every time you say you don't believe in Santa, an elf dies somewhere in Lapland.

Shaking Santa's hand and wishing him and Mrs Claus a merry Christmas, I got back on the bus and went to dinner at Karolinenburg, a wonderful old manor house built in 1836 and run today as a family hotel.

Father wandered around smiling amiably at everyone, mother did all the work, eldest daughter welcomed everyone in an Australian accent and daughters two and three entertained the guests with after-dinner elf dancing.

Much later, I found myself back in one of the cottages at Katinkulta discussing with two women the problems of love. Sadly, by the time we'd found the answer, we were so drunk we'd forgotten the question.

Somewhat confused, I staggered out into the biting cold intending to go back to my own cottage, only to find that a blizzard had sprung up. After half an hour of wandering around, stopping briefly to give two Finns who were even more lost than I was a push to get their car started, I found myself back at the cottage where I had started. By the time I finally made it back to my own, it was five in the morning and I couldn't find any of the light switches.

Few people know this, but the reason the Finns held out for so long against the vastly superior Russian forces during the

Winter War of 1939–40 was not just because they were better fighters. It was because they hid all the light switches.

After quite some time I found a bed that I wasn't in, worked out that it must therefore be mine and fell into it, waking what seemed like five minutes later to realise with a clang of horror that I was due to go on a snowmobile safari into the forest.

Crawling into my snowsuit and staggering out into the blizzard, I found the familiar figure of the chief snowmobile elf.

'Let's go. If I raise my left hand, it means stop,' he said.

'OK. If I raise both hands, it means I've fallen off,' I said queasily as we climbed on matching snowmobiles and bounced off into the forest.

It was all exciting boyish fun, really, like Biggles in the Fridge, I thought as I roared along, struggling to keep down the breakfast I hadn't eaten. After an hour, we stopped at an isolated farmhouse to be welcomed by the farmer's wife with hot glasses of *glögi* and toasted cheese covered with cloudberry jam.

It was the sort of food that made you glad to be half alive, and by the time we got to the next stop, a primitive log cabin with a roaring fire, I was ready for lunch.

Lunch was salmon which had been cooked by the simple expedient of nailing it to the wall behind the fire for three hours, and something which the chef described, worryingly, as elf soup.

Oh dear. I'd assumed when I got off the snowmobile and looked around to find no elves in sight that they were still in the local clink from yesterday's big toboggan bust.

But all was well. He'd actually meant elk, and as I wandered back to the snowmobile later through the snowy forest, several familiar red-clad figures appeared in the gathering twilight. It was like being in the middle of every Christmas card ever made.

Soon it was dark, but there was still plenty of time before dinner for a spot of floodlit skiing. At the top of the first slope I met a Helsinki man called Sauli. Like most Finns, he wore the latest designer spectacles, through which he peered at me briefly before announcing significantly, 'Telemark is fun', then steering himself down the hill in a series of graceful turns while standing on one leg.

'Very impressive, Sauli,' I said after I had got to the bottom with a series of barely controlled disasters.

'If you need any advice, just ask,' he said cheerily.

Thankfully, I didn't take up his offer, for on his next two runs he managed to gracefully demolish a marker pole, his Armani spectacles and the right shoulder of a middle-aged Englishman.

The Englishman's companion, an attractive blonde woman in her late forties, meanwhile, had lost a 500-markka note worth about £66 in the snow and given up any hope of ever seeing it again, only to find later that a teenage snowboarder had handed it in to reception. Very honest people, these Finns.

And courageous, too. On the way home from Kajaani, I spent a few days in the south of Finland with Seija Väyrynen, my oldest friend, with whom I had been a penpal since I was thirteen and she was eleven, and her husband Jarmo.

On the Saturday, we got home from playing in the park to find the feet of their two-year-old daughter so frozen that we had to soak them in hot water for half an hour. Yet she had not uttered a single word of complaint, and neither did their four-year-old son that night when he managed to hammer a nail into his foot. Now, in another country, four-year-olds would be given a plastic hammer and nails, but in Finland they get the real thing.

The hole in his foot was washed and dressed by his mother, and he went back to hammering nails into blocks of firewood with slightly more careful gusto.

The Finns have a word, for that silent, tenacious courage. They call it *sisu*, a word which also sums up the sort of inner strength needed to live in a country which is both beautiful and fatal, as several Swedish, Russian and German armies have found to their cost.

They have an even more legendary quality than *sisu*, though, and that is their drinking ability. Only the Finns, for example, could think of throwing vodka on to the coals of the sauna so that you can get sozzled without even having to open your mouth.

So it is hardly surprising that my enduring memory of that week was not meeting Santa, eating elf soup or even smoking illicit toboggans. It was not even the memory of the monumental feast that Seija cooked us that night, of ham with prunes, codfish, carrot and swede, casseroles, beet-pickled herring salad with sour cream, salmon, cheese, cloudberry jam and smoked reindeer. No, it was running out of the sauna at five in the morning and diving naked into a snowdrift at 20 degrees below freezing.

Some men leave their hearts in San Francisco, but I went to bed at dawn fearing I had left something even more important in a snowdrift in Finland.

We rose at noon, dressed up warm and had a lunatic breakfast at a wooden table in the snow-draped courtyard outside their home, as the neighbours looked over their balconies and came down to say hello. Polish sculptors, Australian actors, French painters came and went, over coffee and cheese, ham and pickled cucumber, dark bread and honey.

And then we walked down by the river in the winter sun, buying lilac cups and slender glasses, and drinking beer in a converted chemist's shop, its dark interior aromatic with old wood and hops.

We drove to Naantali, a village on the coast, where the sudden rain drove us into the Café Antolius, run by Aatos Tapala, a former opera singer who fell in love with a local beauty and became an innkeeper so he could be close to her. There, we drank coffee and ate apple pie, toasting our toes in front of a log fire. The tick of the grandfather clock and the slow flickering of the candle marked the passage of the afternoon as the rain washed the windows and the streets outside. I ordered more coffee and apple pie, and thought that there was nowhere on earth I would rather be. The days stretched by, sharp and golden, aching for the grail of Christmas.

One afternoon we bought birch baskets and wooden brushes, and – by accident – tickets for a Sibelius concert, which is regarded by Finns the way more southern people regard chapel.

That evening we hurried by the river as the evening sky grew dark and the cathedral bell rang six, and as we walked across the bridge and up the hill the last pale light of the day caught and frayed on the wrought iron of the city's highest towers.

Rushing into the foyer, almost late, we passed a flurry of friends in all the washed colours of the rainbow, somehow managing to agree with waves and handshakes to meet in the old chemist's shop afterwards. That evening, I sat at a rough wooden table in the old chemist's shop drinking beer and listening to the Finns laughing and joking in their utterly impossible language, as beautiful and incomprehensible as pebbles in a fast stream, or someone hunting through a cutlery drawer. Time and again I closed my eyes and dreamed that I was in heaven, then opened them and found that I was.

The day after, we drove to a little wooden house in the forest, to have a sauna and dinner with friends. A wonderful place for baring your soul, the sauna. It's difficult to be pretentious when you're stark naked and dripping with sweat. It's also a great place for sorting out the world's problems, especially after a couple of bottles of beer.

For dinner we had the traditional stew from Karelia, Karjalanpaisti, and the little parcels of spiced rice called Karjalanpiirakat, washed down with wine and followed by liqueur made from the cloudberries that glow like tiny suns in the darkness of the forests of Lapland.

In Helsinki, we had coffee in the Kappeli, the café down by the waterfront where Sibelius used come when he was in town to gaze gloomily out across the bay to where I imagine he imagined happiness lay. He should have known that happiness was where he was, sitting at a table in one of the bay windows, as cool and green as an aquarium in summer, and in the winter as warm and welcoming as the womb.

Or in the Finnish Forum of Design, full of objects far more beautiful than words.

Or sitting at teatime in the vaulted waiting room at Helsinki railway station, filled with Finns sitting on the sofas or leaning into conversations across the marble tables, contentedly slurping beer or coffee as they wait for the trains that will take them out of the city to where a rectangle of light marks the welcome of their wooden home in the dark and whispering frost.

Or even standing watching the work of art that is a birch tree, with its silver trunk, its gold and iron leaves.

Seija and Jarmo drove me to the airport, and I hugged them goodbye and took the last plane home to Christmas, feeling sure that I was going the wrong way.

1996

Great Wall (of China, that is)

As the plane began to descend into Beijing, I took out my ticket and searched it in vain for the missing day. You see, we had left Belfast on Saturday morning, travelled for a day and would arrive in Beijing on Sunday night, which meant I had lost a day somewhere. Now, I've often wondered where yesterdays go when we're done with them, but this was the first time I'd lost a today. Even worse, it was a Sunday.

Still, there's no point worrying about todays, since they're just the tomorrows you worried about yesterday, so I put away the tickets, settled back in my seat, and looked around at my travelling companions: seventy-one people who had raised half a million pounds for the mental health charity Mencap, and were now going to earn it by trekking the Great Wall of China, armed only with legs of steel, wills of iron and unlimited supplies of that gastronomic icon of the Ulster traveller, Tayto cheese and onion crisps.

At Beijing Airport, a large sign said 'Warning – no zygotes, embryos or genetically modified organisms may be brought into the country'.

I checked my pockets carefully, found none, and entered China.

There are 1.2 billion people in the country, and most of them were in the arrivals lounge talking at the top of their voices. The rest were outside. Once, all of them would have been riding bicycles with a finger permanently on the bell, but now half of them were driving cars with a hand permanently on the horn.

For the amazing thing about China, as Mao found, is that there are so many people in it that you can remove millions of them without anyone noticing.

In 'The Great Leap Forward' of the fifties, for example, the fat lunatic decided that everyone should build a blast furnace in their back yard in a bid to transform China from an agricultural to an industrial nation. Using up scarce wood, taking farmers off the land and producing steel that no one wanted, the scheme starved up to sixty million people to death. That's the entire population of the UK, give or take Bernard Manning and a few stray cats. It is no wonder that the Mandarin for 'Hello' translates literally as 'Have you eaten?'

As for the Cultural Revolution, along with the People's Liberation Army (that other great oxymoron of twentieth-century Chinese history), no one knows how many millions died.

It is, in retrospect, remarkable how one unhinged fanatic can rule a country through fear for so long, until you realise how many others have been at it: Hitler, Stalin, Ceauşescu, Maggie on a bad day.

Anyway, where was I? Ah yes, on the bus from Beijing, sitting behind a girl who, combined with thirty hours without sleep, jet lag, and the constant jangling of bicycle bells and honking of horns, was driving everyone within earshot close to justifiable homicide.

'It's very flat, isn't it? What are those trees for? What a lot of bicycles. Some of them have motorcycles, don't they? It's very dry, isn't it? The old women seem to sit around and talk a lot, don't they? Is that a mountain?'

Outside, the scene was unprepossessing: dun flatlands broken only by the occasional bright ribbon in the hair of a girl.

In front of simple brick houses with a bicycle leaning by the door, chickens scratched in the dust. It was like Tyrone in a fifties drought.

After several hours we climbed into the mountains and were decanted into a courtyard in front of an office whose various signs announced it to be the Center of Reception, Consulting, Lawsuit and Tourist.

This was the lodge which was to be our billet for the night. I collected a key from the Center of Tourist and let myself into a frozen room in which ten minutes of gurgling, coughing and moaning from the shower finally produced a rivulet of lukewarm water on to the brown tiles.

I washed, shivered, and arrived in the dining room, which was even colder, just in time for the briefing by Lucy, one of the expedition doctors. She looked about fourteen.

'Do take care of your drinking,' she said. 'I'd recommend at least four litres a day.'

I went up to the bar immediately and bought twelve cans of beer, only to find out, tragically, that it was water she was talking about.

With a sigh I left eleven back, opened the other one and had dinner, which was so delicious that it can only be a matter of time before the Chinese start opening restaurants in other countries.

It was 9 p.m., and I had been awake for thirty-three hours. Back in the room, I crawled into bed with my feet dangling over the end, opened *The Chronicles of Narnia*, and fell asleep after two words.

At dawn the next day, I flung back the curtains to reveal the rugged mountains stretching all the way to the horizon and a queue stretching all the way to breakfast. Just ahead of me when I got there were Avril and Janice, who by the look of their carefully coordinated trekking outfits were from Bangor or thereabouts, and who had brought not only unlimited supplies of tinned spaghetti bolognese, but a hot water bottle.

'My feet were still freezing. It's been ages since I did my Duke of Edinburgh. More tea, anyone?' said Janice as we took our seats beside Noel Thompson, the man from the BBC who was recording a radio documentary on the trek.

And so , spag bol and hot water bottles packed away, to the Great Wall.

At the top of the mountain we reached one of the guard towers which punctuate the wall every few hundred yards, straightened our backs and took in the vista for the first time. As far as we could see, along each of the highest and most inaccessible peaks all the way to the edge of the world, snaked the wall, made of bricks cemented by rice flour, a substance so binding that later in the week I was to understand for the first time why so many characters in Chinese novels suffer from permanent constipation.

A signal made by fires of burning wolf dung could be flashed from tower to tower the hundred miles to Beijing in twelve minutes, although all it would say would be 'Cold. Bored. About to be overrun by Mongol hordes. Send help in three weeks to collect corpses.'

The wall itself was an astonishing sight for which no amount of photographs or reading could prepare you, and my heart lifted as much as those of the slaves and soldiers, widows and children, peasants and convicts who built it over a period of two thousand years must have sank as they looked at these same peaks and realised the task ahead of them. Particularly if they knew, as we do, that one of them would die for every yard of its thirty-five thousand miles.

On some sections, such as those built by the fastidious Lord Cai, each inch of the wall took a day to build. His lordship was later beheaded for such extravagance, although when his section was judged the finest part of the wall, he was posthumously rehabilitated, which must have been a great relief to him.

It was impossible to know where the ancient world ended and the modern one began here: in the afternoon, as we climbed down a valley of woods and terraced fields, we came upon an abandoned thatched cottage. Inside was all the detritus of a medieval lifestyle; a wood and wicker yoke, a ladder bound with rope, a wooden bucket. The family had moved a few miles down the valley and built a larger house which was guarded by twin gold and red dragons and an imperiously ruffled rooster.

In a dusty field beyond, two small donkeys with helicoptering ears chewed corn stalks, and a smattering of baffled cows discussed the weather. The family's Number One Son had just finished milking them, and was walking back to the house with two brimming wooden buckets swinging from a wooden yoke.

We downed our packs and slumped against a hedge for lunch, joined by Jason, who had set up the trek. Helicopter pilot turned expedition organiser, Jason was the sort of chap who would have been shooting down Messerschmitts over the Channel two generations ago.

'Been doing much recently, Jason?' I said as I shelled a boiled egg.

'Oh, not really. Just a dog sled race thirty miles north of the Arctic Circle in 35 below. The Norwegians said I'd take five days, if I finished at all.'

'And did you?'

'Absolutely. Two days and a bit. Fifteenth out of forty-four.'

'And the Norwegian teams?'

'Five dropped out. Three got lost.'

Splendid. So if you're ever organising a war, give me a ring and I'll just make sure Jason is on our side.

As the afternoon slid down towards evening, we climbed back down the rest of the mountain to our lodging for the night, to be met by a cadre of souvenir hawkers.

'Hey wa, you buy book, look, beautiful, this photo my brother, T-shirt, look, big size, postcard, look many photo, dragon carving very old, look handmade, necklace, look, for your wife, girlfriend, wa.'

'No, no, thank you very much.'

'No, please, thank you very much, look!'

In the room, the bed was harder than the Great Wall had

been. Below the window, a white box produced noise, but no heat.

In the dining room, which was marginally warmer, I found Linda, who looked like a smaller version of Björk.

'Here,' she said, as I sat down beside her with a plate of beef and noodles, 'how much is 15 yuan?'

I told her.

'Oh dear,' she said. 'I've just paid 15 quid for a postcard.'

I went to bed, and was reading through my *Guide to the Great Wall* when I came across the following disturbing sentence: 'Warning: the ancient path along the Wall to Simatal is only for the brave and fit.'

It wasn't joking: the next morning we rounded a corner and fell silent as we were confronted by an almost vertical climb of several hundred steps.

'Eek,' said Linda, who at a shade over 5ft, was about the same height as two steps.

'Boys and girls,' said Gillian the guide, 'welcome to the step class from hell.'

Kevin, a veteran of previous treks in the Sahara and Namibia, produced a hip flask of Jameson's.

'Alcoholics Unanimous,' he said. 'Fancy a nip?'

'Bit early for me, Smedley, old bean. I'll have a pink gin when the sun's past the yardarm,' I said.

'You'll be doing rightly if you find a yardarm around here,' he said, taking a handsome swig as we set off.

Half an hour of assorted screaming, fainting and heart attacks later, it was a weary bunch who slumped against the wall of the tower at the top.

By now it was lunchtime, and we were glad of it. You are glad of many small things when you are trekking that you do not appreciate in normal life. Like the way your water bottle gets lighter as the day goes on, or the way your daysack weighs less after you have taken your lunch out and eaten it. Of course, you are still carrying the same weight in your stomach, but it is literally a weight off your back.

And we were just about to need it: after crossing a giddy suspension bridge high above a wide green river, we faced a climb which made the step class from hell seem like a Debenham's escalator.

Several of the girls in the group collapsed halfway up and were relieved of their daysacks by some of the more gentlemanly chaps. After several hundred more steps, though, even the most gentlemanly among us were beginning to think it might have been easier to fling the bags over the cliff, particularly since some of them seemed to contain a year's supply of make-up and chocolate bars. It's amazing how quickly adversity can turn you from Gandhi to Goebbels.

Fortunately for the future of chivalry, at this stage we came to the cable car which swayed us, steaming and panting gently, down the mountain under a rising moon.

And after that, it was just a gentle dander through a wood by a lazy river to our five-star hotel, a hot shower and a feather bed.

Only joking. It was a campsite on a grassy plateau, Wet Wipes all round and a sleeping bag. Well, except for Jason, who faced a two-hour trek back up the mountain to retrieve a camera and passport that two of the group had managed to leave behind.

The rest of us sat outside our tents as the sun sank and the full moon rose high above the mountains, rubbing aching muscles and examining painful blisters. Except for the trekking veterans, who had taped up all their toes in advance.

At last, when all were clean and healed, there came from a rise above the campsite the sound of a beer can being popped and chicken sizzling on a barbeque. Fed and watered, we took to our beds and the campsite settled down for the night. The moon sailed on over the ragged peaks across which marched the silhouette of that most admirable and terrible of man's feats, the Great Wall of China.

We slept, silent in the arms of history. Until the entire campsite was awakened an hour later by John returning from the beer tent singing at the top of his voice, 'I wish I was back home in Derry'. A sentiment which, at just that moment, we all profoundly shared with him.

In the morning, the sun rose beyond the mountains to reveal a scene of almost unworldly beauty. And Noel Thompson shaving.

'Noel, you don't need to shave for a radio documentary,' I said.

'One must look one's best for a waiting nation,' he replied splendidly, as from all around came the sounds of the waiting nation waking.

'Bloody hell, I've never been so cold in all my life! Did you sleep?'

'Not a wink. God, it's FREEZING!'

Indeed, they were not far wrong. I had forgotten that unique trekking feeling of washing in sub-zero temperatures with a frozen Wet Wipe, dressing in clothes which crackled with the cold and staggering with hands deep in pockets. I was more grateful than I thought possible for a hot breakfast of that traditional Chinese delicacy, fried egg butties and beef noodles washed down with warm peach juice. Believe me, if you'd been as cold as we were, you would have wolfed down warm cardboard and asked for more.

There were other small pleasures, too, in the frozen dawn, like the heat of the sun on your face as it clears the mountains. Pleasures we forget, in our centrally-heated and double-glazed world.

And out of adversity comes great reward, like climbing late that morning with Elaine, who had struggled with fatigue and vertigo the day before, and who today had climbed an almost vertical cliff face with a pack on her back.

'You know,' she said, 'I lost my mother and father when I was three and six, and I've never had anyone to help me or guide me. When Gillian held my hand for the last hundred yards, it meant more to me than anything that's ever happened in my life.'

She was crying, and it was all I could do not to burst into

tears myself. At the end of the trek, Elaine would say to me in the hotel in Beijing, 'That was the best week of my life. It was worth being born for.'

We stopped for a lunch of cheese and lettuce sandwiches, which had been made by the intriguing method of placing the cheese at one end of the bread and the lettuce at the other, then set off for the scariest bit: the last climb up a crumbling wall to the highest tower of all, walking along a ledge a foot wide with the valley floor several thousand feet straight down. The guardians of this lofty eyrie, as they looked down upon the four horizons of their vast land, must truly have felt the mandate of heaven upon them.

In the afternoon we made our way slowly down the terraced slopes of the valley, past a goatherd calling, 'Wo ka ka ka ka' to his flock.

'What does "Wo ka ka ka ka" mean?' I asked Nikita, the translator.

'It means "Wo ka ka ka ka",' she said sweetly.

Silence fell. Through the dry grass, our boots made silvery whispers, like secret cocktail-party conversations, as we approached the village where we were to spend the night. When Jason came here two years ago, hiking in over the mountains, the village children screamed and ran away, because he was the first Westerner they had ever seen. Today, the strange foreigners are almost normal, and trekkers raise much of the £30 a year it costs to send these children to school. It means so much to them that one girl stays during the week, sleeping in the classroom, and others walk four hours a day to school and back.

Some of them were coming towards us now, skipping and hopping along the dusty path. And although the land was as dry as a priest, they were as bright as Christmas decorations as they passed us, practising their English with a blossoming of bright hallos.

We camped in the village playground and ate goat and noodles under a full moon, while in the classroom behind us, her books under her pillow, slept the little girl who had been given the most precious gift of learning.

It rained in the night, bringing forth from the woods beyond the village the tender scents of jasmine and pine, myrtle and apple blossom. And bringing forth the children, who had walked down the long mountain trails in daisy chains of two or four for the start of their school day.

At ten to eight, as they pottered about their desks putting out their books and pencils, the words of the 'Ode to Chairman Mao' crackled forth from the loudspeakers above No. 2 Classroom.

> He is the sun that rises in the east. And brings light to
> all the land.
> He is the father of us all. And we will love him forever.

'Of course,' said the translator with a nervous smile, 'we do not necessarily believe this any more.'

Then, with a whistle from the headmaster, the children ran out for morning assembly in the playground where, to the breezy air of the national anthem, they saluted the raising of the national flag. At the top of the pole it fluttered gamely, a symbol of a land which is no longer quite communist, but not yet quite capitalist.

Of course, to a child with the mountains all around, the sun rising and the day of their lives just beginning, all that does not matter, and as they trotted and skipped back to their classrooms, laughing and smiling, several of us were close to sniffling as we remembered for a moment what it was like to be alive when the world was brand new every day.

Not me, of course. I'm a tough bloke. Hanky, anyone?

With a last wave, we shouldered our packs and set off reluctantly into adulthood. Even grown up, though, it was a fine thing to step out into the day, strolling between the river and the trees in the warming sun.

Someone among us was whistling the theme tune to *The Great Escape*, and that was exactly what days like this were: a great escape from mortgages and bills, dry rot, rising damp and all the other shoddy cares with which we drag ourselves down from the peaks of youthful ambition.

Ahead of me. Mark was telling Janet that his father taught physiology at East Antrim Institute.

'Here, I think he teaches me,' said Janet. 'What do you call him?'

'Dad,' said Mark.

Just then there came a soft puttering up ahead, and around the corner rode a farmer on an ancient Chang Jiang 750, four baffled chickens in one of his panniers and two white ducks sniffing the air from the other.

Half a mile further on, a dozen other ducks were splashing about in the river, saying to each other, 'Here, isn't it exciting that Hei-San and Li-Jing got a ride on a motorcycle! What time do you think the farmer will bring them back from the market?'

I tiptoed past, looking the other way and humming pointedly to myself.

Compared to the rigorous climbs of the day before, today was a bit of a dander, through little villages where at the sight of us geese stopped splashing, hens paused in mid-cluck, dogs barked up all the wrong trees and the entire population of seven came out to see what the fuss was about. As you would if twenty Chinese people arrived in your village.

At one house, the seventy-five-year-old grandmother invited all of us into the courtyard so she could admire the whiteness of our skin, tell us that our breasts were enormous, especially the women's, and introduce us to her grand-daughters, who were feeding their respective babies from rice bowls.

As we left, Bridget gave the grandmother a bar of expensively luxurious chocolate.

'No, please,' said the old woman, handing it back. 'You are walking all day and you are far from home, so you need it more.'

An hour before dusk we arrived at our lodgings for the night, only to find every shower freezing, so that everyone stomped around in a bad mood for an hour until we were greeted by the sight of Noel Thompson, that most respected representative of Her Majesty's British Broadcasting Corporation, appearing freshly groomed and anointed with expensive unguents.

'Good heavens,' he said, 'the water in my room was so hot it was almost steam.'

He was immediately set upon and lovingly beaten to death with many chopsticks.

The next morning, after much gurgling and wheezing, the reluctant pipes were finally coaxed into giving up their burden of hot water, and we set off, washed and dried, only for the heavens to empty as we made our way down the mountain for the last time.

With the downpour worsening and the temperature plummeting, it was like a summer's day in Donegal as we wound our way down through the little villages of thatched cottages. Hewn out of the same stone as the mountains all around, they seemed to have grown organically out of their surroundings. It seemed as if man and nature, past and present, had melded into one seamless whole.

I mentioned this to Dr Paul, one of the trek medics, and the conversation got on to future trips. He had taken six months off work and was off to Malawi and Cape Town after this, and I was trying to find a sponsor for riding a vintage motorbike from Siberia back to Belfast. And that was how we crossed the line under a dripping Mencap banner in pouring rain, talking of the great adventure that life should be.

In Beijing the next day, the cherry blossoms were blooming in the steel and glass canyons of the new city. I left it behind almost immediately, hiring a rickshaw and plunging into the heart of the old town, where barbers' poles spun, chickens sat in cages awaiting a spicy fate and toothless herbalists sold snake gall-bladder.

On the pavements, repairmen attended to punctures or broken chains on some of the 50 million bicycles which throng the city. There, over the past decade, they have been joined by what seems like the same number of cars, whose surly nouveau riche drivers rush everywhere slowly with their hands on the horn, going nowhere fast except to a heart attack. In the back of limos here and there, through tinted glass, can be glimpsed that newest and most unwelcome arrival in China, the fat person.

Suddenly my thoughts were interrupted as the rickshaw plunged from an alley out into the bright sunlight of one of the boulevards Mao had built during the Cultural Revolution, tearing down ancient and revered buildings with the callous disregard that every dynasty in China has shown for its predecessors.

The lights at the crossing were green for us, but it was of no consequence to the phalanx of advancing cars. We hurtled across them in a cacophony of brakes, pleas, accusations and horns, somehow emerging alive on the other side with several other rickshaw drivers, whose drivers all took to slapping each other on the backs at their good fortune.

I realised that I was near the old silk market, so I paid the driver, stepped out and fell immediately into a medieval world of bartering, haggling and hawking which, apart from the fake North Face jackets, Gucci bags, Rolex watches and Levi jeans, has not changed in six centuries. Ten minutes of polite exchanges with a toothless grandmother produced an exquisite silk Mandarin jacket for Cate. A short walk to the Friendship Store nearby then produced an even more exquisite one.

I could do nothing but buy it too, this time by a Byzantine process which involved choosing the jacket, taking the chit to a cashier behind a Dickensian desk, paying the required amount, then returning with another chit to the salesman, who by this stage had wrapped the purchase beautifully in several layers of crêpe paper.

The entry price for the Forbidden City has gone from instant death to a more reasonable 30 yuan. Unfortunately, I had given the last of my money to the rickshaw driver and a beggar, and was left to gaze up at the bejewelled gates with as little hope of gaining admission as the peasants who stood here for five centuries and wondered at the fabulous life their emperors lived inside.

Instead I set off to walk around the moated walls of the Forbidden City, which took me almost an hour and brought me to Tiananmen Square, best known for the massacre of 1989, an event conveniently forgotten by western democracies in their undignified stampede to get into the country and make several billion fast bucks.

As I retraced my steps back to the hotel to pack for the flight home, the late afternoon sun was playing through the cherry blossoms and dancing in flakes of gold on the water. I closed my eyes and listened for one last time to the sounds of old Beijing: the splish and splash of lazy oars, the rickshaw drivers calling to all and sundry to clear the way, the click of mah-jong counters, the tinkle of bicycle bells calling the city back to yesterday and the honk of car horns calling it forward to a more urgent future.

When I opened them, a small girl with a lilac bow in her hair was standing in front of me.

'Please,' she said, 'I am an artist at Beijing University and we are having our exhibition. I would be very honoured if you would visit us.'

Half an hour later, I walked back to the hotel and left for the airport, in my knapsack a carefully wrapped scroll bearing in scarlet ink on handmade indigo rice paper three Mandarin symbols. Above was the one for family, below was the one for friends, and in the centre was the one for the heart that binds them close. Together, they made up the single word for love.

2002

Greece

In AD 95 the Roman emperor Domitian banished John the Evangelist to the lonely island of Patmos.

'Don't worry,' said John's friends as he set sail armed with a pen, a notebook and his pet frog Fred, 'it's not the end of the world.'

'Huh,' said John, 'that's what you think.'

Arriving on Patmos, the bearded one climbed a mountain, found a cave and, as an act of revenge, penned a scenario in which the Romans and all the other non-believers got their comeuppance on the Day of Judgement. Like the work of that other visionary loon, St Paul, the Book of Revelation has inspired those from the more lunatic fringes of Christian fundamentalism ever since.

John's legacy lives on today as far afield as the militarists of rural America, holed up in the hills with their shotguns and survival manuals, and is preserved closer to its spiritual home by the Greek Orthodox Church, whose latest paranoid pronouncement is that bar codes are the mark of the Beast and part of a Jewish-Masonic conspiracy in fulfillment of Revelation.

However, in St John's cave on the day we arrived, things were a little quieter. An elderly monk was busily polishing the icons with a bottle of Zak and dusting the silver frame of the hollow where the saint laid his head between doom-laden scribblings.

Up the hill in the monastery built in 1088 by the scholar-cleric Khristodhoulos, between a remarkable medieval chapel and a museum holding an even more remarkable fifth-century Gospel of St Mark, sat another monk, the silvery tip of his beard swaying in time with the prayer beads swinging from his fingers. At his feet, a black kitten idly played with the beads, and from the chapel came the song of voices raised in prayer.

We had dinner that night at a little fish restaurant down by the harbour, and as the full moon rose over the bay, wondered out loud that it had only been five days since we arrived at Rhodes Airport where, due to the fact that the baggage handlers had gone home, we were left with two hours to ponder some of the great mysteries of travel.

We finally collected our bags and set off through the streets. All around us were the archetypal sights of Greek life: gnarled fishermen chatted on their mobile phones, yuppie couples drank designer beer from designer bottles and, in spite of the late hour, the traditional island shops such as Marks & Spencer and Harley-Davidson were still open plying their simple wares.

It seemed, now that I thought about it, that Greece had changed a bit since the days when you arrived on the ferry from Piraeus to be engulfed in a Stygian tsunami of matrons, each offering identical rooms containing one chair, one bed and a loo into which you deposited the toilet paper on pain of death.

As a result of all this activity, the Greeks now have more mobile phones per capita than anyone else in Europe, and have dropped from first to fourth worldwide in frequency of sex. Americans are first, since you ask.

However, we still lead the world in drinking, so when we finally arrived at *Anna*, the handsome little motor cruiser which would be our home for the next week, to be greeted by Captain Nicos with an offer of beer, wine or ouzo, we took him up on all three.

The next day, a walk through the old town, with shops selling everything from Rolex watches to Harry Potter beach towels, confirmed our suspicions that Greece had changed.

Heaven knows what the Knights of St John would have thought of it. That merry band of medieval troubadours, having foolishly sworn themselves to chastity and poverty, ended up so bored as a result that they built a fleet and went off sailing around the Med.

Today, all that remains of their courtly, clanking presence in Rhodes is the cobbled Street of the Knights, in which they lived in the Inns of England, France, Auvergne, Provence, Italy, Spain and Germany.

The ground floors, where they stabled their horses, now house sleepy civil servants, who chew their pens, make occasional and languid phone calls with urgent requests for work which will never be done in this heat, and gaze out of the window, dreaming of a more noble calling.

We returned to the *Anna* to find that the other fourteen passengers had arrived, and that every single one of them was German. Apart from the Dutch couple, and possibly us.

Now, I speak German and can get by in Dutch, but a week of starting sentences on a Monday and finally arriving at the verb by Thursday was not my idea of a wild time. Strangely, though, after several glasses of wine that evening, not only did my German improve, but everyone else's English got better.

But not their stomachs, it seemed: at five the next morning, before we had even left the harbour, two of them woke Iolanda, the affable cruise leader, and demanded their money back because they were seasick. She resisted the temptation to throw them overboard, and they were still there that afternoon when we docked at Mandhraki, the little port of Nissyros.

On the wall of the sole hotel, a sign boasted of showers and ice cubes, although not simultaneously. Just down the road was a monastery designed personally by the Virgin Mary, who had apparently appeared to the builder with her ideas in a vision.

Apart from showers and ice cubes, the main tourist attraction on the island is the volcano, which last erupted in 1933, but which still hisses and gurgles spouts of menacing steam into the sulphuric air. Local legend has it that these are caused by volcanic activity, but of course the truth is that they are the groans of Polyvotis, a titan crushed here under a huge rock by Poseidon.

The next day, in Kos, we found the seven-hundred-year-old plane tree which is allegedly the great-grandson of the one under which Hippocrates invented medicine in the fourth century BC. Before that, people didn't know what they died of.

Today, of course, doctors still honour his memory when they

sign the Hypocritical Oath, promising to eat, drink and smoke more than their patients.

That evening, an ice-cream sunset ended the day, as swifts dipped across the still bay, their shadows tangling up the fishing boats in wakes of dreams.

'Groovy chickens,' said Cate. 'Fancy a beer?'

We had dinner under a lemon tree, as at our feet a puppy played catch with its tail.

The next day, lunch was a massive barbecue of some Teutonic jollity, set to Bavarian rap music and Hamburg country and western. Afterwards, all the Germans went swimming and sank immediately to the bottom.

'Don't worry, I will catch them,' said Nicos, the splendidly bonkers captain, heading aft with his fishing rod.

All safely gathered in, we weighed anchor an hour later and set off again across the briny depths – although some are not so briny, since we were passing directly over one of the mysterious freshwater channels of the oceans, which whales use for transmitting messages hundreds of miles.

By dusk we were on Kalymnos, once famous for its sponge divers, who set out in eighty boats every spring and returned with their booty in September. Today, many of them are dead or crippled by the bends, and many of the sponges have been killed by a viral disease, so the sponges in the island shops are mainly Egyptian and Libyan. The island's sponge museum was closed for a holy day, so instead we went for a spongecake and *kaitifi*, a delicious pastry that looks like Dougal from *The Magic Roundabout* doused with honey.

As we walked back towards the boat with our German shipmates, you could see, in the faces of the older men who sat on benches, their walking sticks a legacy of the bends or the war, a palpable bristling at our voices. It was little wonder: during the winter of 1941–2, the German army requisitioned all the food in Greece, and half a million Greeks starved to death. Over one hundred and fifty thousand were shot to discourage resistance. You could see anger in the faces of the old men, and a lingering sadness, too, that while their former invaders wandered around with Nikons and Sonys, they were left with a walking stick, a park bench and a glass of ouzo to kill the empty night.

And yet, in the midst of all the darkness that was the war, there was one small story that shone like a candle. I had heard it before, and remembered it as we stood at the top of the hill in the town of Symi, on the island of the same name. It was here, in December 1944, that the retreating Germans decided to pile all their munitions in the beautiful old Church of the Ascension of the Virgin and blow it up. Unfortunately, they decided not to tell the hundreds of townspeople who lived around the church.

Enter, then, Rudi, a tall, blond Bavarian. As he and his comrades toiled up the hill with boxes for four days in the hot sun, Rudi would stop islanders and say to them, 'Hey, Symiot, when is the celebration of the ascension of the Virgin?'

'Why, 15 August, of course.'

'Wrong. Quite wrong.'

Finally, on the fourth day, when the whole town was talking about Rudi's mystery, anyone who passed him was told, 'Tonight, at eight, the Virgin will ascend.'

All that afternoon, as quietly as mice, the people of Symi moved themselves out: the young ones on foot, carrying what valuables they could, the old ones on piggyback, the babies in baskets, the birds in cages and the cats that had not been eaten padding along behind.

At just after eight, the Virgin did indeed ascend with an earth-shattering roar, taking with it only an eighty-year-old woman named Maria who had refused to move.

The next day, the Germans left on a boat. It sank an hour later, hit by a torpedo or a mine. Of the four hundred on board, only seventeen survived, and Rudi was not one of them.

I looked out for a long time that afternoon at the azure waves beneath which his bones still lie, then went for a walk along the harbourfront at Symi.

In a little bar, Rudi will be pleased to know, Germany were playing in the semi-final of the World Cup, watched by his countrymen and the natives of the little town he saved, sitting side by side at last.

2002

Guyana

Guyana is like the Wild West designed by the Dutch, organised by the British and governed on the same basis as Northern Ireland.

The first because, until 1796, it was a colony of the Netherlands, which built many of the fine wooden buildings which grace the capital, Georgetown. The second because the British, who took over from the Dutch, brought such civilising values as cricket, speaking English, driving on the left and, oh yes, the abolition of slavery. And the third because the country's first reaction to independence in the sixties was to split into two factions, which run the country as an edgy democracy until elections, after which the winners celebrate and the losers riot.

It is not the wonders of Georgetown that anyone comes to Guyana to see though, but the wonders of the interior such as Kaietur Falls, at 741ft the highest single-drop waterfall in the world, to which I flew the next day in a small aircraft.

I was staying at Baganara. This, a luxurious neo-colonial pile on a river island, is an understandable favourite of several celebrities, including Mick Jagger, whose photograph adorns one of the walls.

An hour after I arrived, I had swum, showered and was ensconced in a hammock with a cold beer, watching the sun go down over the trees on the far riverbank. And an hour after that, I was sitting down to a silver-service dinner at a table on the beach.

The next morning, I went walking through the forest, which held such delights as the Arara tree, whose toxic covering is used as an antidote to snake poison. Its bark is worse than a bite, you could say if you were inclined towards dreadful puns. It seemed, in fact, as if every other tree the guide stopped at was a source of food, medicine, poison, musical instruments, weapons, luggage, furniture and building materials. It wasn't so much a collection of trees as a branch of John Lewis – albeit a branch populated by thumb-sized insects, bird-sized butterflies and a tasteful ceiling display of tarantula webs, glistening above our heads like a hammock of horror.

About two miles down the river from the resort is a camp which the British army uses for training. As I sat down to lunch, I couldn't help but think that this was more the sort of tough jungle adventure I preferred: struggling to survive on Banks beer and three meals a day.

In fact, everything was going just about perfectly until Björn sat down opposite me at dinner. I should have suspected the worst when he told me he was a Swedish engineer who lived in Singapore and specialised in deep-bore drilling.

It was a talent he carried through to his private life, as for the next two hours his penetrating voice drilled into my head everything I had ever wanted to know about the courtship rituals of the white-crowned manakin, but had not known who to ask.

Finally, he yawned loudly, having wearied even himself, and picked up his dog-eared copy of Hilty's *Birds of Venezuela*.

'Well, must be off to bed. You have to get up at dawn to catch the really interesting birds, you know,' he said, wandering off into the night.

I looked at my watch. I could have sworn that several years had gone by, but it was only nine o'clock. I ordered another rum, and very carefully destroyed all the brain cells containing any information whatsoever on the white-crowned manakin.

The next morning, I wandered down to the pier to catch the boat to Bartica, only to see as it drew in the dread sight of Björn trotting up, a state-of-the-art telescope draped around his neck and his copy of Hilty tucked under his arm. I stood aside politely to let him board first, then sat as far away as possible, lest he suck the will to live out of me like a sort of emotional black hole.

At Bartica, I breathed a sigh of relief as he stepped ashore and disappeared into the jungle. I headed in the opposite direction, down the village's only thoroughfares, loftily named First and Second Avenue, lined with bars filled with lumberjacks and gold miners happily spending their pay.

It was only mid morning, but the temperature was nearly 40°C. I waited for the next boat downriver in the shade of a dockside bar, surrounded by locals drinking rum and watching a Pakistan vs India cricket match. It was like being an extra in a Bacardi advertisement rewritten by Graham Greene.

Inevitably, as the boat appeared, so did Björn, looking pleased with himself at a sighting of the lesser bowlegged sandpiper or somesuch.

'You should sit over this side. Better view,' he shouted above the roar of the diesel, patting the seat by his side. I mimed a cheery deafness, and sat several yards away.

An hour later, the boat pulled in at a little wooden jetty, and I saw with relief the car waiting to take me to the Cara Lodge Hotel in Georgetown. I slipped gratefully into its air-conditioned chill, only to look around and see, to my horror, Björn jumping in beside me.

'You know,' he said, resetting his chronometer, 'that journey took exactly fifty-nine minutes and thirteen seconds. You don't mind if I share your lift, do you?'

Thankfully, for the entire journey he talked to the driver, Belinda, about the lack of litter and chewing gum in Singapore. I watched her carefully in case she nodded off and killed us all, until suddenly a dreadful thought struck me.

'Björn,' I said as casually as I could, 'what, er, hotel are you staying at in Georgetown?'

'The New Tropicana. Look, there it is. My wife thinks I'm crazy to stay at cheap places, but to me, a bed is just a bed,' he said.

I breathed a short prayer of thanks to God, Allah, Buddha and the Seven Sainted Sisters of Constantinople as he got out, informed me in passing that the car journey had taken 1 hour, 10 minutes and 28 seconds, and strode into the foyer in search of fresh victims.

At the Cara Lodge, I had the blissful experience of dinner on my own, several beers and no information whatsoever on the mating habits of any birds anywhere in the universe, and the next morning I left for the interior: an eight-hour drive down a dirt road, through blizzards of suicidal white butterflies who whirled towards the windscreen like snowflakes.

Our destination was Iwokrama, a wildlife research station deep in the jungle at which we were met by the splendidly named resident biologist Waldyke Prince. His assistant was called Edghill.

'My mother actually called me Adrian, but the priest who baptised me was deaf,' he said by way of explanation.

'Anyway, you're just in time for a refreshing stroll up the mountain,' said Waldyke cheerily. I dumped my bag in a log cabin, sprayed myself all over with insect repellent and followed him into the jungle.

Almost immediately, the sunlight disappeared. Far above our heads, vampire bats slept, awaiting the destiny of the night. In front of me, Waldyke waved a stick to stop us accidentally logging on to a tarantulas's website.

'Careful of that bullet ant,' he said, pointing to an inch-long creature sitting on a branch. 'It's called that because that's the effect its sting has.'

An hour and a half later, we finally reached the top of the mountain to find a view of the following: an electrical storm raging over the Venezuelan mountains on the horizon; millions of trees; one river; and a reflection of me in the water bottle, weary and soaked with sweat. As experiences go, it was almost as good as the shower and beer when we got back, in increasing order of both coldness and satisfaction.

Dinner was served on a terrace by a shy Makushi teenager. As she padded to and fro with rice and chicken, bats flitted above her head, an emerald green insect crawled up the wall, and there came from the short-wave radio in the office the hiss and crackle of fractured signals from the distant, alien civilization of the modern world.

The next day, I found myself eating chicken soup in a native village, watched intently by a three-year-old called Michael.

'Are you going to the jungle?' he said.

'Yes, later.'

'Big, black snakes in the jungle.'

'Oh dear. How big?'

'This big,' he said, holding his finger and thumb as far apart as he could get them.

As I finished my soup, three donkeys appeared in the doorway, followed by Milner, the head man.

'Right,' he said brightly, 'time to walk to the camp. Only two hours.'

I sighed, shouldered my pack, assured Michael I would watch out for big, black snakes, and set off. Just before dark, tired and soaked in sweat, we arrived at a hut by a river and put up the hammocks and mosquito nets. Oh well, I thought, at least I can have a swim in the river to cool off.

'I wouldn't do that if I was you,' said Milner as I stripped to my shorts and trotted down the riverbank.

'Why not?'

'Piranhas.'

It grew dark. We ate chow mein and crept into our hammocks, surrounded by the sounds of creatures waking, going out for a refreshing stroll in the moonlight, and eating each other.

After five minutes, I realised I needed to go to the toilet. I reached down for my torch, something unidentifiable ran over my hand, and the torch rolled out of reach. Below the hammock, I could hear more unidentifiable things scurrying about. There was no way I was putting my feet out there without the torch. And a pair of Kevlar wellies. All night long, as I lay awake, the howler monkeys wailed with a sound like a banshee convention.

Next year, I thought as dawn broke over the jungle, I may well stay in the Ritz.

2004

Honeymoon

I have a confession to make: I have slept with a married woman. My only excuse is that I was far from home, and she was lovely. Oh, and she was my wife.

Anyway, the circumstances were made for romance: a turreted castle in the Slovenian mountains, a circular bed 10ft wide and a bottle of vintage champagne chilling on ice.

It was the first night of our honeymoon, and the setting of Castle Mokrice, a medieval pile on the Croatian border, could not have been more romantic. In fact, it was so perfect that we drove past it twice, thinking we could not possibly be staying there.

When we finally realised we were, they showed us up to a circular room in one of the turrets, so big that to go to the bathroom, you brought your passport and crossed two time zones. Not only that, but it came with a series of antechambers, in one of which was to be found a grand piano.

We drank some champagne, had that most delicious of adult feelings of dressing and going down to dinner in a grand hotel, and the next morning woke to sunlight and church bells through the open window.

Butterflies flitted between sunflowers and a fox loped across the road into a cornfield as we wandered aimlessly, stopping to potter by rivers and lift our faces to the sun. Above our heads, the birches whispered and the swifts were tossed to and fro by the dying breaths of the *borja*, a wind which every September gathers itself up in the Aegean, vents its rage on hapless sailors in the Adriatic, dries the washing of grateful Croatian housewives, crawls over the top of Mount Sneznik and finally falls exhausted on the rolling hills of southern Slovenia.

This, like much of the country, is a pocket paradise in which the view in any direction has all the elements of a children's fairy-tale illustration: the village, its gardens awash with flowers, the white church with its terracotta spire, the wooded mountain topped by the turreted castle. All you do is bring your own prince or princess.

In the lilac dusk, we found ourselves in the thirteenth-century church of Pleterje. Vespers bells rang in the cool Gothic spaces, and behind the monastery walls beyond, the monks flitted to and fro, lost to the sight of all but God. We bought a bottle of their plum brandy from a little shop nearby, and escaped to more secular pleasures.

And the next day, even more so, in the shape of two hours of pampering in the spa at the Hotel Terme. Honestly, it was all I could do to drag myself to the bar afterwards.

After such sloth, the least we could do the next day was to go for a hearty walking tour of Ljubljana, a capital so Ruritanian that old ladies still grow vegetables in the centre, and a kindergarten sits in the middle of the grand embassies of the diplomatic quarter.

It was hardly surprising, then, that when we arrived at Lake Bled the next day, we emerged from the toytown railway station to find the stationmaster tending his cabbages.

In a land of picture-postcard beauty, Bled is the ultimate snapshot: as if the surrounding forest and the castle on the clifftop were not enough, in the middle of the lake sits a wooded island topped by a white church. It is to this island that young Slovenian grooms row their brides, then carry them the ninety-nine steps up to the church, and either call for an ambulance or ring the bell three times and wish for a happy and successful life together.

Remarkably, being neither young nor Slovenian, I managed the ninety-nine steps in one go. Ah, there's life in the old knees yet, I thought, carrying Cate across the threshold of the Okarina, the nearest restaurant, to celebrate.

In fact, we celebrated so splendidly that at three the next morning we found ourselves with Leo, the owner and manager of the Villa Bled, plotting to blow up the Vatican. I was not a well man the next morning when we set out for the drive across the high mountain pass to Soca, built by ten thousand Russian prisoners during the First World War.

We arrived at our destination, an isolated farmhouse in a valley, as the moon rose over the mountains. Fortunately, it was surrounded by other isolated farmhouses and an isolated inn, and as we were sitting down to dinner at a rough table, I was approached by a tall man with a congenial air about him.

Naturally, he turned out to be William Blackley from Cookstown in County Tyrone, on a mountain hiking holiday with his mates from the patent office in Munich.

'I was living in Edinburgh, but I was getting too settled, so I moved to Munich and got too settled there instead,' he said by way of explanation.

Lost in the mountains, we passed the next few days in medieval pleasures: admiring horses, petting goats, improving our archery, eating roasted pigs and carousing.

Descending heavily at last to the sea for a spell, we wandered for a day around lovely old Piran, then caught the boat to Venice: glorious, doomed Venice, forever sinking under the weight of its own decadence while admiring itself all the while in an ornately carved mirror.

And after days of living like lords for pennies in Slovenia, we staggered from St Mark's Square, muttering in shock,

'Twenty-five euro for two coffees? 17 per cent commission at the bureau de change? Good grief!'

We took refuge in a walking tour, letting facts wash over us until we realised they were no longer facts, but raindrops. Drenched, we hid in the Piero Mauro, a little jewel of a corner bar, all mahogany and brass and mirrors, and spent the rest of the perfect afternoon there, steaming gently over hot chocolate and brandy. Outside, the thunderstorm sent Japanese tourists in fluorescent macs fluttering to and fro, like a species of tiny, endangered butterfly. We returned to our room at the Duodo Palace Hotel, a painstakingly restored hymn to opulence, and spent the early evening, before we went out to dinner, sitting on our balcony watching gondolas whisper to and fro.

The next morning, a varnished launch took us direct from the hotel to Santa Lucia station, where, high above the echoing concourse, the clickety-clack board was showing the most evocative of departures: Venice Simplon-Orient-Express, London via Paris.

I felt the same thrill as I had when, about three decades earlier, I had stood at London Victoria, an InterRail pass in hand, looking up at the departures board with my heart full of the infinite possibilities of life.

We boarded and were organising ourselves in our little compartment when Bruno, the steward, stuck his head around the door.

'Listen, the room next door is empty,' he said, opening the adjoining door and giving us a suite.

After a while we made our way along the train to a languid lunch. Which was followed at length by afternoon tea.

It was the most sybaritic of pleasures, even if being on the Orient Express leads you into the strangest of conversations.

'Sorry I took a while, dear. There were three of them, with knives.'

'Were you hurt, darling?'

'Good grief, no. Although the last one was obviously a black belt in dim sum trained by the great master Shi-Tsu.'

'Good heavens. Did you throw him off the train?'

'No, I'm saving that for after dinner.'

In between times, we read, or, wrapped up in a cocoon of luxury, simply gazed out of the window at the modern world flashing by, like a parallel universe to which we never wanted to return.

As darkness fell, we returned to our compartment and found Bruno lighting the wood-fired stove at the end of the carriage for heat and hot water.

And so, the honeymoon ended as it had begun: dressing up and going down to dinner with my wife, as beneath us, the tickety-tack of the rails sang to us with the rhythm of paradise on earth.

2004

Italy

500,000 years BC
Neanderthals arrive and swan around in designer mammoth furs with matching clubs, setting standards which have remained to this day.

736 BC
Greeks arrive, bearing vines and olive trees. Italians make wine and olive oil, then sit around scrubbed wooden tables waiting for pasta to be invented.

600 BC
Rome invented by Romulus, Remulus and a working party of wolves, starting an empire which will last almost a thousand years.

65 BC
Julius Caesar crosses the Rubicon and takes the city, only to be murdered by Brutus. Mark Antony takes over, gets distracted by Cleopatra, loses battle of Actium and commits suicide, to be followed by Caligula, Claudius and Nero, best known for his hobby of persecuting Christians.

3rd century AD
Christianity gets its own back by being named state religion.

455
Roman Empire ends, ushering in centuries of assorted popes and emperors.

1401
Filippo Brunelleschi invents perspective, allowing people to walk to the end of the street for the first time, and ushering in the Renaissance, in which all the geniuses in the world seem to live in one block.

1886
Italy decides to become an empire again by invading Abyssinia and Eritrea.

1886, half an hour later
Campaign's a disaster. Italians give up war.

1939
Mussolini persuades Italians to have another go, helping Hitler to take over the world.

1945
War ends in disaster. Italians string Mussolini and mistress upside down from petrol station in Milan, then give up war for ever and go back to designing cars, motorbikes, clothes and furniture, in between sitting around scrubbed wooden tables laughing and drinking in pasta advertisements.

Rome and Florence

The mist was draped seductively over the hills, the rising sun caressing the slopes and sliding towards the dark woods below. As the plane sank towards Rome, it was easy to see why

Italy was a country where art is love, and love an art.

And talking is a performance.

It is impossible to speak Italian with your hands in your pockets, and waiting at Rome airport for a transfer to Florence, it became obvious why: although Italy stretches from the frozen Alps in the north to shimmering Sicily in the south, the population is about the same as the UK. That's because everyone is waving their arms around so much that there's no room for any more people.

The Italians are also indelibly stylish. It is quite normal, I hear, for families to leave ugly or badly dressed relatives out in the heat to die in the same way as the Eskimos leave the elderly out in the cold.

Alternatively, they can just leave them in the street to be run over. For anyone who says that Italian drivers are a bit mad is a liar. They are, in fact, raving.

Simultaneously engaged in a stormy marriage with the throttle pedal and a passionate affair with the brake, Italian drivers view pedestrians with the same sort of hungry scorn that lions view three-legged wildebeest. Hardly worth the effort, but may as well kill them anyway.

A foot sticking over the edge of the kerb? Fair game, *grazie*. A spot of lane discipline, old chap? Not today, *signore*. One hand on the wheel and an air of languid machismo? *Si, si*, that'll do nicely.

After fifteen minutes of a car chase which involved only our taxi, we screeched to a halt, paid the driver and, trembling slightly, went into the Grand Hotel Baglioni, a magnificent pile with buttery ochre walls, ancient oak doors, arched vistas, a rooftop restaurant with a view of the famous Duomo, and a stiff drink in the bar. The latter was the most welcome.

My room had a bathroom with ancient brass fittings, a toilet flush which was like a bell push set into the wall, and a huge, soft bed. I checked it for taxi drivers and, finding none, decided it was safe to go to sleep.

The next morning, lightning rent the sky and thunder rattled the terracotta roof tiles. Splashing through the narrow streets towards the Duomo, it was easy to see why when Stendhal first came to Italy at the start of the nineteenth century, he staggered around Florence in a perpetual stupor of delight, fainting regularly and having to be revived with copious draughts of the local brandy.

The art, the culture, the intense, almost spiritual devotion to beauty. And that was only the shoe shops.

When you finally stand in front of the Duomo, the shock of its brightly patterned marble exterior is so arousing that you feel you will have to go home and confess to your wife that you have become a duomosexual.

The interior is as plain as the outside is extravagant, which helps calm you down enough for the delicious experience of wandering through the streets in the torrential rain, sniffing air redolent with the nutty aroma of coffee curving out from cafés here and there. And then arriving at the green river and walking along, deliberately not looking back at the Ponte Vecchio until you cannot resist any longer the temptation to turn and drink in the view.

Objectively, the Ponte Vecchio is just an ancient bridge holding up a collection of patchy ochre, dun, orange, terracotta and duck-egg blue jewellery shops which have been there since 1593. But subjectively, like everything else in Italy, it fills you with the joy which comes from having each of your senses filled to the brim first thing in the morning then topped up all day.

Who knows what causes it? The light on the crumbling paint, the statues everywhere. The food, the clothes, the happy, relaxed marriage which Italians have had with beauty for three thousand years.

Not the rain, which in 1966 fell for forty days and nights and flooded the city – some believe in divine retribution for letting England win the World Cup – and which by now had become so heavy that we jumped on a bus up the mountain in a vain attempt to get above the clouds.

On board, by a complete piece of serendipity, Paul, one of the group, met Susan, a friend from Dublin who was in Florence studying history. Although she had only been in Italy for ten days, she had already acquired a patina of ancient romance, wearing a great black rain-pearled cloak wrapped around a *quattrocento* air of noble frailty.

She took us to the Ristorante Mario in the piazza at Fiesole, where we had salami, crostini, panini, ravioli and fettucini washed down with chianti until we were completely stuffini.

Outside, the sky was slowly clearing, and the drying, opalescent light dripped through the window on to a wooden trolley whose wheels were hooded in curved chrome, sitting on an ancient tiled floor. Beauty, everywhere you looked.

Up the hill, the Monastery of San Francesco offers a stunning view, in colours which seem to reach out and embrace you, of the basin in which Florence sits. It is a view which has changed little since the sixteenth century, seen daily by the monks, still padding about in brown habits and sandals, who have changed little since the sixteenth century either.

Even older is the three thousand-seat Roman amphitheatre and baths just around the corner, which have apparently been around since Roman times. They come complete with vomit-orium, the stone trough in which hedonistic guzzlers deposited the contents of their stomachs before returning to the feast.

Still, at least they enjoyed themselves, which is more than could be said for John, one of the group who had spent the morning moaning to the tour operators because they had given him a free diary halfway through February, because the flight had been too long, because the hotel hadn't had rashers for breakfast, and because it was raining.

'You wouldn't have a spare tie, would you?' he said after we had returned to a city washed clean by rain, under a sky the colour of shotguns and buttermilk. 'Apparently we need one for the bloody restaurant tonight.'

I dug out my favourite tie and handed it over.

'It's a bit loud, isn't it? Doesn't really go with my jacket,' he said.

'Here, take this one, then,' I said, giving him the one I was wearing.

'I hope they don't give us too much for dinner. I'm stuffed enough as it is,' he said, knotting it begrudgingly around his neck.

Before I could offer to help him tighten it, the woman standing beside us suddenly noticed that she had torn her tights. Luckily, I had a spare fan belt with me.

Sitting before dinner with Alessandro, the manager of the Plaza Hotel Lucchese, it was easy to see why almost every woman in the world wants to sleep with Italian men, although not necessarily to marry them.

Alessandro was wearing an olive linen suit, a powder blue cotton shirt and a silk ochre and burgundy tie, and was so genuinely warm, contented and stylish that although I am profoundly heterosexual, it was all I could do not to go over and snuggle up to him.

If you are the sort of person who loves dressing up and making a special occasion out of life, for heaven's sake come to Italy. You can drape your cashmere coat over your shoulders, adjust your fedora to a suitably rakish angle and feel perfectly at home, since everyone else will be doing much the same thing – except with such a genuine love of life that they make the equally stylish French seem frigid and stuffy by comparison.

You may mock the Italians for wearing fur coats and fedoras on a wet Tuesday morning, or claim that their army is more interested in the design of their uniforms than their guns, but more power to them, I say. Their dressing up has all the happy, guileless innocence of childhood, and if every army paid more attention to suiting than shooting, we'd all be a lot better off, hurrah.

That night, possibly as a result of several grappas at the Plaza Lucchese, I dreamt that I went to see Michelangelo's *David* in the nearby Galleria dell'Accademia, but when I woke up I was still in bed, and when I went to see the real thing I discovered that it was half-term holiday and half the schoolchildren in Italy were standing in the queue for the Galleria.

The other half were standing in the queue for the Uffizi, thus denying me the chance to see Italy's finest collection of paintings by Botticelli, Leonardo da Vinci, Michelango, Titian and Piero, who lived in a house that was never cleaned, kept a garden that was never tended and ate nothing but hard-boiled eggs.

There was nothing for it but to take the train to Rome through countryside so seductively curved and lit that if it was a woman you would want to marry it and have its children, never mind the pain.

At Rome station, the taxi driver raced off as usual, then screeched to a halt in the middle of a busy intersection, leaped out and, ignoring hoots and gesticulations on all sides, helped a bus reverse around the corner.

'I was a bus driver myself for ten years,' he said by way of explanation as we sped away through streets with cars squeezed into spaces so small that the people inside could not get out, and were reduced to gesticulating wildly at each other.

Parking is such a problem in Rome that the inhabitants have taken to driving around in smaller and smaller cars like the Fiat Bambino, a wonderful little car so utterly Italian that it would look perfect painted in patchy ochre with laurel-green wooden shutters.

Or in new city cars with a single seat.

Or, best of all, in the ubiquitous Vespa scooters, which even in the early hours of the morning can be heard buzzing everywhere like a storm of angry bees. They are, naturally, ridden without helmets, since that would ruin one's hair.

Hordes of Japanese tourists were taking photographs of each other outside the designer shops before whipping out their trembling credit cards and diving in en masse, emerging several hours later laden with bags.

The reason why most of Europe is filled with Japanese

tourists is very simple. It is because Japan is so overcrowded that there isn't room for everyone to be there all at once, so the government has set up a system where at any given time half the population is touring around Europe.

At least the fact that they were in Gucci, Versace *et al* meant that the Vatican was empty. To get into this monumental tribute to man's sense of his own importance, you have to pass through airport-style scanners which remove all traces of Protestantism, before being frisked by armed nuns for Orange sashes, King Billy campaign medals and up-to-date Democratic Unionist Party membership cards.

Inside, the scale of St Peter's is almost as stunning as a souvenir shop where the Italians' normally impeccable sense of style has momentarily deserted them. Here, you can buy everything from 3ft-high plastic virgins to holograms which turn from Jesus to Mary and back again.

From far above, if you listen, you can hear God weeping quietly.

Much better to be at the Trevi Fountain, where Anita Ekberg cooled off in *La Dolce Vita*. Like everything else in Rome, it is better than even the most gadabout optimist could imagine.

Well, almost everything. Later that night we found ourselves at the Fantasie Theatre, where on stage several chaps in drag and women in authentic polycotton peasant costumes were singing Italian marching opera folk pop songs to an audience which consisted entirely, apart from our table, of Japanese people politely chewing salami.

It was so surreal that the only answer was to drink several glasses of wine very quickly and slide under the table as all around members of one of the most ancient, civilized nations in Asia, who had abandoned their spiritual inheritance for a pair of Gucci loafers and a Burberry scarf, watched as members of one of the most ancient, civilized nations in Europe, who had abandoned their cultural inheritance for a pair of yellow stockings and brown velvet knickerbockers, belted out 'O Sole Mio' into a Sony microphone.

Still, the best thing about it was that it wasn't really Rome. Rome is walking around a corner in the cobbled moonlight to be stunned to your bones by two things. The sight of the cool silvery water in the Trevi Fountain splashing on the marble below the warm lamplight on the terracotta and ochre buildings around the square. And the realisation that you are about to be mown down by the phalanx of Vespas which has just appeared around the corner.

1996

The Amalfi Coast

In England, graffiti invariably refers to the lonely nocturnal proclivities of Jones minor, the strongly held belief that carefully selected football teams are more deserving of honour than others, or the dimensions, in imperial measure, of even more carefully selected regions of both the male and female anatomy.

But the flamboyant white text on the side of the tumbledown farmhouse on the road south from the airport had none of that.

'*Ti amo, Mozart,*' it simply said. 'I love you, Mozart.'

It could only have been Italy.

In Salzburg, the composer's birthplace, such an untidy proclamation of affection would have been met with thinly pursed lips and a wire brush.

But in Italy, there is only one thing more important than love, and that is the love of love. After all, 99 per cent of their songs are about the first, and the rest are about the second.

And when you get too old for all that, there is always the love of pasta. At dinner on my first night in the Bajamar Hotel, a dark and brooding establishment on the breezy coast which is know as the Riviera of Ulysses – not because the Greek paragon ever visited there, but because the local authorities thought it sounded nice – we were served with so many different types that I ran out of fingers counting off the kinds of pasta which Italians eat in enormous quantities. This still does not explain the mysterious process by which Italian women, who are universally slim, delicious and fashionable when they are young, wake up the morning after their wedding night as completely spherical mammas dressed in old black army blankets.

Or, indeed, the equally mysterious process by which Italian men, who before their marriages are popularly perceived to be demon lovers with 18in hips, afterwards become impotent in such large numbers that in March 1993 the national newspaper, *La Stampa*, devoted a large article to the subject, offering no more helpful advice than that the chaps affected should listen to more music.

Indeed, I often find that there's nothing like the soundtrack to *The Sound of Music* by the Dagenham Girls' Pipe Band for getting me in the mood.

Perhaps the problem for Italian men is that they always compare their wives to their mothers, and no one wants to make love to their mothers in case they end up in a Greek play with everyone laughing at them.

Anyway, where was I? Ah yes, at supper, where the British guests were eating their pasta by laying their napkins very properly on their knees, then spending the whole meal wishing they had brought a hand mirror so they could check their chins, shirt collars and new linen suits for sauce splashes.

The Italians, much more sensibly, tucked their napkins into their collars like huge self-empowered toddlers, covered the rest of their bodies with any other napkins which happened to be lying nearby until they looked like carelessly abandoned piles of laundry, then tucked in with enormous gusto, in between talking about cars, families, outsmarting the taxman, love, betrayal, football, shopping, soap operas, food, health, superstition, politics, bureaucracy, corruption and several other national obsessions.

Each of them was studied and discussed with the effervescence, known in Italian as *allegria*, which shows that it is not for nothing that the word 'company' comes from the

Italian *con pane*, or with bread, meaning to break bread with friends.

In fact, so animated did the discussions become that after a while the outside of each trembling mound of napkins began to flicker and glow so that we shrank back in alarm, fearing that we were about to witness the first ever case of self-immolation by enthusiasm. It transpired, however, that it was just the reflection of the fireworks across the bay to mark the start of the annual festival of Erasmus, the diminutive sixteenth-century Dutch humanist who, for reasons which in spite of some investigation I never discovered, had been adopted as patron of Formia.

It seemed as baffling a moment as any to go for a walk on the beach and fall into bed, where I woke at half three, switched on the television and found a choice which included a dusty professor demonstrating differential equations on a blackboard, *Bonanza*, Alec Guinness in *The Lavender Hill Mob*, *Star Trek*, and an erotic chat-line advertisement which consisted of a series of rather too earnest nymphomaniacs grimly gyrating under a large declaration saying *'Non sono una puttana'* (I am not a whore).

I zapped the remote control and fell asleep again, vaguely troubled by the fact that according to official government statistics, if everyone in Italy actually got up, walked over to the TV and switched it off properly rather than leaving it on standby, the country would save enough electricity to build a new power station every year.

But then, if God had meant Italians to walk, he would never have invented Alfa Romeos.

The next day began badly.

I killed a mosquito at dawn, then realised that I was in Mafia country, and spent the rest of the morning worrying that as I was eating lunch, or enjoying a post-prandial grappa this evening, a petite black limousine would draw up and several mosquitoes, dressed in immaculate dark suits and with little fedoras pulled down over their diminutive sunglasses, would emerge and, with a set of exquisitely matching machine guns, unstitch me at the ankles with a hail of tiny bullets.

The Mafia, or more correctly its sister organisation the Camorra in this part of Italy around Naples, has been around since the beginning of the nineteenth century, waxing and waning, but never going away.

In Sicily, the birthplace of the Mafia, it almost disappeared under the Fascists, then was restored by the Allies, who relied on Mafia intelligence in the battle for Sicily in 1943 and maintained political control of the island by entrusting sixty-two of its sixty-six districts to mafiosi or their kin.

Today, the Mafia controls more than half the world's heroin trade from Palermo and deals with official purges much as it has always done, by killing the officials involved and leaving behind a trail of what the Italians call, with moribund elegance, *cadaveri eccelenti*, or illustrious corpses.

But none of this explained, as we drove away from the hotel that morning, why I was worrying so much, when I normally worried less than anyone I know. Maybe I was worried about being forty-one and not having 2.54 children, a Labrador and a Volvo estate bought on one of those strange schemes where you pay for the car for two years then give it back to the dealer.

Or maybe I did have 2.54 children somewhere that I didn't know about. But then, I'd always practised safe sex by keeping my eyes closed when I was doing it.

So there was little point worrying about anything, really. Maybe I should just worry about worrying, and cut out the middleman.

Thankfully, at this stage my metaphysical reveries were interrupted by our arrival at Sperlonga and its well-known mausoleum, which is, as we all know, where German mice are buried in tiny vaults, which they reserved by laying down their beach towels several years earlier. In between their discreet cadavers lie the remains of Monazio Planco, founder of Lyon and the governor of this part of Italy under Julius Caesar.

The most important Roman site in the area, however, is the

nearby villa of Tiberius, uncovered when workmen building a road in 1957 started digging up enormous marble legs, arms and torsos buried underground like the aftermath of a massacre by giant mafiosquitoes.

Tiberius moved here in AD 14 at the age of fifty-five to get away from an ancient nagging mother in Rome, surrounding his new villa, grotto and swimming pools with statuary representing the adventures of Ulysses, like a sort of pop-up Odyssey.

Magnificently reconstructed in 1958 by the winner of that year's Italian 3D Jigsaw Open, it is now the centrepiece of the simple, refreshing Sperlonga museum, which also possesses a wonderful film of the 1957–8 excavations, showing excitable workmen holding up a bust, shouting 'Head, head', then all rushing off in a group to see if it fits on the torso they discovered that morning. If you can, get an interpreter to sit through it with you – the script is spontaneously hilarious.

Just down the hill are the walls and floors of the slaves' and soldiers' apartments, the pools, and the terrace where Tiberius and his guests would take their regulation forty paces after dinner to aid digestion.

Of course, Tiberius wasn't the only out-of-town obsessive to visit the area – in 1541 Il Barbarossa sacked the entire coast on the instructions of Suleyman the Magnificent to find and bring back to Constantinople the legendary beauty, Princess Julia Gonzago of Fondi. Tens of thousands died in the subsequent war, and only thirty-seven escaped, among them the Princess.

At various stages before and after that, this part of Italy was in the hands of the Etruscans, the Greeks, the Romans, the Barbarians, the Byzantines, the Lombards, the Franks, the French and the Spanish, before Italian unification in 1871.

Today, the only invasion is from ten squillion German tourists every summer, but in late spring the little square at the heart of Sperlonga village is only half empty, or half full depending on whether you're an optimist or a pessimist, and is a perfect spot for sitting outside the Nibbio *gelateria*, tucking into one of its famous ice creams and a café latte while watching the plums, figs and peaches slowly ripen on the market stall nearby.

Sperlonga itself is a pearl among places, cradled in the palm of the mountains and perpetually offered to the blessing of the sea below. But if you can bear to tear yourself away and plunge inland, you will be well rewarded by the Circeo national park, full of migrating birds who arrived and never left, filled with a combination of Mediterranean torpor and fear that the moment they cleared the park's boundary fence, an Italian sportsman, dressed in the most exquisite tweeds and bearing an intricately worked Purdey 12-bore with a walnut stock, would blast them to pieces.

At one end of the park, and a fine venue for lunch to boot, is the rather exclusive hotel of La Stiva, which possesses the most automated toilets in Italy. I walked in and the light came on. I put my hands under the tap and water came out. Then the water stopped and was replaced by hot air.

I should explain at this juncture that I always wash my hands before going to the toilet, on the basis that since I have been out and about doing all sorts of things with them, they are actually much more filthy than the part that I am just about to touch with them, which has been innocuously nestling in freshly laundered cotton minding its own business all the while.

Anyway, after I began performing my micturations and the urinal started flushing, I half expected a pair of mechanical hands to reach out of the wall, give me the regulation two shakes, tuck me away and zip me up, but in the end I had to do it myself, sadly.

So it was that, fed and watered and with everything back in place, I drove south down the coast, following the route of the Appian Way and passing from time to time shops with signs outside saying 'Mozzarella di Bufala'.

Now, someone had actually told me once that proper mozz-arella was made with buffalo milk, and I had dismissed it in the same way as when someone told me that the Israelis were going to set up an official dairy industry and call it Cheeses of Nazareth.

Now, it appeared that it could actually be true, but it was difficult to know how to ask someone. If it was the case, they would think I was stupid for not knowing something so obviously true, and if it wasn't, they would think I was stupid for asking something so obviously untrue.

Still, if I was stupid it was too late to do much about it now, so I did ask, and it is true. Which leads to yet another question: how on earth do you milk a buffalo? By some sort of miraculous process, presumably, similar to the one which according to local legend caused the cliff at nearby Gaeta to split into three at the very moment that Christ died on the cross.

Fifteen hundreds years later, a chap from Cassino named Filippo Neri abandoned the ways of the world and came to live, not in the biggest split, which was too draughty, nor the smallest one, in which you could not even have swung a German mouse, but the middle one, which was just right.

Today the site is, naturally, a shrine and a chapel which combines the worst features of Renaissance, Gothic and baroque architecture, and which is best avoided if you suffer from good taste.

Outside, stalls sell little glass bowls which when turned upside down engulf tiny plastic popes in a flurry of snow. It is strange how the Italians, normally such paragons of style, occasionally fall into such black holes where their entire sense of beauty is sucked off whole, like the souvenir shop in the Vatican.

But then, you only notice the rain when you've been standing in the sun, I thought as I walked down the hill to the much more impressive medieval Chapel of the Immaculate Conception and its matching orphanage, which has in the middle of one wall a night safe for children in which distraught mothers would place their unwanted bundles. The nuns, hearing the infant's cries, would flutter down the stairs like doves to fling open the wooden doors and reveal their latest tiny burden.

Although Gaeta was mightily pillaged in the Second World War, this chapel was saved by an enlightened German officer who arrived ahead of his troops, fell in love with it, and planted ersatz '*Achtung – Minen!*' signs around the building.

Although his name has been lost, the embodiment of his spirit lives on in not only the building, but in an interior which contains a deeply moving sixteenth-century series of panels depicting the life of Christ, and which shows that the dialogue between different architectural styles need not always descend into argument.

Unless, that is, it involves the Neapolitan architect Guarinelli, who in 1848 was asked by Ferdinand II to design a magnificent cathedral, using only the finest of materials, to replace the little church which had stood on the hill above the Chapel of the Immaculate Conception for centuries to celebrate the 1222 visit to Gaeta of St Francis of Assisi.

Instead, Guarinelli used half the King's money to build a magnificent villa nearby, then invited the King to the villa-warming party.

'Nice pad, eh, King?' he said when the King sauntered up halfway through the evening.

'Do you take me for an [expletive deleted]?' replied the King.

As a result of Guarinelli's duplicity, the facade of the cathedral is, indeed, a splendid hymn to marble, but the rest was built with the cheapest local rock. You'd better see it soon, before it falls down. Or even better, treat yourself to the luxury of returning to your hotel by the evening boat, as I did, leaving behind a town on which the soft golden light of early evening was blessing, one by one, buildings painted variously the salmon pink of the eighteenth-century Bourbon dynasty and the buttery yellow of the popes.

And, in the harbour, a collection of strange white pointed objects which were slowly bobbing ashore. A day which had begun with the threat of death by mafiosquito was ending with the threat of death from the underwater division of the Ku Klux Klan. It was, it has to be said, a good time to leave.

In the morning, I took the ferry from Formia to the Pontine Islands. The hydrofoil docks at the hillside village of Ponza, painted in the delicious Italian colours of faded terracotta, buttery ochre, indigo and white, so that all I wanted to do for a while was collapse into a café chair, admire the view and ask for a cappuccino and *acqua con gas*, while all around indolent teenagers prowled with an air of what they hoped was brooding menace but which actually looked like the result of premature haemorrhoids.

Except there was no gas.

'*Solo senza gas*,' said the proprietor with a sympathetic shrug.

The island was having a bubble crisis, so we were reduced to drinking still water, while in the villas in the hills behind the village, disenchanted widows presumably sat tapping their dessicated fingers impatiently on the marble edges of flaccid jacuzzis.

Beside the café where we sat, at the end of a row of the usual tourist shops, was an interesting establishment selling scuba-diving equipment and, quaintly, a black plastic sack with a nozzle attached describing itself as a solar shower.

'Simply rinse with one teaspoonful of baking soda, fill with water, leave in direct sunlight, and after three hours you should be able to have a relaxing hot shower,' said the instructions on the front.

Below that was a discreet pile of bright yellow packets of something called laundry tablets. Did you eat them then watch the molecules of grime leap off your shoulders like lemmings?

Sadly, I was never to find out, for at this moment a grizzled veteran in a South Sea Islands shirt and brown trousers turned up and offered us a chance to potter around the coast in his boat for a fiver each.

It seemed too good an offer to refuse. We explored deserted inlets and coves over the next couple of hours. From time to time there would speed past fat speedboats of the sort advertised in American boys' comics, driven by men in dangerous sunglasses.

In their mysterious wake as they unzipped the tranquil surface of the Tyrrhenian Sea, they left huge waves which almost engulfed our tiny craft, leaving us in turn gazing down into the bottomless blue then up into the endless sky, and although most of us on board were indifferent Protestants, leaving us crossing ourselves and praying to Neptune, St Erasmus, Our Lady of the Aquatic Grottoes, Robert Maxwell and anyone else connected with disasters at sea who might be able to put in a good word for us.

Miraculously, when we opened our eyes, a deserted beach had appeared before us. We splashed ashore, fell to our knees, partly in gratitude for our lives and partly because walking on sharp shingle is an art which requires years of practice, and undressed for swimming, each according to our nation.

The Dutch flung off all their clothes without a thought, flung guttural consonants over each other to ward off the cold – with that peculiar Dutch way of speaking which in an Amsterdam accent sounds like someone trying to swallow a reluctant goldfish and elsewhere sounds like small hedgehogs being beaten to death with cucumbers – and flung themselves in the water.

The English undressed so slowly, taking such infinite care to cover every inch of flesh with towels, that by the time they were ready it was time to leave and they had to content themselves with a quick paddle.

And the Italians draped themselves so elegantly with a single white towel in the manner of Augustus addressing the Senate that by the time you had finished admiring them they had magically donned swimming costumes so up-to-date that by the evening they would be unfashionable and would have to be replaced.

They were led into the water by Gigi, our guide, a noble, white-haired patriarch, so magisterial that as he breaststroked across the bay he looked for all the world like Moses parting the Red Sea. Rather than take the boat back to Ponza for lunch, we simply walked after him down a corridor of water lined with baffled bream and fretful octopus parents on one side, who had temporarily become separated from their little octopi on the other.

We shuffled hastily by with eyes averted, knowing that we were going to eat their second cousins for lunch, in a dockside restaurant in which as the meal went on, the noise levels from the tables around us gradually rose to the level which in other countries would have had someone reaching for either earplugs or a handgun.

But Italian is the most beautiful language to listen to, unlike other languages such as German, in which most words ends with a plosive sound, which leaves the speaker in such a state of tension that they can never relax except by driving their Porsche faster and faster down the autobahn until they crash into a Trabant in a welter of torn metals and slowly deflating egos, and which leaves the listener with such a feeling of being violently besieged that even if someone says 'I love you' in German, your immediate reaction is to punch them in self-defence.

In Italian, however, each word is stressed on the penultimate syllable, a stress accompanied by a slight raising then lowering of the shoulders, which for the speaker creates the feeling of cycling up a gentle hill on a fine summer's afternoon – on the latest designer racing bicycle from Turin, naturally – pausing briefly to admire the view, then coasting gently down the other side.

For the listener, meanwhile, the inevitable reaction is to fall into a hypnotic torpor in which they want to remove all their clothes and be made love to with beautiful, almost unbearable tenderness for the rest of that same summer afternoon.

Tragically, there was no one around to make beautiful, almost unbearably tender love to, so I had to content myself with a tour around the island.

The island of Ponza was inhabited in turn by Romans, monks, no one and Bourbons, whose two thousand descendants drive around in quaint three-wheeled vans while wearing woollen bobble hats, both of which have been banned from the mainland for not being stylish enough.

Highlights of the splendid coastal drive include the cliffs from which Lucia Rosa, a beautiful local girl, threw herself because her rich parents disapproved of her lover for being so penniless that he could not even afford a bobble hat, never mind a Reliant Robino.

Other strange forms of transport on the island include Citroën versions of Second World War German Kübelwagens and a red Fiat Strada convertible whose interior the owner had imaginatively replaced in its entirety with wicker.

On the hydrofoil back to the mainland one of the more unusual passengers was a 9ft swordfish in a body bag, obviously the innocent victim of the feud between the mafiosquitoes and the Ku Klux Klan underwater division which I had predicted the night before.

'I'll never forget the halibut I had in Kiev,' said Gerbert, the man from Amsterdam who was sitting opposite me at breakfast.

He was silent for a moment, becoming as misty-eyed as a Frenchman would about his first mistress, an Englishman would about his Morris Minor and … well, a Dutchman would about a halibut.

We were discussing our trip later in that day to Naples, a city so close to social meltdown that only a few years ago hospital patients having a seizure would pick up their mobile phones and dial the emergency number 113 rather than waiting in vain for a nurse doing her rounds. Not only that, but there wasn't a decent halibut to be had in the whole city.

Even before then, the city was once so decadent that for a couple of centuries it was the sex capital of Europe, giving rise to syphilis in such quantities that the expression 'See Naples and die' took on a much grimmer meaning than originally intended.

Today, Naples is returning to normality, although of a sort so chaotic that Neapolitan drivers say there are only two types of traffic lights in the city – those that are there for decoration and those that are merely a suggestion.

To get to the city, you drive through countryside where more escaping British prisoners of war were caught than in any other European country. Their home-made suits fooled the Germans, but the Italians took one look and knew that not even Germans could dress that badly.

We arrived and decamped at Garibaldi Square, where it is said that at any one time, one in three of the occupants are major criminals, and the other two haven't been caught yet. And indeed, as we got off the bus, two youths on a Piaggio were being frisked by a *carabiniero* while his colleague and a sniffer dog checked their scooter for illicit halibut.

Standing nearby with an expression which suggested that he had seen this all before was Antonio the guide, who with his shaven head, luminescent green eyes and slightly pointed ears, looked like the result of a night of unexpectedly illogical passion between Sinead O'Connor and Mr Spock. Indeed, so otherworldly was he that he established an immediate telepathic link with my preconceptions about his city, and began to apologise for them before I had said a word.

'It's a bit unfair,' he said. 'No matter what the city's social and political problems are, it had a very cultured and civilized reputation until after the Second World War.'

Sadly, my concentration on his subsequent eulogy about the city's moral worth was disturbed at this stage by the sight of a passing pigeon so devoid of self-worth that it had given up flying and was hitching a lift on top of a bus.

'Of course, you must be careful with your belongings when walking around,' Antonio was saying. 'It's understandable – we have a large number of unemployed people, and they can't eat air. And another thing ...'

Tragically, what he was just about to say – that we were standing in the middle of the Galleria Umberto I, an astonishing *fin de siècle* plaza in marble and mosaic now occupied by an eclectic mixture of shops and businesses, including one intriguingly advertising 'Intercontinental Investigazioni Private' – was drowned out by the piercing whistles of a passing march of policemen protesting about low pay.

'Since Antonio Bassolino was elected as mayor in 1993, things have become much better in the city,' Antonio was saying after the din died down. 'For example ...'

Tragically, what he was about to say – that Bassolino had attracted the G7 summit in 1994, cleaned up the city centre, dealt effectively with its traffic problem and was tackling the stranglehold of organised crime – was drowned out by a group of well-dressed businessmen nearby shouting at each other at the tops of their voices while waving their arms around so extravagantly that it could only be a matter of time before one of them took off.

'What are they arguing about?' I asked Antonio.

'They are not arguing. They are discussing last night's football match,' he said. 'Did you know that ...'

Tragically, what he was about to say – that Napoli had won the Italian championships in 1987 and been celebrating ever since – was drowned out by a rattle of paperwork as a traffic policeman booked a passing motorist for stopping at a red light, thus causing such a cacophony of horns that we had to step into the Church of Gesu Nuovo for a bit of peace and quiet, only to find a wedding taking place in the midst of a riot of baroque which was the visual equivalent of the noise outside.

Paradoxically, though, the most silent object in Naples is also its most menacing – the brooding, truncated hulk which sleeps under a blanket of cloud to the east of the city. Vesuvius.

The volcano, apparently the only one in the world designed by Germans, since it has erupted with clockwork regularity since it buried Pompeii in AD 79 and is just about to pop again, as a result of which a team of scientists monitors it twenty-four hours a day.

Although twenty thousand people lived in Pompeii, most of them had scarpered after several days of ominous rumblings, and it was only the city's two thousand optimists, who put the noise down to indigestion and were in any case reluctant to leave a town containing twenty-five brothels, who were left.

What the eruption did leave behind, apart from eighteen thousand smug pessimists, was the world's most perfectly preserved Roman town, buried under 27ft of soft ash which, like an early neutron bomb, killed the people and saved the buildings.

And happily, the optimists did not die in vain because even their most gloomy counterparts today are bound to be astonished by Pompeii, with its almost complete forum, basilica, baths with detailed stucco and frescoes, its streets of shops once staffed by Greek slaves, its amphitheatre, gymnasium and stadium where Gladiators II vs Barbarian Thirds would draw capacity crowds every week.

You cannot help but be astonished – by its scale, by its beauty, by the spooky feeling as you round every corner that you will come chest to face with a fully armed centurion, looking just as surprised as you do. But there are no living people in Pompeii today, apart from the tides of tourists who ebb and flow. There are just the plaster casts of the bodies caught as they swam or napped, or curled up to escape the fatal rain of ash.

Strangely, many of them have a peaceful expression which can only be gained from the sort of optimism which takes the rumbling of a volcano as a spot of indigestion.

And which believes that you can find a decent halibut anywhere outside Kiev.

1997

Japan

660 BC
Emperor Jimmu founds country, which over the centuries adopts and adapts Chinese script and Buddhism.

794–1185
Heian era of peace and poetry

1185
Start of Kamakura era established by Minamoto no Yoritomo, the first shogun, who rules over a spartan military regime of feudal lords and their samurai, known for quaint traditions of ritual suicide and chopping heads off anyone who annoys them.

1274 and 1281
Mongol hordes of Kublai Khan driven back by typhoon, which Japanese christen kamikaze, or divine wind, a name which will return to haunt American sailors centuries later.

1549
Portuguese missionaries arrive, bringing religion and guns.

Japanese, more interested in latter, take them away and, in a sign of things to come, improve them.

1637
Realising that Christians are taking over the country, Japanese expel them, shutting the country off from the outside world until 1853.

1853
US commodore Matthew Perry arrives with fleet of black ships and forces Japan to open its doors to foreigners, resulting in the end of the shogunate in 1867.

1868–1912
Meiji era, ending feudal and class system and bringing huge modernisation and a craze for all things Western, including beef, christened 'mountain whale'.

1926
Inauguration of Emperor Hirohito, who chooses the name Shōwa, or Enlightened Peace, for his reign, then invades Manchuria and attacks Pearl Harbor.

1945
Atom bomb brings defeat and American occupation. Japanese, unused to both, take a deep breath and decide to make the best of it, eventually creating sixties economic miracle, symbolised for Japanese families by the 'three sacred treasures' of fridge, TV and washing machine.

1980s
Three treasures become 3Vs – video, villa and vacation abroad.

1998
Recession. Japanese smile inscrutably and wait for new technology and internet boom.

Hai! I had finished the 3,564-page manual on bowing, graduated with honours from the four-year degree course on ways to avoid saying no and finished the evening classes on the correct way to hand over a business card.

I was a black belt in origami and could kill a rhinoceros at forty paces with a carefully folded sheet of foolscap.

I'd had the lyrics to 'Yesterday' and 'My Way' tattooed on the inside of my eyelids so that I could go out to karaoke bars and sing with the best of them.

I could work twenty-eight hours a day making widgets for a Nissan Sunny, drink whisky all night and pick up a single grain of rice with a pair of oiled chopsticks.

In fact, I was absolutely indistinguishable from most Japanese people, apart from being 6ft 7in and blond.

So why was I so nervous?

Perhaps because the more I read on Japan, the more baffled I got. It was a paradox, in a country full of them.

A country of sumo wrestlers and women like reeds in the wind. Of monstrous urban architecture and the delicate beauty of a tea cup.

A country which loves nature and the changing of the seasons, but which pours millions of tons of effluent into Tokyo Bay annually.

A country where Buddhism advises the letting go of all earthly desires, but which buys 40 per cent of everything that Chanel produces, and where the profits from selling the grounds of the Imperial Palace in Tokyo would buy California.

Perhaps I was nervous because I was standing at the end of a very long queue of people trying to get on to the overbooked BA flight from London to Tokyo. All around me were tiny Japanese women clutching Louis Vuitton purses and Prada handbags, and Japanese men in the navy suit, white shirt and sober tie of the salaryman, except for one, who was dressed from head to foot in English tweeds, complete with deerstalker.

Miraculously, I got on the flight. Even better, I got an upgrade. Delayed for three hours by fog, we finally rose into the evening and tilted east.

Below us, earnest Scandinavians munched pickles and downed vodka in their saunas, while outside the night gathered around and inside the food and club-class champagne passed to and fro so that by the time the brandy and chocolates arrived I had convinced myself I was quite fluent not only in Japanese, but also in Sanskrit, Swahili and left-handed Urdu.

It was a conviction increased not only by watching all of *Braveheart* in Japanese, but by a successful transfer of business cards with my neighbour, Shigehito Kawasaki, according to the rigid rules of Japanese business etiquette – hand card over with both hands, English side upwards so that you pay the other person the compliment of accepting that he can read English, bow slightly deeper than he does, which is difficult, since he's trying to pay you the compliment of doing the same thing, accept his card with both hands, study it carefully, feel the paper and nod approvingly at the quality, graciously accept his denial that it is anything special, place his card lovingly in your wallet, and when you thank him profusely, do not look him in the eye for too long, since it will be seen as a sign of arrogance.

In fact, by the middle of the night I had become so Japanese that I stood for three minutes outside a toilet which turned out to be unoccupied, quite unable to push the door in case there was someone inside who had forgotten to lock it and to whom being discovered in mid-ablution would be such an unaccept-able loss of face that they would rush to the cockpit, wrest the controls from the pilot and send us all plunging to our deaths.

There's a lot to be said for politeness, I thought as I finally fell asleep, vaguely troubled by the fact that although I was app-arently cocooned in an endless limbo of blankets and brandy, I was in fact hurtling across Russia with Vladivostok just emerging over the lilac horizon.

And beyond, already dimly lit by the rising sun, a land chaotic with impregnability.

However, possibly the thing that was troubling me most was that I had just realised I was going to the most expensive country in the world and had somehow forgotten to go to a bank and get some money.

Dawn broke to reveal the Japanese Alps below in bright sunshine and the pilot telling us that if we looked out of the starboard window we could see Mount Fuji.

I looked, but all the mountains seemed the same.

However, it was hardly surprising in a country which values harmony above individuality and where even the smallest Japanese schoolchild knows the proverb that the nail which sticks up gets hammered down.

As we landed, I was for some reason still incredibly nervous. I couldn't think why – after all, I was only arriving tall, blond, penniless and almost illiterate in the most expensive, alien, cultured, vertically challenged and trichologically Stygian country on earth.

A quick phone call to Seiko Taniguchi in the Japan National Tourist Office in Tokyo to explain that I'd been delayed, a successful raid on a bank and I was off to Tokyo on a bus, a song in my heart and a page of directions to the JNTO in Japanese for a taxi driver.

This may seem superfluous, but in Tokyo houses either have no numbers, or numbers which refer to when they were built rather than their position in the street. As a result, addresses go something like 'Turn left at the train station, go past the soft drink vending machine, right at the post office and third left at the little noodle shop on the corner.' The handy thing is that you can use the same directions for almost any house in Tokyo.

At Mrs Taniguchi's office, I was served a bowl of green tea by an office lady who was probably better educated than I was, but due to the male domination of Japanese office life, was destined to spend her working days serving tea to people like me until she married that nice salaryman in the corner, preferably before her twenty-fifth birthday, after which her friends would start calling her Christmas cake, since it's no good after the twenty-fifth either.

The unfortunate state of Japanese women is pretty much the fault of Confucius, who set down the strict hierarchy of obligation which still governs Japanese society. The seventeenth-century Confucian scholar Kaibara Ekiken set down the following maxims after his master: 'A woman should look upon her husband as if he were heaven itself. She should never dream of jealousy. If her husband be dissolute, she must expostulate with him but never either nurse or vent her anger. Should her husband become angry she should obey him with fear and trembling.'

Yes, quite.

Mrs Taniguchi, who was obviously not a Confucian, was making three phone calls at once in four different languages and simultaneously handing me huge wads of cash to pay for the inns in which I would be staying.

For a people so rich, the Japanese have a strange distrust of credit cards, preferring instead to walk around with loads of dosh sticking out of their wallets, a habit which makes them very popular with pickpockets when they go abroad.

And so it was with a thousand quid in crisp yen secreted about my person that I bowed carefully and set off, suddenly nervous again.

For I had just realised that I was about to experience the Tokyo subway at rush hour.

Still, in Japan, even the subway is polite.

The machines thank you for putting your honourable ticket in them, and once you are on a train a cheery female voice and a series of brightly lit arrows make sure you know where you're going.

You'd better be sure, because once you're on in the rush hour, there's no getting off.

Everything they say about the Tokyo rush hour, like the white-gloved attendants politely shoving ten thousand people into a space designed for three men and a small dog, is not only true, but falls far short of the truth. If you can imagine being stuck up to your chest in quicksand, unable to move your arms to wipe the sweat trickling down your face because you've been stupid enough to wear an overcoat, you have some idea what it is like – and I wasn't even on the busiest line.

I looked out over the packed glossy blue-black heads, and felt like a daffodil in a bowl of olives. On one side of me, a girl who had been clever enough to get on with her hands in the up position read a picture comic called *Be Love*, and on the other side an advertisement for Guinness suddenly appeared on a station wall, as surprising as the face of a dead friend at the window.

At Asakusa station, squeezed to 3in wide and 9ft high, I was borne by the crowd to the exit beside Thunder Gate, which marks the entrance to Asakusa Temple.

Built in AD 628, it is the oldest temple in Tokyo and contains a 4in gold statue of Kannon, the Buddhist goddess of mercy, that was allegedly hauled from the Sumida river in the same year as the temple was built.

However, by this stage my armpits felt as if they'd been around for a lot longer, and what I really needed was a bath at the Ryokan Shigetsu.

Ryokan are traditional Japanese inns, where you sleep in a simple room with sliding paper shoji screens and tatami matting on the floor, upon which the maid will lay your futon at night. And like everything else that is simple in Japan, ryokan are very complex. When you enter, for example, you take off your shoes, leave them pointing towards the door and are given a pair of slippers which you wear at all times when you are in the ryokan.

Oh, except for in your room, where you are only allowed bare feet or socks on the tatami.

Er, and in the toilet, when you put on a special pair of toilet slippers.

Ah yes, and outside, for which you get a special pair of outdoor slippers called *geta*.

Anyway, where was I? Ah yes, at the reception desk, behind which stood a small, exquisite woman wearing a small, exquisite kimono.

'*Konbanwa. Hiru desu,*' I said, surprising both of us.

'*Ah, Hiru-san. Irasshaimase,*' she said, since she'd obviously read the same phrase book.

Exhausted by having used up practically all my Japanese vocabulary in one go, I sat down and started to take off my shoes.

'Oh, *Hiru-san,*' she said – '*Hiru*' being the closest you get to Hill this far east of Belfast, and '*san*' turning me into an honourable Hill – 'you don't need to do that.'

I laced up hastily and was whisked in a space-age lift to a room which contained a normal bed, carpet on the floor and a TV in the corner.

Oh well. At least there was a beautiful blue and white *yukata* on the bed. Light cotton kimonos for throwing over your shoulders after a bath, these are not to be confused with *yakuza*, the Japanese gangsters identifiable by flashy suits, permed hair, tattoos and a little fingertip missing as a punishment for a minor misdemeanour like not killing enough people in a gang fight.

Try throwing a *yakuza* over your shoulder after a bath and you'll lose a lot more than a pinkie, dear.

But first – the bath! Tying my *yukata* left over right in the approved manner, I strode manfully up to the sixth floor for a dunk in the *o-furo*, '*o*' being the respectful prefix which is also attached to rice and chopsticks.

Japanese baths, naturally, come complete with their very own set of rituals. God forbid that you should actually wash yourself in one; that's all done beforehand, sitting on a little wooden stool and soaping yourself all over, and then rinsing from a wooden bucket and tap or a shower.

Most modern Japanese baths have a soap detector sensitive to one part in a million and linked to the nearest police station, so that should you enter the bath with the merest whisper of suds behind your ear, the local cops will nip around and drag you stark naked and screaming to the airport for the next flight home for being such a barbarian.

So, rinsed thoroughly, you ease yourself down into a communal bath in which the water is just on the right side of scalding. There, you lay your head on the edge, watch the neon of Tokyo twinkle over the rooftops, and imagine that you are the hero of a post-modern James Clavell novel, just about to elope with the receptionist downstairs, live in a little wood-and-paper house in the mountains, swim naked in forest pools every morning and have fifteen children with blond hair and olive skin who give themselves a happy surprise every time they look in the mirror.

And after you've dreamt all that, you can go downstairs, glowing gently, make yourself a nice bowl of green tea and come over all Japanese.

After a while I pulled a padded cotton jacket over my *yukata* and went for a walk, finding myself sitting in the shade of a moonlit cypress tree watching a woman in a pale blue kimono making an offering at the shrine below the great squatting roof of Asakusa temple, her head bowed in silent prayer.

Nearby, a white cat snoozed inscrutably in spite of the fact that it was the dog-walking time of the night, and assorted poodles, collies and Rottweilers were passing within feet of its nose.

A day which had begun in the turmoil of a late arrival in Tokyo, a battle through the subway and a sincere desire that I had stayed at home and got a proper job, had ended in peace.

Breakfast the next morning was delicious, whatever it was. Mind you, the fish looked even more surprised than I did – but then, I'd never eaten a whole fish with chopsticks before.

From sneaking a glance at the people kneeling at the next table, who were slurping down beer, noodles and pickles with relish, it looked like the correct technique was to work back along the spine from the head to the tail, finally leaving something on the plate which looked like the piscine equivalent of *Thunderbird 2*.

The rest was spicy miso soup, glutinous rice, pickled this, that and the other, tiny strips of dried seaweed, cubes of tasty tofu and steaming bowls of *o cha*, or green tea.

Stuffed, I had to sit in the lobby of the ryokan for a while before I could make it up to my room. Framed by the open front door was a white wall, a simple red lantern, a black wooden beam and the autumnal branch of a maple tree.

Suddenly, into this rectangular poem strode a passing salaryman, a Japanese white-collar worker, on his way to another brutal twelve-hour day at the office. As his footsteps receded, the scene began to slip back into the past, not stopping as it reached one hundred years ago, or two, or even three.

In Japan, life is art and the past is the present. Every day is filled with moments of the most extraordinary beauty, and you are often uncertain which century you are in.

Later that morning, I stood at the shrine in Yoyogi Park built in 1920 for Emperor Meiji. Like almost every shrine in Tokyo, it had been burnt down during the war and rebuilt to the last detail.

A traditional Shinto wedding was taking place, with the bride wearing a flawless, white silk kimono and cowl and the groom in layers of black and grey. They were flanked by two huge wooden drums, below which sat four white lanterns and above which two black rooks spiralled in a clear blue sky.

At the entrance to Shibuya Park, only ten minutes away, a young woman in a kimono hurried below a giant TV screen blasting out continuous pop videos, while just down the street two red, British telephone boxes stood outside the Walt Disney store.

Everywhere, old met new and east met west, nodded peremptorily to each other and went their separate ways.

Six hundred feet above our heads, visitors to the Metropolitan Bureau building were enjoying the staggering view. Or rather, they were thinking how staggering the view would be were it not for the smog. On a clear day, they say, you're not in Tokyo.

After a few minutes not admiring the view, they made their way to the lifts, where white-gloved attendants made sure they were all gathered safely in, thanked them for their honourable custom and wished them a pleasant descent.

Most then made their way to the Imperial Palace. The palace itself is only open to the public on Emperor Akihito's birthday, 23 December, and New Year's Day, so for the rest of the year visitors must content themselves with 100 acres of punctiliously trimmed grass, black pines and a lake filled with the imperial carp.

Carp are much admired by the Japanese because of their tendency to swim against the current, probably because most Japanese people spend their lives doing exactly the opposite. But since there is no current to swim against in the imperial lake, the carp just amble aimlessly about, bumping absentmindedly into each other then bowing and apologising.

The emperor, who has nothing much to swim against either since his father, Hirohito, was forced to renounce his divinity at the end of the war, has applied himself a little more diligently than the carp, working hard to make the royal family a little more human. However, no matter how low-key he becomes, he is unlikely to break his father's record for the understatement of the century, when Hirohito went on live national radio after the bombing of Hiroshima and Nagasaki and the unconditional surrender of the Japanese armed forces and announced, 'The war situation has not necessarily developed to our advantage.'

By this stage, too, the daylight had not necessarily developed to my advantage, and as darkness fell I returned to the ryokan. A nightclub doorman asked me in Japanese what height I was.

'*Ni hai*,' I said, meaning two metres. I'm not sure if it was grammatically correct or not, but it was quite comforting to know that although I was the tallest person in sight, I was still only *ni hai* to a Japanese person.

Back at the ryokan, I found on the television a cookery

programme in which a man who looked like a Japanese Marcello Mastroianni was sailing out of mist-shrouded harbours to hunt shark, plundering fish markets at dawn in search of giant crayfish and crashing through aromatic forests to dig up mysteriously phallic mushrooms, accompanied all the while by stirring music and a babe from heaven in a mini-skirt, who took photographs of him while he cooked the lot then ate it with astonished gasps and sensuously quivering sighs.

Like most Japanese women, she had no bottom, which probably explains why most women in the rest of the world feel they have more than enough bottom to be going on with.

Another thing the Japanese have very little of is the word 'No'. According to Michihiro Matsumoto, an expert in the matter, there are 145 different ways in which the Japanese can say no without actually saying no.

Even Richard Nixon, no slouch himself at being economical with the truth, complained when he visited Japan in 1970 that President Sato failed to live up to a firm promise.

But as Sato explained, what he had actually said was, 'I'll handle the matter with prudence.'

In the morning, I rose at the stroke of nine and set off to Tokyo's Ueno Park intent on going straight to the Shitamachi Museum of Life in the old town and calling in on what the guidebook referred to quaintly as the zoo logical gardens, which presumably meant that the animals were arranged in alphabetical order and the zebra was always last to be fed.

But then I got waylaid by Mr Wadaka.

It happened like this. I was standing listening to an outdoor karaoke and wondering how the same singer could tunelessly murder John Lennon's 'Imagine' then produce a tone-perfect rendering of an old Japanese folk song, when an elderly man who was wearing a floppy hat and listening to a Grieg piano concerto on his Walkman came up and bowed.

'So sorry, but would you like me to explain what's going on?' he said.

'Ah, certainly, please, yes,' I said, having apparently become illiterate in English as well as Japanese.

'It's karaoke. It will be the death of us yet,' he said with a grin. 'Let me buy you a beer.'

Mr Wadaka had learnt his flawless English in junior school before the war.

'We learnt English properly then, but after the war young people didn't really bother,' he said, tucking into the Sapporo and pickles he'd bought us from a noodle stand.

'During the war I was in the army in Indonesia serving as a mechanical engineer, then when we lost I worked for the American Air Force.'

After that he spent fifteen years with the Nippon Electrical Company and ten years selling cancer insurance – the Japanese, with their almost exclusively seafood diet, have one of the highest rates of bowel cancer in the world.

'Now I get up at five every morning and walk for four hours listening to music. My wife complains she never sees me, but she should come with me, especially in the autumn when the trees are changing so beautifully like this.'

'Your English is perfect, Wadaka-san.'

'Thank you, thank you. But I'm seventy-six now, and I think I will die soon. Bit of a shame, since I'd really like to visit Norway and Finland for some reason. Still, in a couple of weeks I'm off to Sendai in the north to visit my brother.'

'By train?'

'Oh no, I have a Suzuki l00cc motorcycle. Bit small for 400 kilometres, but it'll get me there. The milk's very good up in the north, and the beer's even better.'

He drained his Sapporo, shook my hand, bowed and set off at a brisk pace for the remaining two hours of his walk around Ueno.

In the national museum at the end of the park, they were having a special exhibition on flowers, in which I spent a happy hour wandering around studying displays of *ikebana* and impressing the Japanese people around me by breathing in sharply through clenched teeth, nodding wisely then muttering, 'Ah, *astanubate*,' a nonsense word I had somehow remembered from phonetics at university.

At the other end of the park, upstairs in the Shitamachi Museum, you'll find a wonderful collection of everyday artefacts like fridges, tin toys, televisions, comics, early Sony tape recorders, Godzilla posters and Pentax cameras. Downstairs is a small but perfect recreation of the maze of tiny streets, wooden houses, tatami mats and shoji screens which was Tokyo until the great earthquake of 1923 and the firebombing of 1945.

Take off your shoes, sit on a cushion on the tatami in the prescribed knee-twanging position, and you could be one of the characters in James Michener's *Sayonara*. Except, that is, for the thunderous noise of the open-air rock concert on the other side of the lotus pond, so loud that it made old ladies on their bicycles wobble in the gaps between the cedar trees.

Perhaps, in spite of all its perplexing past, Japan is just the same as other countries – young people playing bad music too loud, and old faithfuls like Mr Wadaka wondering why they can't get up at five and listen to Grieg like any civilized person.

But enough of Tokyo. It was time to take to the mountains, by bullet train, mountain train, funicular and boat.

To Hakone, specifically, a popular Japanese getaway since 1590, when Toyotomi Hideyoshi first ordered hot springs to be opened there for his samurai to rest their battle-weary bones. The last part of this journey starts on a little train which has been puffing and panting its way up the mountains since 1919.

All around us on the steep journey up, the trees burned with autumn fire, and in the near distance the black mountain steamed with white smoke-wraiths. Looking like a Hokusai print, it was the strangest of sights – the cold trees looked hot, and the hot mountain looked cold.

From Soun-zan it was a giddy cable-car ride across the yawning valleys to Owakudani, where I had a lunch of black eggs boiled in volcanic mud – repulsive, it has to be said – and that canned Japanese soft drink peculiarly known as Pocari Sweat, as all around the mountain boiled and steamed, and a few miles away that most famous of Japanese symbols and home of the world's highest Coke vending machines, Mount Fuji, made a rare public appearance from behind the cloud which normally shrouds it.

Burping gently from the volcanic reaction the eggs had caused, I swayed onwards across another valley then, to a chorus of cheery 'Harros' from schoolchildren in the cable car going the other way, descended into Togendai and took the ferry to Moto-Hakone, settling back in a clean seat with a freshly laundered cotton headrest as a female voice on the intercom informed us all that we were on a ferry of the Izu-Hakone Railway Line, pointed out that the ferry operated all year around so that we might fully appreciate the changing seasons on beautiful Lake Ashi, added by the way that the traditional Japanese pile on our left was the Hazone Prince Hotel Annex, which was perfectly asymmetrical, and urged us to relax and enjoy the rest of the voyage.

Which I did, as burnt orange Shinto arches rose out of the dark waters to a backdrop of forests which were a peaceful riot of colour.

Come to think if it, I had had a perfectly asymmetrical day – travelling by bullet train, mountain train, funicular, cable car and boat, arriving nowhere near where I'd left and still feeling at home.

It seemed appropriate to round it off on foot, docking at Moto-Hakone and toddling down the Tokaido Highway, the ancient route used by shogunate samurai, but today only a little side road filled with memories, falling leaves and the occasional Toyota Corolla.

I bought some noodles and checked into the Moto-Hakone Inn, only for the innkeeper to vanish before I could borrow some chopsticks off him, reducing me to sitting on a bench outside eating the noodles with my toothbrush and inventing a new Zen koan riddle in the manner of 'What is the sound of one hand clapping?' – 'What is the sound of one chopstick eating?'

Replete, I went up to my room to find a shrink-wrapped telephone and a strange electrical plug with a small foil package attached to it. It looked for all the world like an electric condom warmer in the same tradition as that other great Japanese invention, the heated toilet seat.

And so, with a full belly and an empty mind, safe from the threat of cold pregnancy and hot pursuit by samurai, I had a beer and fell asleep on the futon, in a perfectly asymmetrical sort of way.

The bullet train, which I found myself on again the next day, was originally conceived in March 1941, but the little matter of a war put it off for more than two decades. Finally, after months of slow-speed trials, the engineers were given the go-ahead on 3 March 1963 to sink the pedal to the metal – which they did, setting a new world rolling-stock record of 160mph and leaving behind the light plane that had been sent to record the event.

On the Tokaido line between Tokyo and Osaka, the bullet train makes 230 runs a day carrying three hundred thousand passengers. On several occasions the network has moved one million people a day, and the system has not had a single fatal accident. You can also set your watch by it, whereas in some countries you'd be lucky to get away with a calendar. Not to mention the fact that your ticket tells you precisely where to stand on the platform for your carriage, and when the train pulls in, the white-gloved stationmaster trading a formal salute with the driver, the door stops opposite you to the nearest inch.

At Utsunomiya, the ticket collector followed me all the way to the platform to make sure I got on the right local train to Nikko, home of several dozen historic sites, the quaintest of which must be Deity with Sedge Hat presiding over Prayers with Deadlines.

And just up the hill from that is the Toshugu shrine, built by fifteen thousand artisans in the 1630s. The home of 42 build-ings, 5,147 carvings, 2.25 hectares of gold leaf and 3 monkeys, the shrine was in questionable taste when it was built, and goes so completely against the Japanese grain of chaste minimalism that the effect of suddenly seeing it at the top of an avenue flanked by quiet cedar forest is as shocking as if a nun's habit had slipped aside to reveal a scarlet basque.

Among its more wonderful sights are two elephants sculpted by an artist who had never seen one, and which look like what you'd get if you threw all the animals in the world into a pile, picked out the fattest and ugliest bits, and glued them together.

Slightly more realistic, and part of an allegorical series depicting the life of the monkey, are the original 'hear no evil, see no evil, speak no evil' threesome.

In the innermost courtyard, though, was a sight more beaut-iful than wonky elephants or indifferent monkeys. It was the shrine attendants in snowy robes and deep red overskirts, covering the sacred offertories with pure white cloths, then taking out brooms almost as tall as themselves to sweep the temple grounds.

I wandered off into the forest by the river, where the air was damp and sweet with the afternoon rain, past modern houses where fathers were outside tinkering with recalcitrant motor-cycles, wives were inside kneeling on the tatami setting the table for supper and children were playing in the road with that mad, excited joy for life that children have before they are sent to school.

And on into the aromatic gloom, until even the ubiquitous vending machines had vanished. On, as the road became narr-ower and darker and the houses became wooden ones with folding shutters of the sort which have been built in Japan since the time before time.

It was the twilight time of day when colours seem brighter if you look away from them a little, so that the forest seemed to burn darkly as I walked on until the houses vanished and I was alone among the trees, sure that time had been unmade and I was standing in a Japan where the present had not yet happened.

A Japan in which the hurtling sound from around the corner was a Tokugawa samurai – galloping back in a fury from a fruitless meeting with a member of the *bakufu*, the shogunate civil service, in an attempt to get planning permission for his bonsai – who would decapitate me in about five seconds for not being prostrate in the ditch as he passed.

Which probably explains the stupid expression on my face as a white Toyota estate appeared around the corner and sped past on its way into town before the shops shut.

In the morning, on the train to Kyoto, the girl opposite me was carrying a knapsack bearing the timeless legend 'Flash Bowl American Football', like a leopard finding a game. We are longtime friend of sportsmen, let's form a scrummage together.

While this may seem strange, it was not, for the Japanese are one of the most cultured, civilized and literate people on earth – until it comes to their slogans, which are a fascinating mixture of nostalgia, postmodern angst and gibberish. Over the twelve days I was there, examples I saw included:

Tissue of kitten – on a box of paper handkerchiefs
Funk the peanuts – radio station jingle
Every day you need goods, Junior In Bag, For boy and girl
    young beet – on the side of a leather bag in Tokyo
Shot at close range – a hunter's sweatshirt
This is the White Corner. It's the bright, fantastic and
    sophisticated urban life – sign on cigarette machine
Let's Kiosk – name of a railway-station shop
Moto Fizz motorcycle good Napoleon Air Valve System – on
    a punk's knapsack
FIDS: Fresh Information Delivery Service – on the back of a
    tracksuit
Spilt coffee has a sad remembrance of old – on a shopping bag
I like two wheels. Have a nice life with motorcycle and
    scooter – plastic motorbike cover

Fall in love with Twinkle Heart and she become charming,
    happiness for a while – on the side of a vacuum flask
Live Asahi for Live People – beer vending machine

One I missed, as spotted by Mark Gauthier, author of *Making It in Japan*, was: 'Women are making bread on Sunday with the high quality milk and powder lie on their face and turn up their sleeves sweat is falling down on the trough women's finger, hand, and body hot just like burning their blouse seems to be burst swing their rich breast' – on a bread wrapper.

The trouble is, it's catching. In a ryokan in Tokyo one night, I found myself muttering 'Yokohama mamasama. Oh yes, I'm running around like a lovely young chicken, then I'm going to bed to have a fine rich time, isn't it?'

Anyway, where was I? Ah yes, on the train to Kyoto, where that evening I found myself on Gion Corner, watching the most expensive women in Japan for nothing.

They were geisha and their apprentices, maiko, dressed in the most formal style of the country's most formal city – from their elaborately coiled hair held up by antique ivory pins to their snow-white faces and cherry lips, to kimono and obi in the most understated silks, to their simple white-cotton *tabe*, split socks and lacquered *geta* sandals. They were on their way to appointments, and they do not come cheap.

If you want them to dance and sing a little, to pour your sake as you eat and to laugh from behind a politely raised and perfectly manicured hand at your bad jokes, it will cost you at least £600.

And, naturally, money alone is not enough to procure the company of these most refined hostesses for the evening. So sorry, honourable guest, but you will also need an introduction from a patron.

The institutions to which they were tripping were probably specialists in *kaiseki*, or stone-on-the-stomach cuisine, named after the warm stones Buddhist monks held against their stomachs to fend off hunger during the long hours of meditation, and which developed into plain meals with tea, and then into one of the most ritualised forms of eating in a country where ritual is all. In the best of establishments, the bill per person is unlikely to be much short of £300.

You can see why I was sitting on a fence with an £18 ticket for the Gion Corner Theatre in my back pocket. Gion Corner, an evening of traditional arts, is the poor man's night out with a geisha, down a back alley which was so tricky to find that I finally asked at a police box. This is always a good way to get directions in Japan, except that no one ever knows how to get to the police boxes.

First onstage, after a lot of relaxing plinky-plonky music from a traditional thirteen-string *koto* – not to be confused with the relaxing plinky-plonky music from the three-string *shamisen* – was the tea ceremony. Not to be confused with nipping out to the kitchen for a cuppa during the commercials, this was perfected in the sixteenth-century by a Zen priest called Sen no Rikyu as a means of achieving inner peace through simple surroundings and graceful ritual.

However, since the original ceremony took place in a small four-and-a-half-tatami room, the surroundings just disorderly enough to seem uncontrived, it is difficult to achieve the desired serenity in a theatre filled with foreigners with big feet, itchy beards and trains to catch. You might as well try to read a poem at a football match.

After some more relaxing music on the *koto*, there was a display of *ikebana*, or flower arranging. There are about three thousand schools of *ikebana*, from vastly complex ones involving entire forests and gardens, to the school we were to see this evening, *nageire*, where the flowers are literally thrown in.

If you ever want to make a joke at a Japanese dinner party, study a large *ikebana* display which obviously took several years to arrange and then announce wisely, 'Ah – *nageire*.' This will either have your hosts doubled up with laughter, or have you doubled up with pain after they give you a dig in the dongles.

Next onstage was a *bunraku*, or puppet theatre in which

although no attempt is made to hide the puppeteers, they soon become invisible to you as you are wrapped up in the story of Kichiza, a page boy, and his sweetheart, Oshichi, whose love finally overcomes their parents' attempts to marry them off to someone else.

I do like happy endings, I thought as I wandered home, had some noodles and beer with a Dutchman living in Washington, a Frenchman living in Uppsala and a Swede living in Berlin, and went to bed under a Kyoto moon.

At nine the next morning, waiting outside the inn just as she had promised was Sei the guide, a slim, exquisite girl in her twenties who was here to take me on a walking tour of Kyoto. Autumn is the perfect time to do this, in an ancient city full of stories as sad as the falling of the leaves.

There is no greater symbol of that order than Nijo Castle in Kyoto. The feudal lords, or daimyo, got no further than the outer reception rooms, where wall paintings of ferocious tigers and leopards gave no uncertain message that they were to stay in their place.

More trusted daimyo were allowed deeper and deeper into the building to be granted an audience in rooms where the paintings were designed to relax rather than intimidate them.

In every room used by the shogun, bodyguards sat permanently behind ornate doors set into the walls, and even the corridors between the rooms were specially designed so that the floors creaked to warn of intruders.

Today, the so-called nightingale floors are still creaking; even when the Japanese do something badly, it seems, they do it well.

The most impressive room in the building is the huge inner sanctum in which only the most trusted lords would be allowed to gaze upon the imperious figure of Tokugawa, alone in his frugal majesty on a raised platform at the other end of the room.

We walked away across the creaking floors, and had lunch in a little inn nearby. As I handed Sei the noodles, our hands brushed, and our eyes met, for exactly a second too long.

'What fine hands you have, *Hiru-san*,' she said.

Nijo is in its way a sad indictment of the fretsome nature of power, especially when compared to the Katsura Rikyu villa built in 1624 for the emperor's brother, Prince Torihoto, where the gardens are a miniature landscape of chapels and tea houses, and which has possibly contributed more to the ascetic elements of contemporary architecture than anywhere else in the world.

Each of the tea houses is the very essence of restful simplicity – a little entrance, four and a half tatami mats and an alcove for the display of *ikebana* or calligraphy.

One house is designed so that you can sit and enjoy the moonlight on the waves of the pond.

'How beautiful it would be to take tea there on an October night, wrapped up in a padded cotton robe against the autumn chill,' said Sei.

She was right. There is a sense of immense peace to be gained from this type of architecture, without the Cripes-can-I-afford-it syndrome which you often get when confronted with the best of Western design.

It is a sense of peace continued elsewhere in Kyoto at Daitoku-ji Zen temple, where I arrived to find the wonderfully mad abbot singing '*Deutschland über alles*' to a departing German tour group, giving them a quick V-for-victory sign and wishing them '*Auf Wiedersehen*' individually as they left.

When he heard I was from Ireland, he whipped out a remote control, pressed a button and brought an illuminated globe descending from the ceiling with a hum as he launched into a word-perfect rendition of 'It's a Long Way to Tipperary'.

Funny old thing, Zen, I thought as I went into one of the gardens and watched the sun set through the trees, casting ever-changing shadows on the raked sand. It is very difficult to explain in words the feeling you get when looking at a Zen garden, which is probably why attempts to explain Zen since it was established in the twelfth century have been met with snorts, guffaws and claims that it is a huge fraud. But being in the presence of it creates such a sense of peaceful contentment that you can only feel that whatever it is, it must be right.

We said goodbye to the abbot, who saw us off with a cheery rendition of 'The Soldier's Song', and finally, as darkness fell, we found ourselves at the temple of Jakko-in.

For some reason I was thinking of a sad sight I had seen two days before in Kamakura – hundreds of tiny grey statues on a hillside overlooking the sea of Jizo, the patron saint of children. Many of them had been draped with unused baby clothes by women who had lost a child and who came there in the misty morning or in the long shadows of evening, bearing with them their unbearable burdens of a futureless past, then walking away down the desolate path, as alone as it was possible to be.

As we walked away, I looked at my watch. It was coming up to eight.

'Sei, may I buy you dinner?' I said.

'Of course,' she laughed.

We found a little restaurant, and had beer and teriyaki, and talked and laughed, and then she walked back with me to the inn.

'You know,' she said, as we stopped outside, standing close together in the breathing dark, 'we have a saying in Japan that when we travel, we leave shame behind.'

'I have heard that,' I said, looking at her and knowing exactly what she meant. 'But I am travelling, and you are at home.'

'Not tonight,' she smiled.

I looked at her, thinking how stunning she was, and then thinking of my girlfriend back home.

'Oh Sei, you are lovely, but I cannot,' I said.

She smiled again, kissed me on the corner of my lips, and walked slowly away.

I watched her disappear into the night, honour and desire

wrestling in my heart, then went into the inn and slept the sleep of the just, but only just.

I said right at the start that Japan was a land of contrasts, and I could not have asked for a greater one the next day, when I went to see Cecil.

Cecil gets free beer, free lodging and free massage, but I wouldn't trade places with him for all the tea in Japan. For when you look at Cecil, you are looking at two thousand of the most expensive steaks in the world.

He is, in fact, one of the famous Kobe cattle bred by the likes of Mr Kakushi Ikeda, who collected me at the train station in a small green floppy hat which seemed to deny his status as a millionaire, and a very large black BMW which seemed to confirm it.

Ikeda-san, a big cheese in the cattle world, is the current holder of the award for the best beef in Japan, as he proved to me when we arrived at his farmhouse by producing not only a diploma containing a photograph of a huge slab of beef, but the breeding certificate of the bull which produced it. A sort of passport for dead cows who want to travel abroad, this contains all the details of their mum and dad, favourite beer and a large black and white rectangle which looks like the tributaries of the Ganges but is actually an ink print of a bovine nose.

Ikeda-san buys Kobe calves for £2,000 each, spends thirty months breeding them then sells them at auction for up to £31,000. Translated into steaks, that works out at £30–£60 a shot. Translated into Mr Ikeda's bank account, it means the manager stands up when he walks in.

We leaped out of the BMW and wandered around the cowshed with Chijiki Imura, the interpreter. A huge yellow, green and black spider scuttled through the rafters, and all around us, black, furry cattle the size of small elephants sat around munching finest quality American corn and wheat blended to Ikeda-san's secret recipe, looking at us with damp, oily eyes as he discussed their relative merits.

'That's Cecil in the corner. Eh, that's a nice fat arse on him, like a pig, don't you think?' he said as Number One Son arrived back from the winery in a new pick-up truck. For not content with bringing home the beef, Ikeda-san is now producing the wine to go with it. Over eighty thousand vines have already been planted, a small research laboratory built and Ikeda-san junior packed off to France to learn his Chablis from his claret.

With the way the Japanese usually go about developing original ideas, I'd give it about ten years before we're all sitting around at dinner parties chattering away about how Tesco are doing a lovely little Chateau Kobe 2004 for only a fiver, darling.

'Here, let me show you around the winery,' said Ikeda-san, ushering me into the BMW and tearing off up the lane, only to become distracted on the way by the sight of the Kobe Beef Pavilion, inside which we found a series of wall posters showing the intriguing process of embryo transfer, in which the startled expression on the face of the receiving cow can probably be explained by the fact that the eggs are stored at minus 196°C before transfer.

I wrote politely for twenty minutes as Mr Ikeda explained in great detail the whole messy business, then realised that the only reason Mr Ikeda was still talking was that I was still writing.

I put my notebook away and stared politely at a grove of plum trees, then we both gave a sigh of relief and walked across the road into the local pottery, where small, wonderful women were producing small, wonderful pots.

And so to lunch, where the local wine proved as soft as a Mazda gear-change and where Cecil ... well, I'm afraid Cecil turned out a bit like Prince Andrew must have felt about Sarah Ferguson – very sweet, but slightly fat and not worth the expense in the end.

Ikeda-san, meanwhile, was asking me increasingly complicated questions about agriculture in Ireland, to which I gave such increasingly obtuse answers that I'm sure by the time dessert arrived he was quite convinced that our main exports were DeLorean cars filled with mangoes and driven by Kashmiri goats.

We drove to the station, bowed deeply to each other and left in different directions and similar confusions.

At the station, Chijiko asked me where I was heading next.

'To Osaka, to catch the Midosuji-line tube to Namba,' I said.

She sucked in her breath sharply, as Japanese people do when faced with anything very difficult or upsetting.

'*Ah so desu ka?* Osaka subway is very complex, *ne?*' she said, giving me directions which went something like this – take *shinkansen* to Shin-Osaka, local train to Osaka on Kobe line, go down steps, turn right, cut through food section of Daimaru department store, take sharp left at radishes, slow down for chicane through persimmons, handbrake turn at those little green furry things from New Zealand, straight on at sour plums, exit at pickled ginger then sharp left through Hanshin store and look for door beside women's perfume counter.

She drew me a map which looked like the wiring diagram for Apollo 13 and left, still shaking her head at the unutterable complexity of the Osaka subway system.

When she was finally out of sight, I dropped the map politely in the bin, took the train to Osaka, followed the signs like everyone else, and found myself eventually at the Ebisu-so ryokan, an inn so gloomy that the two ancient women who ran it seemed to have become almost transparent, like those spiders that live in very deep caves and never go out. I asked one of them about the possibility of breakfast the next morning, a suggestion which reduced both of them to helpless cackling.

When they finally straightened up again, one of them led me up a dark and creaking staircase and down an even darker corridor to a three-tatami room which contained walls apparently covered in fur and a black Bakelite telephone with no dial.

I sat on the floor and wished that I had followed Mrs Imura's directions and got lost after all. It served me right for being so ungrateful to her. But after a while I decided to make the best of a bad job and go out for an evening in Osaka. Osaka is the Birmingham or Glasgow of Japan – miffed that Tokyo is seen as more important, and determined to look, talk and act bigger than the capital.

Walking through it even on a Monday evening, you get the impression that half the people of the city have been told they're going to die in the morning and they should dress up, go out and enjoy it while it lasts, and the other half have been ordered to use up a year's worth of electricity before dawn.

Beneath entire buildings covered in moving neon and giant TV screens, shops were selling everything it was possible to buy, *pachinko* arcades plinked and plonked and cigarette vending machines urged me to 'Speak Lark'.

Men in Armani suits huddled together on street corners in flickering wreaths of cigarette smoke, asking each other how much they had earned today, and women wearing outfits just in from Paris rode to and fro on shiny bicycles, languidly discussing on mobile phones which date to accept for the evening.

I went back to my room, had a hot dog and a beer and slept fitfully, dreaming that I had forgotten to cut my nails.

But in the morning they were fine. I checked out and walked away down the street in the morning sun, the plastic dog on the doorstep barking at me all the way to the corner.

And then I took a train to the mountains to see some monks.

Funny chaps, Buddhist monks. You'd expect them to spend their time either sitting meditating or wandering about with little bowls begging for alms. Yet from the eleventh to the sixteenth centuries, the Japanese ones were a right bunch of mad buggers, either burning down the temples of rival factions or showing their disapproval of shogunate policies by rampaging down from the mountains and slaughtering everyone in sight.

But then, they were members of the Pure Land school, for whom salvation was simply a matter of nothing more vigorous than repeating the phrase '*Namu Amida Butsu*'.

Having thus saved themselves, and with nothing to do all day but wander around the mountains occasionally chanting, 'Save me, Amida Buddha', just to keep their spiritual insurance payments up to date, and checking the north-eastern horizon where evil spirits were supposed to dwell, it's hardly surprising that they found themselves twiddling their thumbs and wondering what else they could get up to.

Finally, one soggy autumn evening in the eleventh century, Kakujin, the thirty-sixth bishop of the Enryaku-ji monastery, stuck up his hand and said, 'Here lads, what about forming an army just in case we're attacked by someone?'

Human nature being what it is, of course, it wasn't long before the monk-soldiers got a bit bored sitting around waiting to be attacked, and decided the best policy was to get their defence in first.

Finally, in 1571, Oda Nobunaga got fed up with them. Storming into the mountains, his samurai burnt thousands of temples, killed the monks and left eight centuries of history in smoking ruins.

Today, at holy sites like Koyasan, high in the mountains, there are 120 temples where once stood one thousand five hundred.

And the only way that visitors get killed is with kindness.

As I arrived by train and took the cable car, the glorious weather of the morning had broken, bringing rain slanting down from a leaden sky as I caught a local bus up the narrow mountain road and finally squelched through the low wooden gateway of Haryoin temple, sat on the front step and took off my sodden shoes.

A young monk, his head shaved and his feet bare, brought me in and padded in front of me down a polished hall as I schlipped and schlopped behind, leaving huge, damp footprints all the way to a simple room with a view of a garden dripping with rain.

We exchanged bows and I went inside to unpack, listen to the rain on the roof and drink green tea from a little pot in which the leaves were already damp, since the Japanese believe that the best tea is made from leaves which have already been used more than once.

And by then it was time for supper. Kneeling on a cushion in front of a low table, I was served a delicious combination of food grown and cooked by the monks. Known as *shojin ryori*, it lacks meat, fish, onions and garlic, but neither quality nor quantity.

After half an hour of huge portions, I slowly began to realise two things.

One was why the Buddha's belly is so big.

And the other was that I couldn't stand up because both my legs had gone to sleep.

After five minutes trying to work out how to make a dignified exit from the dining room, I gave up and limped slowly backwards on my knees to the sliding door, which was thankfully open, bowed deeply and muttered, 'Delicious, thank you so much,' in bad Japanese, much to the enjoyment of everyone in the room.

After retreating to the hallway and wriggling my toes until I could feel them again, I decided to celebrate being able to stand again by going for a walk. And although it was still chucking it down outside, it seemed the perfect night to visit a cemetery.

Borrowing an umbrella from the monk at the gate, I caught a local bus to Okuno-in, where the body of Kobo Daishi, who founded Koya-san in 816, is enshrined.

Twenty minutes later, as the tail lights of the bus disappeared into the pouring night, I turned and plunged into the deep, wet blackness of the cypress forest, walking along a winding path lit only by guttering stone lanterns. Behind them lay the ashes of thousands upon thousands of abbots and priests, bonzes and acolytes who had come here to spend their days on the mountain, to live and then rest at last beneath the tall trees in wait for the western paradise which Buddha had promised them.

A wandering dog joined me, and since he spoke English we

walked on together, leaning into the rain.

He was the first to stop. And then I heard it too – the faintest tinkling, deep in the forest somewhere ahead. It grew and grew, and then suddenly from the flickering dark, carrying tiny bells or lanterns on wooden staffs, came a file of elderly pilgrims dressed in white, as if the dead had risen.

Dog looked at me, and we both shivered, and agreed that it was time we went our separate ways home to bed, where I was lulled to sleep by the rain washing off the roof and the wind howling in the eaves.

And awakened at dawn by the time-honoured temple greeting of Diana Ross and the Supremes. Eh?

Closer inspection revealed that it was only 2 a.m., and that one of my fellow pilgrims was suffering from insomnia and was either determined to share the experience with us or had forgotten that the reason Japanese walls are paper-thin is because they are made of paper.

Several hours of Motown later, interrupted by bouts of stentorian nose-blowing, the real dawn arrived and it was time for morning prayers in the temple's candlelit inner sanctum. Prayers began with a gentle dusting all over with powdered incense – which left me carrying around, for the rest of the day, the delightful aroma of chicken korma – followed by half an hour of chanting punctuated by the sonorous tolling of a bell and occasional bouts of spirit-exorcising by the abbot, who at last summoned me forward, bade me kneel in front of the sacred flame and wash the purifying smoke over me, then dipped his fingers in the still-glowing embers, blessed the back of my neck and bowed me out.

At breakfast, my noisy neighbour turned out to be an Englishman with a wild look in his eye and a crumpled Burberry raincoat over his shoulders, who wished me a hearty 'Good morning, sah!', then proceeded to go over to the table of everyone else who came in, bow deeply, announce, 'My woman – Japanese!' and share their tea. Noisily, naturally.

It was one of those moments when you know it is time to

leave. Sneaking quietly out the door, I pulled on a pair of shoes still sodden from the day before, bowed to the monk on farewell duty and took the first cable car down the mountain to catch the local train.

Down and down, into a scene in which at first the only colours were the white of mist, the sharded green of pine and the bitter red of maple, accompanied by the glorious, living smell of a forest after rain.

And then at last the muddy olive of workers' faces as they boarded the train on their way to work in the valleys.

But best of all was the fact that the train along the coast to Shingu had a stream of hot air blowing out from under the seats which had my feet toasty in no time. As they say, you only appreciate dry and warm when you've had cold and wet. Bliss.

I tilted my seat back and slept all the way along the edge of the Kii Peninsula, passing in happy slumber the ancient training grounds of the ninja, as in turtles, the birthplace of the poet Bashō, as in haiku, and the home of Minakata Kumagusu, as in presenter of 300 papers to the British Museum, identifier of 70 new Japanese fungi and master of 19 languages before he died in 1941. Not to mention the building in Shinawa bearing the legend 'Fukodo: Bone Setting', which summoned up a curious vision of the people of Shinawa regularly falling over and muttering, 'Oh heck, fractured my leg in three places again. Better hop down to old Fukodo and get it sorted out.'

Any time I tried to sit up and take more of an interest in my surroundings, however, I fell asleep again. It was all the fault of the muzak section of Japan Railways. Even the jingles preceding announcements that the next stop is approaching are so relaxing that they're liable to make you nod off and miss the stop.

In keeping with the Japanese belief that nothing is more important than *wa*, or harmony, they seem to say 'So sorry to disturb you, honourable travelling guest, but we at Japan Railways are as happy as teddy bears that you have decided to join us this morning. Please feel free to tilt back your honourable seat, loosen your honourable tie and relax. Please be kind to old people, and if you miss your stop, please do not trouble your honourable self, for was it not Buddha who said that it will take many attempts to arrive at our chosen destination?'

It was, in fact, with a considerable effort of will that I dragged myself off the train at Shingu, a seaside resort where I was booked into the Station Hotel, a Western-style establishment where I'm ashamed to say I ruined my perception of myself as a cosmopolitan by bouncing up and down on the bed in my room for five minutes saying, 'Springs, springs, springs – hooray!'

It was obviously time I got back to being Japanese, which I did first thing the next morning by inventing a koan riddle all on my own:

Q: What do you do if you've got a town so old-fashioned that everyone's leaving it?
A: Turn it into a town so old-fashioned that everyone wants to visit it.

Tsumago, one of the post towns on the Nakasendo Highway, which ran between Kyoto and Tokyo between 1603 and 1867, fell into disuse in the early part of the twentieth century. Then, in the late sixties, the citizens had the bright idea of preserving the entire town as an open-air museum to the extent of keeping TV aerials and electricity poles out of sight. And today, millions of Japanese people, who when they lived in the country couldn't wait to get out of it, flock to Tsumago every year to see what they have lost.

There are two ways to get to it. One is to take the local bus up the mountain from Magome, but the best way is to come upon it as daimyo, or feudal lords, and their retinues would have done in the seventeenth century, hiking for hours up the old highway and spending the night in an inn before moving on.

When I arrived at Magome I found that I was two months late for the daily delivery of rucksacks from there to Tsumago, and was forced to walk up the mountain in the manner of a grumpy snail, rather than in the manner of a feudal lord.

At first, all was well. Bright fritillaries fritillaried about, enabling me to use up all my butterfly vocabulary – 'Ah, a cabbage white! And look, a red admiral!' – while all around the afternoon sun glowed brightly on orange persimmons, red maple, yellow birch and green cedar trees.

But after an hour's steady climbing, dripping and with a huge blister on my big toe, I was beginning to regret my impetuosity. I was beginning to wonder, in fact, why it was that God had made me a Calvinist, halfway up a mountain with a rucksack, when he could just as easily have made me a hedonist, lying in a bath in a Tokyo love hotel surrounded by girls covered in soap.

But then, as I sat on a wooden bench and mopped my damp brow with an even damper hand, two apple-cheeked farmers' wives with their heads wrapped in white kerchiefs and their teeth elsewhere came out and gave me a brimming bowl of milk. Perhaps, I thought as I sipped it gratefully, since I was incapable of kneeling and meditating for hours on end without my legs going to sleep, climbing mountains was the rigorous discipline which would lead to my own moment of Zen enlightenment.

So, filled with fresh milk and fresher vigour, I leaped up and plunged into the cool and cypress-sweet forest. The sweat dried, and above my head the setting sun fell on the tips of the trees, painting them greenish-gold.

I pressed on, keenly aware that for almost three hundred years daimyo and samurai, priest and pilgrim, merchant and peasant alike, had walked these very steps, looked up at these same trees and wondered if they would find their inn by nightfall.

What a boyish adventure it was, to walk through forests in the footsteps of such heroes and villains.

And then, finally, as darkness fell, to stagger gratefully up the steps of the Koshinzuka Inn, to have the hottest bath I have ever had in my life, in an ancient cedar tub.

To be given a bedroom whose shoji screens slid back to reveal a pond flickering with moonlit carp, and the river tumbling in the dark forest below.

And then to have dinner in an old wood-beamed room, of tempura of wild vegetables and a rare moss which can only be plucked a little at a time, otherwise it dies. Of pickles, potatoes, buckwheat noodles, baked fish from the river outside. And *kurumimochi*, the local delicacy of pounded sweet rice dipped in ground walnut sauce and baked over the *irori*, the open fire in a sandpit in the centre of the room, over which a blackened kettle hung from a cantilever of bamboo, pine and plum wood. And then, at last, *umeboshi*, tiny sour plums.

After dinner, the woman who owned the inn showed me the old family album, from the pages of which gazed her grandfather, the ancient white-bearded keeper of this same inn, who had made the table at which we sat – a 5ft-wide slice from a three hundred and fifty-year-old chestnut tree.

Some of the photographs were fading badly, not so much because of their age but because as the evening wore on the room had been filling so completely with woodsmoke that it was quite some time before I realised that my host had actually gone to bed and I had mistakenly been exchanging pleasantries with the stuffed boar in the corner.

In the morning, walking down the mountain from the inn was like being awake at the dawn of creation: dewy grass sparkling in the warming sun, woodsmoke rising against the forest green and the barking of dogs echoing through the valley as I came to Tsumago itself, the little town preserved exactly as it was during the Edo period of 1603 to 1867.

It was a strange place. Outside the ancient wooden buildings, lazy waterwheels turned, carp flashed dimly in dusty pools and women washed their faded white smocks in wooden troughs with a rhythmic splash and slop.

And inside, in the Edo gloom, were shelves of Fuji film.

At the top of the town, the street narrowed and rose, and I

found as it turned the corner a garden of grass and moss, with an overhanging rock to which a small maple clung.

And so to Matsumoto, home of a famous castle which was built in 1595 and is entirely black and white, since they didn't have colour in those days. Near the castle is a museum of Japanese folklore, which contains a magnificently batty collection of hundreds of clocks donated by local businessman Chikazo Honda. I stood there for quite a while thinking of what a strange place Japan is, but I am afraid I cannot tell how long I stood for, because in a room filled with hundreds of clocks, every single one of them had stopped.

It was now my last few days in the country, but at least I had finally discovered the secret of why Japanese women had such lovely little bums.

Noodles.

After two weeks of eating little else, my own had shrunk to a state of such pert splendour that I quite fancied it, and had to keep slapping myself to keep my hands off it.

I took the next train out of Matsumoto, passing on the way to the station several people wearing face masks, not because of pollution, but in case any of their friends spotted them going to work at the unacceptably late hour of 8 a.m.

It was a bright, cold morning, perfect for warming your hands on some station-platform vending-machine coffee. Who would have thought that you could become addicted to coffee out of a can, I thought as I boarded the early train, from which the view as we proceeded north was quite baffling.

The fields below had rice drying in what looked like midsummer sun, the trees beyond were rioting with autumnal colour and the mountains beyond that were heaped with winter snow. I almost expected to arrive at Yudanaka and find the cherry blossoms in bloom.

But then, it hardly mattered what season it was any more, for I was on my way to find the key to salvation.

The key is contained deep within the inner sanctum of the Zenko-ji temple in Nagano. To get to it, you pass through an immense wooden gate, walk past a No Smoking sign almost obscured by the clouds billowing from the incense burner, and climb the steps into the Hondo, or main hall.

Ninety feet high and the largest thatched building in Japan, the Hondo contains statues of the Buddhist trinity of Amida Buddha, Kannon and Daiseishi Bodhisattvas. However, in 642 Empress Kogyoku decided that the images were too sacred for human eyes, and since then no one has been allowed to see them. Even the copies are only brought out for viewing every seven years.

At the very front of the hall is the *naijin*, the innermost sanctuary, and to the right is a flight of steps leading down to a winding, pitch-dark corridor beneath the altar. Somewhere along its twists and turns, on the right hand wall, a lock is hung, and on that lock is a key. If you find it as you grope your way along, you are guaranteed entry to the Buddhist paradise.

But first let me tell you about a strange little creature from Japanese folklore called Tanuki. He resembles a badger, an animal which crops up quite often in the country's mythology. Tanuki, usually depicted wearing a straw hat and clutching a bottle of sake, has a reputation for saving people by suffocating their enemies with his scrotum, which is of legendary size. The reason I mention him at this juncture is because when I finally encountered the key, it was with the part of my anatomy least prepared to deal with a large piece of metal sticking out of the wall.

Rather than me being saved by a scrotum, mine had found salvation all by itself. Painfully fumbling my way to the exit, I emerged with a deep bow, which the monks kneeling there took as a gesture of immense respect and bowed back, but which was actually an attempt to walk upright.

Uncertain whether I had got to heaven or not, I decided to go to hell instead and have a bath with some monkeys.

Jigokudani Onsen, or Hell Valley Hot Springs, lie in the mountains above Nagano. At this time of year, wild monkeys come down just after first light to bathe, preen and escape the cold.

First you take the train to Yudanaka, looking out of the window and realising that virtually every spare inch of the Kanto plain between Tokyo and Kyoto is cultivated – to the extent that you can reach out from the train window and pluck a passing peach.

On the train, a woman came up and gave me a tiny, succulent mandarin, and behind the Uotoshi Ryokan in Yudanaka, where I was staying, I found a session of Zen archery underway.

Wearing plain white kimonos and black overskirts, the archers stood on a wide cedar platform using unadorned bows almost 7ft long. They invited me in to drink green tea, and then they began again, using a ritualised series of slow and graceful movements.

I sat and listened to the creak of the huge bows being drawn, the *phhht* of the polished bamboo arrows being released, the silence as they arced over the long carp pond and the thwack or plunk as they either hit the small targets or sank into the soft sand 100ft away.

Either way, it did not matter. The important thing was the stillness arrived at through focus and repetition.

An hour passed by, unnoticed. The moon rose above the mountains, splashing silver on the stream tinkling into the pond. At peace, I left, bathed in a hot cypress tub, ate a little, and slept the sleep of the blessed.

And woke before dawn, to take the bus to Hell Valley. A farmer's wife got on, gave me a plum, then got off after a while, leaving me the only passenger as we rattled up the tortuous mountain road.

At last I got off and walked for an hour through the forest, while geysers steamed and spiders sat on dewy, trembling leaves. To sit, and wait, until finally the monkeys came – pink-faced macaques padding down through the trees and over the rocks in an orderly procession.

'After you, Yuriko-san.'

'No, please, you put me in a difficult position, honourable friend.'

'But really, I insist.'

'Ah, this will never end.'

In their dozens they came, to bathe and preen, looking around from time to time with their almond eyes.

I left them in peace, went downstream a little, took off my clothes and walked into the hot spring for humans. With my head frozen and the rest of me being boiled alive, I was, as any statistician will tell you, at the right average temperature.

In hell, I was in heaven – a koan riddle which ensured that although I had not discovered Zen, I would at least leave Japan as baffled as I had found it.

1995

Killer Dormice of Slovenia

6th century
Slaveni arrive from Carpathian Basin and create Slav Duchy,
which lasts about ten seconds before arrival of Franks,
Magyars and Hapsburgs.

16th century
Reformation leads to publication of first Slovene book and
grammar. Counter-Reformation leads to both books being
burned before the ink is dry.

18th century
The Enlightenment. Art and culture flourishes. Baroque buildings
spring up all over Ljubljana with surprised looks on their facades.

1809–13
Four years of rule by Napoleon gives Slovenes a taste for
liberté, égalité and fraternité with their fellow Slavs.

1914–18
Four years of First World War gives Austrian Slavs a taste of

164

fighting Serbian and Russian Slavs, resulting in mutiny and
the formation of the Kingdom of Serbs, Croats and Slovenes,
including Bosnia, Montenegro and Macedonia just to be on
the safe side.

1929
Locals, fed up taking all day describing where they're from,
rebrand kingdom under snappier title of Yugoslavia.

1945
Yugoslavia becomes Communist-lite nation under Tito.
Citizens, for example, allowed to travel abroad freely.

1980
Tito dies. Anarchy. In Slovenia, revolution led by artists,
journalists and a punk band called Laibach.

1992
After a ten-day war in which twenty-one die, independence
declared. In careful leaps and bounds, Slovenia transforms
itself from communist satellite to democracy, joining NATO
and EU and finally adopting euro.

In Slovenia, dormice were once hunted all year round, until
they became so scarce that the dormouse hunting season was
cut back to a single week every autumn. A short but intensive
period of activity which marks the beginning of a long, dark
winter, especially for the dormice, this culminates in Dormouse
Night, an evening of carousing, dancing and boasting about the
one that got away.

To recreate the effect in the privacy of your own home,
simply drink several bottles of wine, hold your finger and
thumb a few inches apart, and repeat after me, *'Bil je talo relik'*
('It was this big').

As the plane descended towards Ljubljana in the afternoon
light, the mountains all around were draped seductively in snow,

forest and cloud, as if they couldn't decide what to wear that morning and had simply put on everything in their wardrobe.

Somewhere down there, killer dormice huddled in the shelter of trees, communicating with tiny walkie-talkies as they plotted their small but deeply satisfying revenge.

At the airport, Manja the guide was waiting. Like most Slovenians, she was tall, finely sculpted and fluent in 486 languages, plus dialects.

'You know,' she said, as we drove away, 'when I was younger I couldn't wait to get away, but the more I travelled, the more I loved Slovenia.'

I could see what she meant: as Slovenians will always point out to anyone who cares to listen, they're part of bright, modern, efficient Central Europe, not the down-at-heel East or, God forbid, the turbulent Balkans.

'Anyway, Manja, tell me about the dormouse hunting,' I said, as we passed a string of shiny new Volkswagens and Audis.

'You know about dormouse hunting?' she said, her eyes widening. 'Well, we hunt them at night and when we catch them, there is much singing and dancing and, of course, drinking.'

'Of course. What do you hunt them with?' I said, imagining tiny rifles exquisitely hand-made by Italian mountain dwarfs.

'With nets. We cannot damage the fur or we would not be able to make coats with it.'

'Good grief. How many dormouse furs does it take to make a coat?'

'Oh, lots,' she said, which will hopefully teach me to stop asking stupid questions.

'And are we going to get a chance to go dormouse hunting?'

She gave me a strange look, but I gave it back, since I have enough of my own.

'Maybe tomorrow. Anyway, here we are at the ski factory,' she said.

When the Slovenians are not stalking dormice, they are

skiing. Forty per cent of the population can ski, and 60 per cent of the country is covered in forest. Since that leaves nothing much for dormice, they have gone underground, nibbling out vast bunkers lined with little Kalashnikovs for their Day of Revenge.

The first man to ski down Everest in one fell swoop, for example, was local hero Davo Karnicar, and, of course, he did it on Elan skis, which, along with wine, beekeepers and dormouse coats, have been the country's most famous exports since the factory opened in 1945.

Inside, in a room lined with symphonies in poplar and ash, fibreglass and titanium, the firm's Matjaz Sarabon, a former downhill racer, was talking about the future of skiing.

'Today's skiers are more interested in fun than technique. They are less fit than before and just want an easier time,' he said, with a palpable air of regret for the days when only men of steel could hurtle down mountains.

The future is even stranger: Elan has already patented a fusion ski in which the bindings are part of the ski so that the whole construction curves together, making turning easier.

'By 2005, separate skis and bindings will be history,' said Matjaz confidently.

The factory is also experimenting with fabric-based materials to make skis. So, the next time you see a farmer hurtling down the Sperrins with a pair of Aran pullovers strapped to his wellies, do not mock, for he is at the cutting edge of ski technology.

On the way back to the car, laden with ski brochures, Manja dropped her keys in a snowdrift.

'*Tri sto kosmatih medvedov*,' she cried.

'What does that mean?' I said, bending to dig them out from the snow.

' "Three hundred hairy bears". It's the worst curse in Slovene. Apart maybe from "Duck on the lake" and "You are the mother of a chicken". We don't really have any swear words in the language, to be honest.'

And so, the next morning, to the slopes of Kranjska Gora, with the added excitement of wearing my very own ski boots, finally bought the week before after several years of dithering.

Sadly, I was admiring them so much in the queue for the ski tow that it found me first, with a whack on the side of the head which bled all morning.

'Good grief. What happened to you?' said Manja when we met for lunch.

'I was attacked by a rabid dormouse in the woods,' I said, ordering the soup.

'Yes, they get very annoyed at this time of year because all their friends are coats,' she said.

'When are we going hunting them so I can get my revenge?'

'Maybe tomorrow.'

We were in the sort of traditional inn that features lots of meat, potatoes and strudel served by high-cheeked waitresses in low-cut dresses. It was like being an extra in a Hammer horror movie, except that Christopher Lee didn't stride in and sink his teeth into your neck after the pudding, which I find always takes the edge off a meal.

After lunch, I waddled back to the slopes to continue admiring my new boots, which were enabling me to crash so much faster and more comfortably than before that, by the end of the day, I was able to bury myself in snowdrifts with only the skis protruding.

Satisfied, I went back to the hotel, bled all over the bathroom and went out for a dinner of goulash with extra dumplings.

Afterwards, my stomach lapping over my belt like a high tide, I found myself in a pub called Papa Joe Razor. Inside, several people were dancing to a Slovenian pop song.

'What do the lyrics mean?' I asked Manja, who had appeared with two beers.

'They mean, more or less, "Let's drink until we feel like partying, then party till we feel like drinking some more",' she said.

At the bar, a girl with bright red locks was talking to a boy whose hair looked like a series of wheat sheaves springing from scorched stubble, below a ceiling from which hung a variety of agricultural implements.

I tried to think of this for a while as a metaphor of Slovenia's postmodern exodus from its rural past, then I stopped thinking and had another beer.

The next morning was Sunday. Church bells rang out in the clear, still air, and on the mountains, waterfalls froze like witches' hair.

Considering what my head had done all the day before, it was rather appropriate that we were on our way to Bled. Now in an ideal world, Bled would be twinned with Transylvania, but it is, in fact, a stunning lakeside town where the former Yugoslavian royal family – and later Tito – spent their summer holidays in the monolithic pile which is now the Vila Bled Hotel.

My suite was so big that it came with its own boardroom. I had a bath, then got a taxi back to the bedroom and fell asleep.

The next day, realising by now that I was never actually going to get dormouse hunting, I took a cable car up Mount Vogel and spent the day hurtling down from the mountain top, proving yet again the Micawber principle applied to skiing, that 100 per cent speed and 99 per cent ability equals disaster.

By the time I finished, the setting sun was painting the peaks rose pink, and the mirrored flat of Lake Bohinj far below was the colour of midnight. The evening came, as cold as ether, and I walked up the hill in Bled to the baroque Church of St Martin for an organ recital.

All the way up the path, candles flickered in the snow, and underneath the blue and golden arches as I stepped in, soprano Janja Hvala was singing 'Sveta Noc', the Slovenian translation of that most memorable of Christmas hymns. Outside, after the concert, all was still in the cold, dear air, and it was, indeed, a silent and holy night: in the stars above my head, in the candles at my feet and, most of all, in the sight out there in the dark of the moonlit spire of the church on the island in the middle of the lake which is to Slovenians more than anything else a symbol of their country.

It is to this church that they row out, to break the holy silence with its bell, and wish for the appearance of children, the health of grandparents or the love of strangers. Manja's own mother had come here, after childless years of marriage, wished for a daughter and become pregnant within a month. They come and make their wishes and then walk back down the ancient steps, their hearts full of hope.

And, as they do, they pass the little chapel of St Maria, in which a statue of the saint sits between two adoring cherubs, her hands a few inches apart, in exactly the manner of a dormouse hunter describing the one that got away.

2003

Llama trekking

'Right,' said Marion on the phone from Austria, 'you'll need some sturdy boots for the trekking with llamas, training shoes for the cycling and salopettes for the skiing.'

I looked at my watch. It was the middle of summer.

'Skiing? Llamas? Austria?' I said.

'The skiing's on a glacier. Burgli will tell you about the llamas when you get here,' she said.

'Burgli?' I said, but she had gone.

On the plane to Innsbruck, I had a bacon sandwich and thought about the llamas. What on earth were they doing in Austria, where the only indigenous mammal is the yodel?

There was only one explanation. They must be descendants of the elephants which Hannibal had used to cross the Alps. Left to their own devices when he returned to Carthage, they became smaller over the centuries through lack of food, and furrier through lack of heat. Today, they are almost indistinguishable from real llamas, and the only way to prove their illustrious ancestry to the Carthaginian elephant is to offer them a currant bun.

However, all that was not until Friday. This was only

Thursday afternoon, and I was standing halfway up a mountain with Burgli. And Dave from Essex.

'Funny,' Dave was saying, 'the last time I was here was skiing with a mate. He broke his leg on the first day, and I went out drinking that night, met two nymphomaniac sisters from Southend, and only got back to the chalet three days later. He was lying in bed in plaster, and hadn't eaten or been to the toilet since day one.'

'Are you still mates, then?' I said.

'No, we're not, funny enough,' said Dave.

'Right,' said Burgli, just as I was about to ask her about the llamas. 'Time for some gorge trekking.'

First, though, we had to walk around her calves, for she was one of those healthy outdoor Austrian types who had been climbing mountains since she was knee-high to an edelweiss, and had the legs to prove it.

For the next two hours, we followed them through deep gorges and past splashing waterfalls and ice-dark pools, until we emerged at last into a sunlit paradise of lake and meadow.

Trout pottered and frogs sat stolidly in the shallows, bright-blue dragonflies darted about, and on the slopes above, sturdy calves only slightly smaller than Burgli's grazed and tinkled.

It was all so impossibly idyllic that at any moment you expected Julie Andrews to come cartwheeling down the mountain in a habit.

When we discovered a little lakeside cabin selling Magnum ice-cream bars, I began to suspect that I had actually died on the flight over, and had gone straight to heaven.

However, I was to discover the next morning that I had only got as far as purgatory, in the shape of a golf lesson.

W.C. Fields described golf as a good walk spoiled, but it's more the art of trying to get an impossibly small ball into an impossibly small hole an impossibly long way away. With an impossibly thin club.

The man who was attempting to show me how to do this was called Richard. He was from South Africa, but his coaching technique was from somewhere east of Moscow: the ball went precisely here, your feet went precisely there and the angle of your shoulders was precisely this.

Unfortunately, I am from the intuitional school, in that I am instinctively bad at golf rather than precisely bad, and after felling several middle-aged Innsbruck housewives with a series of wild hooks, I gave up, sat on a bench and watched the gliders from the Kaprun Flying Club circle lazily overheard.

Kaprun, a sleepy village of three thousand souls, is famous for year-round skiing on the local glacier, and infamous for the funicular fire of 2000 which killed 155 people. Today, looking up the mountain, you can see the mouth of the tunnel which they entered that day, never to see daylight again.

The funicular is still closed, but in the winter Kaprun and its large neighbour, Zell am See, buzz with skiers. In the quieter summer, the visitors are still mostly retired British colonels and their wives, but you will see more and more young whippersnappers who are realising that this is the only place in the world where their digital holiday photos can show them skiing, mountain-biking, windsurfing, golfing, parascending and snogging llamas before going out drinking all night.

Indeed, talking of mountain-biking, I was due to pick one up and go for a cycle around the lake with a chap called Steve.

It was years since I'd ridden a bicycle, but it's a bit like riding a bicycle, really, and within minutes I was pedalling along merrily with my hands in my pockets, whistling Schubert's *Trout Quintet* and recapturing that most childish of pleasures of riding for miles without using your hands.

And then, afterwards, other forgotten pleasures of childhood, of swimming in a lake and feeling the grass between your toes as you towel yourself dry in the sun.

On the way back, I heard a thump behind me, and turned around to see Steve lying on the ground bleeding profusely with his bike on top of him.

'Sorry. Wasn't paying attention,' he said.

'That's all right. At least you can tell everyone you were attacked by a complete cycle path,' I said.

Laugh? He was in stitches. Four, in fact, as I discovered when he got back from the hospital.

'Still, the doctor was gorgeous,' he said, rubbing his head. 'Come on, I need a drink.'

At some stage, much later, we seemed to find ourselves in a bar playing a game which involved hitting nails into a log with the wrong end of a claw hammer. If you think this is almost impossible after a few drinks, you're being generous.

Above our heads, posters advertised everything from go-go mädchen to a band called Mastic Scum (Guaranteed Noise Entertainment).

I came back from the toilet at one stage to find Steve explaining to a blonde chalet girl how he'd damaged his head.

'Luckily, though, I was able to push the two little girls and their mum out of the way of the truck before it hit me,' he was saying.

I sighed, tried for the 4,876th time to hit the nail, and went up to the bar to get another two pints of banana colada. They were on special offer, you see.

The next morning, suffering from the world's first banana hangover, we staggered out of the hotel to bright sunshine and villagers wearing shorts and T-shirts, and half an hour later had the surreal experience of skiing down a glacier on the mountain 8,000ft above the village.

'Your skiing is a triumph of power over technique,' said Frank the instructor, as he dropped me back at the hotel.

I was trying to work out whether that was a compliment or not when Burgli arrived in a large car.

'I have come to take you to the llamas,' she said.

The llamas were in a meadow outside the village, looking faintly baffled. Close up, they resemble incredibly tall sheep, so that you expected them to suddenly start swapping high fives, talking jive and dunking basketballs.

'What exactly are we going to do with them, Burgli?' I said.

'We are taking them for a walk,' she said, handing me a lead on the other end of which was a benignly truculent beast who went by the name of Attila.

All went well for the first half hour. Until the thunder started. And the lightning. And the torrential rain.

So if you were one of the pensioners driving through Austria that Friday afternoon and saw several people and seven llamas crushed into a bus shelter, there was no need, after all, to change your medication.

An hour later, soaked to the skin and smelling of damp wool, I deposited a disgruntled Attila back in Burgli's llama park and returned to the hotel bar.

For a dry martini, naturally.

2003

Microlighting to the Shetlands

Day one
Oxford to Carlisle

Gordon Pill, the owner, managing director, sole proprietor and tea boy of Thruster Air Services, screeched to a halt in front of the factory in his 300hp Audi Quattro, which he had customised with overhead underhang and a diagonal steam-trap connected directly to the bonglesprockets.

At least I think that's what he said.

In the back, Victor and I crawled out from where we had slid to the floor and peered out into what was a perfectly ordinary Oxfordshire farmyard, apart from three small details.

On our left was a hay barn in which several bits of crashed aeroplane lay dotted liberally about. On our right, three earnest-looking chaps were busy constructing another aircraft. And in front of us was the third aeroplane which Gordon, in a moment of misplaced generosity that he was now regretting, had lent us to fly to the Shetland Islands.

We were barely in the air before Victor, who the year before had agreed to teach me to fly and been similarly regretting it ever since, handed me the controls.

'Here. You fly, I'll navigate,' he said, pulling a set of charts from the voluminous pockets of his flying suit, as we set off to attempt the first ever microlight flight to the Shetlands.

Two and a half hours later, entirely numb from sitting in one place for so long, I carried out possibly the worst landing in the long history of Lancashire Aero Club, which has been based at the little grass aerodrome of Manchester Barton since 1922.

We bounced to a halt beside the fuel pumps, and emerged bent double as a grizzled attendant appeared, bearing an expression which suggested that we were possibly the first two hunchbacked pilots he had seen in a long career.

I asked him to fill her up, and when he had, limped painfully across the grass towards the venerable brick clubhouse. Bearing my first-ever fuel chit through the hallowed doors like the Gutenberg Bible wrapped up in the Dead Sea Scrolls and signed by Michelangelo, I handed it over proudly to the girl behind the counter.

After that I signed the visitors' book with a gay flourish where it said Name of Pilot, then sauntered out into the sunlight and through the little wooden gate marked 'Warning: Aircrew Only', my soul awash with Bigglesworthiness.

On the grass ahead of me, Victor was peering inside the cockpit of a yellow Tiger Moth, and overhead a little Christen Eagle biplane puttered lazily downwind.

Ten minutes before I could not have been more miserable, and at this moment I could not have been happier.

There came a ringing sound, and Victor pulled from another pocket of his suit, bringing forth a bright cascade of Werther's wrappers, a mobile phone. It was Gordon from Thruster.

'Lucky buggers, you two,' he said. 'Started lashing it down five minutes after you left and hasn't stopped since.'

We took off, tilting north towards the Lake District in the golden light of evening. By eight we were curving down towards the runway at Carlisle, beneath our port wing a Vulcan, Lightning and Vampire sitting on the grass and wondering how, even with the finest navigation equipment, they had ended up so precisely in the middle of nowhere.

As I straightened up to land, I realised that I had lost all feeling in my right leg. Douglas Bader would have appreciated the landing, even if Victor did turn white.

We got a lift from the airport with Joseph, a scatological taxi driver with a shock of white hair and a theory that the recent foot and mouth epidemic had been spread by MAFF disposal men, who had driven around flinging bits of infected cows willy-nilly into fields all over the country.

'Why would they do that?' I asked guilelessly.

'Because they make a f***ing fortune, the f***ers. The c***s have legs, you see.'

'Eh?' said Victor from the back seat.

'Legs. Legs and tongues and tails. Farmer lives down the f***ing road from me found a f***ing leg in one of his f***ing fields with no f***ing cow attached to it. F***ing farmers are no better, pouring boiling f***ing water into cows' mouths to blister them. Same f***ing symptoms as foot and mouth, and they make a f***ing fortune, cos the poor f***ing cows are worth more infected than walking around f***ing healthy. Can you believe what sort of a f***er would do that to a poor f***ing cow?' he said as we pulled up outside The Steadings, a picturesque farmhouse which was the only place we could find a bed for the night.

Tragically, it was a picturesque farmhouse which served neither food nor drink.

'F***ing f***,' said Joseph with feeling, racing off at speed to a restaurant he knew down the road, only to find it had shut at nine.

'What kind of f***ing restaurant closes at nine o' f***ing clock, eh?' he said as he got back in the car.

We had no answer.

Finally we ended up in Carlisle, at an establishment which served until all hours.

'It's crap, but it's cheap,' said Joseph.

He was not wrong on either count. I ordered a Spitfire Ale, since it seemed appropriate, with bangers and mash.

Still, it was a lot better than the previous time I had stayed near Carlisle twenty years before, when I had slept in a phone box in the middle of the country, only to be woken at four by a man who wanted to phone his mother.

Even worse, I had lent him 10p for the privilege.

Day two
Carlisle to Stranraer

A fine feeing it was too, to open the little creaking gate at Carlisle airfield and walk across the dew-damp grass to your aeroplane, leaving a glistening trail of the memory of youth. In the hangar just after the dawn, the air was cool and heavy with that smell of oil and metal that always makes me think of my father's garage in Tyrone where he worked on his racing motorcycles, and which always seems to me the smell of what it means to be a man.

We left Carlisle in golden light, only to arrive an hour later at the military airfield of West Freugh, near Stranraer, with visibility of about a foot in every direction.

'Victor, I can't see the runway,' I said in a voice which was meant to sound calm and authoritative, but came out like a gerbil being liquidised.

'Well, according to this we're right on top of it,' he said, peering at the chart.

I looked out of the left-hand window and realised that we were actually flying alongside it.

Sideslipping carefully into my worst landing since the last one, I taxied slowly to the fuel bowser past four parked RAF Jaguars. Two of the pilots, looking impossibly chiselled and clean-shaven, gave us a baffled wave. They had seen me land, and were probably surprised that we were still alive, and that something could fly so slowly and still stay up.

As the Thruster was being refuelled, they wandered over for a chat. They were, it transpired, just back from being shot at day and night over Iraq.

'Can't shoot back, that's the problem: they hide all their

anti-aircraft batteries in towns and villages, which are outside our rules of engagement,' said the smaller of the two, whose badge identified him as Chin and who had been flying Jaguars for about thirteen years, even though he looked several months short of his GCSEs.

They were waiting for two tonnes of fuel to be taken off each of their planes so that they could take off – it takes a Jaguar about a mile to get airborne – and fly back to Cottishall.

'Where are you chaps heading?' said Sasso, the taller pilot.

'Hoping to get back to our home field, Mullaghmore in Northern Ireland, and set off from there for Shetland, if the weather lifts,' said Victor.

'Why don't you wander over and have a word with the Met man?' he said, indicating a Portakabin beside the control tower. 'He'll only be sitting over there with his thumb up his bum and nothing to do.'

We walked over, knocked politely and went in. Victor introduced himself, sat down and looked wisely at several computer screens. After a while he picked one, and the Met man, one of those chaps who wears a vest under his shirt even in summer, pressed a button and produced a printout.

I took it gingerly, hoping that he was holding it with a different thumb to the one Sasso was talking about, and we walked back to the plane.

As we did so, the four Jaguar pilots came strolling out of the hangar in all their complicated finery. They had run out of fuel containers, so one was simply going to sit on the runway and burn off his two tonnes of fuel.

'Here, that's our taxes!' I said plaintively.

'Yes, dreadfully sorry about that,' he grinned.

Above our heads, the fog was slowly burning off with the heat of the day. We climbed into the survival suits stowed in the back of the plane in case we came down in the water, although the way I was landing it could only be an improvement.

We looked like two giant orange frogs.

'I assume we'll be taking our traditional route, Kermit?' I

said as the four Jaguars took off and came roaring back in a low pass down the runway, giving us a little waggle as they shot by. They may have been wasting our taxes again, but it was very kind of them.

'Right,' said Victor, 'I'll just give Mullaghmore a ring to check it's OK there.'

He listened for a minute, then hung up.

'Bollocks. It's raining, and they can't even see the trees on the other side of the runway.'

We climbed out of the suits, dragged a couple of old armchairs from the hangar and sat like Spitfire pilots waiting for a scramble. Against a nearby wall leaned two ancient black bicycles of the same vintage as the armchairs.

Funny old things, airfields. We had just watched four supersonic jets take off, yet here we were in a scene unchanged for half a century.

Which was, it seemed, how long it was going to take the weather to clear over Mullaghmore. Further calls elicited the information that the trees were now visible, but not the hills, and that the rain had become mizzle, which is just drizzle in a dither.

By late afternoon the drizzle still hadn't made up its mind, and there was nothing else for it but to give up for the day and repair to a hostelry.

'Here,' I said. 'do you think the RAF would mind if we borrowed these two bicycles?'

'No, except yours has a flat tyre.'

A search of the hangar failed to find a pump, so we got a lift down the road with a passer-by, and half an hour later found ourselves in the bar of the County Hotel in Stoneykirk.

'Wanted: Good woman who can clean and cook fish, sew and owns boat and motor. Send photo of boat and motor', said the sign above the barmaid, who turned out to be called Elizabeth Patterson.

'Here, aren't you Geoff Hill from Omagh?' she said, handing me a pint of ale.

'No, I'm Olaf Studmuffin, the famous Norwegian aviator,' I said.

'You can't fool me. I went to school with you,' she said.

Not only that, but I walked into the restaurant that evening and met a man I knew from Belfast, then a friend of Victor's walked in with his wife.

I'd say it's a small world, but I normally avoid clichés like the plague.

'Here,' I said over a dinner of so much dead cow that had it been alive it would have taken John Wayne three days to drive it across the Rio Grande, 'how long would it take us to burn two tonnes of fuel?'

Victor was silent for a moment, chewing thoughtfully on a leg.

'Two hundred and fifty hours,' he said at last.

After dinner, as midnight came winding by, we applied ourselves to the almost impossible task of walking off dinner. A fat moon sat in the branches of a cedar tree, and a hedgehog came waddling down the centre line of the road. I lifted him into the safety of the hedgerow for the night, and we turned and went home to our own warm beds.

Day three
Stranraer to Islay

To be the pilot of a microlight in the UK, you need to become a Zen Buddhist, to be in the eternal now and to realise that when you expect nothing, everything is a gift.

Otherwise you would kill someone by lunchtime, what with looking at the sky, trying to guess what the wind and clouds are doing, making endless phone calls and paying even more endless visits to the Met man, who today was sporting both the vest and a natty pair of grey shoes.

In between, we spent the morning kicking our heels, reading old flying magazines in the aircrew room at West Freugh and chatting to three pilots who had flown a bunch of dignitaries up from London the day before for a night of wining and dining.

At lunchtime the dignitaries arrived looking suitably corpulent and climbed aboard. Their aircraft lined up, trundled down the runway and lumbered heavily into the air.

Finally, a call to some air-traffic controller or other – I forget which, from the several thousand we phoned that day – elicited the information that the sea fog had lifted to 500ft off the deck.

'Right,' said Victor. 'We can fly under it. Let's go.'

I looked across to where the windsock was trying to tear itself off the pole, sighed, and began to clamber into the survival suit, into the various pockets of which I secreted a *Pooley's Guide*, an emergency location transmitter and other essential equipment such as a Swiss Army knife and a packet of Werther's.

We took off into a howling wind and proceeded west at a height, by my estimation, of eight and a half feet, crossing the coast in a sky which seemed like an upturned bowl of semolina. Or possibly farina.

The horizon was somewhere in Victor's imagination, but we were able to get a rough idea of where we were going by shouting up at passing fishing boats and some of the more intelligent seagulls.

Neither of us spoke. By now I was in a cold sweat beneath my suit. I twisted around to see if any land was visible. Nothing. In front, more nothing.

After the longest half hour either of us had ever experienced, Victor broke the droning silence with a single word: 'Land!' I looked, but could see nothing. He was obviously suffering from a sobriety-induced hallucination, in the manner of nuns who have been too long at sea.

But then I saw it too: the shadow of a ghost of a mirage of the Copeland Islands. I took the tiniest of breaths, but like a miser of hope saved the big one until the coast slipped below our port wing.

'Now I know how bomber pilots felt when they saw the white cliffs of Dover,' I said.

'Here, you take over while I get Aldergrove on the blower,' said Victor.

We angled north-west for Mullaghmore, bounced from hill to dale by gusts and squalls, then followed the river north until at last we saw the four chicken sheds and then the dear little clubhouse of our home airfield, bless its cotton windsock.

And there was Cate's car, and her standing beside it, looking up. I have to confess that at that moment a manly tear sprang to attention behind the steely visage of my aviator's sunglasses.

We circled in and curved down to land, feeling like Lindbergh when he arrived at Paris. Heavens, they must have been lining the runway three deep down there, even if there were only two rows of them.

We taxied in and climbed out to hugs and a feast which Cate had brought up in a wicker picnic basket.

'Are we going on to Islay tonight?' I said to Victor through a mouthful of pork pie.

'No bloody way. Not in that stuff. Any chance of some more of that ham?'

I trudged glumly over to the phone to cancel the hotel, only to pause in mid-sentence.

'Here, the hotel on Islay says it's gorgeous there.'

Victor looked out of the clubhouse window.

'Tell you what. We'll take it out to the coast at 500ft. If it's clearer there, we'll give it a go.'

We said a tearful goodbye to our loved ones, and took off. At the coast, it looked even worse. I began to turn back, then out of the corners of our eyes we both saw it: a glimmer of light to the north.

'Wait,' said Victor 'Head for that, but keep the coast in sight.'

We turned towards the light, and a horizon slowly formed.

'Keep going,' said Victor.

We trembled north at 400ft. The engine coughed politely, once, and my heart stood still.

'Carb icing.' said Victor. 'It's clear now.'

Twenty long minutes crawled by. We passed a solitary sea-
gull. Did that mean land? Or was that a myth?

'Look,' said Victor, pointing. It was the tip of the Islay coast.
I glanced at the chart.

'The Mull of Oa.'

'It's pronounced O.'

'Ah.'

'Funny language, English. Like Worcester. What's that all about?'

'Or sauce, come to that.'

I followed the angry cliffs around the long bay, and there
was the glorious sight of the crossed runways of Islay airfield.

I curved around into wind, managed a passable landing, switched off the engine and took a very deep breath.

Victor reached over and shook my hand.

'Well done that man. Now let's go and have a Laphroaig.'

And you know what, that's exactly what we did. In fact, we
liked it so much we had several more.

And I don't remember much after that.

Day four
Islay to Oban

They say that criminals always return to the scene of the crime,
so it seemed appropriate that we woke with the most appalling
hangover to find Iain Henderson, the manager of Laphroaig,
waiting to take us on a tour of my vast holdings in Scotland.

You see, some years before, as part of a Laphroaig
promotion, I had acquired a lifetime lease on a square foot of
Islay, with the promise that should I ever care to visit it, I
would be supplied with a dram of whisky, an umbrella, a
warm scarf, a pair of size 12 wellies and two pieces of string to
bind my trouser legs against inquisitive stoats.

'The bad news, I'm afraid,' said Iain, opening the wellie
cupboard with a melodious creak, 'is that marauding sheep
have savaged the scarf, but we've replaced it with a copy of
War and Peace.'

'Of course,' I said, taking the book and following him out to my plot, which lay in a little wood. I didn't half come over all funny standing on it, I don't mind telling you, even if my feet did stick into next door.

Mind you, I wasn't quite as overcome as the Japanese barman who planted a flag on each corner, took a photograph, then cut the grass with nail clippers and took it home to Tokyo.

Back at the airfield, we suited up and took off, only to be confronted by the unfortunate combination of descending cloud and rising ground. Disgruntled, we returned to Islay, where I'm delighted to say Victor made a complete horlicks of the landing after getting his hand caught on the edge of the *Pooley's Guide*.

'Well, Mr Mitchell, I'm sorry to tell you that you would have passed your General Flying Test but for that atrocious landing,' I said as we taxied in.

His reply was not printable.

By the time we had refuelled from the little filling station up the road, the sky had cleared, and we set off, threading our way north over mist-shrouded islands. Through gaps in the white we could see sailing boats cossetted by harbours and damp children in bright pullovers walking down summer lanes.

An hour later, we rounded a leafy promotory and landed at Oban to find a small clubhouse filled with three friendly pilots, all called John.

We settled into a sofa with some old flying magazines, a cup of chicken soup and the club's black Labrador.

'Who owns the dog?' said Victor.

'John,' said John.

John, meanwhile, was looking out of the window, a favourite occupation of pilots. Although I was only a novice aviator, I was already beginning to realise that 90 per cent of flying was bollocking about, and only 10 per cent was actually flying.

'I can see Mull, so it's going to rain,' he said.

'Because if you can't see it, it's already raining,' said John, just as it started raining.

'Don't think you fellows are going anywhere today,' said John, 'but there's a hotel at the end of the runway. It's our equivalent to the restaurant at the end of the universe.'

We called to book a room, and returned to the clubhouse sofa. In the evening, by which time it was too late to go anywhere, the sun came out over the bay.

'Come on,' I said, 'let's go for a spin.'

Ah, the pleasure of just jumping in and starting up without survival suits, lifejackets, rafts, baggage, Met men, air-traffic control and flight plans. We rose over the sparkling sea, danced around the little islands, and I managed my second perfect landing of the day, even if only by the definition that we were both alive and the aircraft was reusable.

We put the plane away, wandered down to the hotel, poured ourselves a large Laphroaig and had steak pie and ale for supper.

As non-aviating days go, it hadn't been a bad one at all. Even if I did lose the toss for the double bed for the second night in a row.

Day five
Oban to Cumbria

On the breakfast TV weather map, the bank of cloud looked like a truculent sheep covering most of the field that was Scotland.

'Bollocks,' said Victor, and went back to sleep.

Two hours later we were wandering down the runway, our feet crunching on the shells dropped on the tarmac by seagulls for supper.

'Still, at least the microlight bunch here are really friendly,' I said.

'Aye, if they were light-aircraft bods they'd be a bit snotty. Worst of all are British Airways pilots. How do you know if you meet a BA pilot at a party?' said Victor.

'Don't know.'

'He'll tell you. And what's the difference between God and a BA pilot?'

'Give up.'

'God doesn't think he's a BA pilot.'

We arrived at the clubhouse to find John pre-flighting his plane, the process all pilots go through to make sure there are two wings, three wheels and a noisy bit on the front.

'John's printed out the Met reports for you,' he said.

Victor walked in, picked them up and flicked through them.

'Seven-eighths cloud at 300ft. Mist, drizzle, 3k vis.' he muttered darkly.

On the clubhouse TV, *Star Trek* was just starting. 'This is the five-year mission of the Starship Enterprise: to boldly go where no man has gone before,' intoned Kirk gravely.

At this rate it looked like it was going to take us five years to boldly go as well. As we sat around looking at the overcast sky, a large motorbike roared to a halt and its leather-clad owner strode in.

'Hi, I'm John,' he said.

'Thought you might be. Is it compulsory around here?'

'Apart from Dave. Funny thing is, there's a hang-gliding club near here where everyone's called Bill,' he said.

On the TV, the weekly forecast came on. An unremitting landscape of rain, cloud and low pressure passed before us as the days rolled by on the screen.

When they got to the gale warnings, Victor, who had been slumping lower and lower on the sofa, turned to me.

'Let's get out of here. Our only way out of it is south,' he said.

The great Shetland expedition was off, and now our only concern was whether we could return the plane to Oxford.

Two hours of merrily bouncing around later, we found ourselves at the Kirkbride Aero Club in Cumbria, which during the war was the huge RAF airfield to which pilots, like the entertainer Hughie Green, flew thousands of planes from Canada and the USA.

It was inhabited on this particular afternoon by a bluff Yorkshireman, a bluff Yorkshireman's wife, two bluff Alsatians and the chief flying instructor, who managed the remarkable feat while we were there of talking non-stop for half an hour about bearings.

By the time he had finished, it was too late to go anywhere, so we climbed in and taxied to the former officers' mess at the end of the runway, now a hotel. It was closed.

The chief flying instructor, who turned out to be called Ian and an entirely pleasant chap in between bearing conversations, disappeared around the side, then emerged through the front door.

'They're open again. You're the only customers, so when they leave for the night they'll lock you in,' he said.

We stepped into a lobby in which a noticeboard listed forthcoming attractions. A single small piece of paper pinned to it advertised organ tuition by D.A. Shaw.

A small receptionist in a large blouse showed us up to our room, passing on the way the Velvet Suite, in which could be glimpsed a four-poster hung with chintz and a sunken bath beyond.

'How much is our room?' said Victor as she unlocked the door.

'Haven't a clue,' she said.

We unpacked our meagre kit and went down to dinner to find the bluff Yorkshireman and his wife already dining, the chief instructor having disappeared to check his bearings.

The concept of nouvelle cuisine being unknown to this part of the nation, Victor and I were presented with half a lamb and half a small cow, thickly sliced and served with Yorkshire pudding.

The bluff Yorkshireman's wife had salmon. It was also served with Yorkshire pudding.

The bluff Yorkshireman had fish and chips, which he ate while breathing through his nose to a rhythmic clickety-clack from his false teeth, so that the overall effect was like dining in the buffet car of a small but determined steam train.

When we finished and sat back in a state somewhat beyond replete, the waitress took the plates away, sprinkling peas willy-nilly over the brown floral carpet.

Hauling ourselves heavily to our feet, we set off for a constitutional around the airfield.

In the gold-grey light of of a late summer evening, flat fields of barley stretched all the way to the horizon, punctuated by the sleeping hulks of vast hangars.

We rounded one, and came knee to jaws with three giant Alsatians. A visceral growl dribbled from the largest, while the other two bounded over and began sniffing our ankles enthusiastically.

We were just about to be either savaged or shagged to death when a man appeared from the gloom in ragged socks and a T-shirt that had been boiled once too often.

'We're pilots,' I said in answer to the question he hadn't asked us.

'Oh, that's all right then. Don't touch the big bugger or he'll bite you.'

We retreated to the centre of the airfield and what was left of the control tower, a little brick and glass turret through the heart of which spiralled a graceful staircase. Beyond was the main runway, a mile of undulating tarmac. We stood there in the gloaming, looking across to the Commanding Officer's elegant brick house, built to standard RAF bourgeois specifications, and to more hangars beyond that.

It was not too difficult a feat of imagination to see in the crepuscular gloom the ghosts of the several thousand airmen and gunners, navigators and radio operators, fitters and electricians, mechanics and clerks who had once kept this great heart of darkness beating. And to hear, as night finally gathered around, the somnolent throb of a Beaufighter sliding down from a moon-dark cloud at the end of a long flight from Canada, with Hughie Green taking that long, deep breath that every pilot takes when his field is finally in sight.

Day six
Cumbria to Oxford

As the sole occupants of the hotel at the end of the runway sat down to breakfast, the sole member of staff came pottering up.

'Would you gentlemen like the full breakfast?' he said.

'What's in it?'

'Everything.'

Some time later, we waddled out of the front door, walked, oh, at least five yards to the plane and flew south to Manchester Barton, which with its gently undulating runway was like landing on a sea of grass – skip, skip, skip, boing, hurgle and burgle.

'Bloody hell, we're alive,' said Victor, the unappreciative sod.

In the clubhouse, the menu advertised soup and barm cake.

'What's a barm cake?' I asked the man behind the counter.

'A what?'

'A barm cake. It's on the menu.'

'Oh, that. It's a barm cake.'

'Aye, but what is it?'

'Well, it's a barm cake.'

'But what is a barm cake?'

He sighed, shook his head, went down the back and returned with a plain white bun.

We had two, and flew south, passing on the way the vast chimneys of Sellafield making clouds.

The reason, of course, that the Government allows everyone to believe that these are power stations is that if the truth were known we would demand the removal of all clouds and come to believe, in the resulting permanent sunshine, that all this time we had been a Mediterranean people betrayed by geography and politics. The holiday industry would collapse and we would all give up work and spend our time gathered around large wooden tables eating pasta washed down with red wine and olive oil while wearing dark suits, fondling our grandmothers' bottoms and machine-gunning the neighbours.

Also, without weather, we would have nothing to talk about.

We would therefore become the world's first silent Italians, lapse into decline and die of terminal contradiction in the same way as Greta Garbo when she started making movies and found she was expected to be a talkative Swede.

Anyway, where was I? Ah yes, landing in the the meadow beside the Thruster factory and handing the keys back to Gordon.

However, we still had one more mission to complete before the expedition was truly over.

You see, when I was a boy, I had promised myself that when I finally learned to fly, I would buy myself a proper Second World War flying jacket.

Which is why, five minutes later, we found ourselves hurtling south in Gordon's borrowed Land Rover to the factory at Thruxton where Irvin jackets are still made.

If I had expected the factory shop to be an emporium where rows of flying jackets hung like ripe chestnuts while chaps discussed their requirements with a member of staff – 'Need an extra pocket for moustache wax, old boy?' – I was to be disappointed. It was, in fact, a largish broom cupboard, and the staff was a carefully flamboyant man called Terry in a faded pink Marks & Spencer polo shirt.

Still, he measured me up, declared that what I needed was a 46 extra long with an extra inch on the body, told me it would be in the post in two weeks, and relieved me effortlessly of four hundred quid. But then, a promise is a promise, especially to yourself.

As we closed the door and walked away, I checked the expedition kitty and found that it contained just enough to get us into the Army Museum of Flight just down the road.

There, we spent a happy hour pottering around Sopwiths and gazing with regret at the dead and smiling faces of men we had never known on the Royal Flying Corps wall of honour.

At last, having gone backwards through the museum by mistake, we found ourselves in 1911, looking at a quotation from General Sir W.G. Nicholson, Chief of the Imperial General Staff.

'Aviation is a useless and expensive fad advocated by a few individuals whose ideas are unworthy of attention,' it said.

2001

Namibia

Let me give you two pieces of advice. Never look a leopard in the eye, and always put collapsible water bottles away where you can find them again.

But let me explain. The previous year, I had walked across the Sahara with 123 other lunatics from Northern Ireland to raise £250,000 for Mencap.

Every day, we walked 20 miles in temperatures of 40°C, facing blisters, sunstroke, heat exhaustion and 2000ft-high dunes.

Every night, we faced sub-zero temperatures, the life or death struggle to find a bed next to someone who didn't snore, and the horrific realisation while halfway across the dunes to answer the call of nature in our bare feet, that scorpions only come out after dark.

Every morning at dawn we were dragged out of warm sleeping bags to wash with a tin mug in a bucket of freezing water.

So why, when that nice Ciara Gallagher from Mencap phoned up to ask me if I'd fancied an even tougher trek across the deserts of Namibia, did I accidentally say yes?

Sighing deeply, I made my way up to the study, found a guidebook on Namibia, made a nice cup of tea, and sat down to find out, among other things, that you should never look a leopard in the eye, because it really annoys them, and you should avoid male elephants when they are sexually aroused, which I generally do anyway.

The politics, meanwhile, sounded even more complicated than Northern Ireland: groups vying for supremacy over the past few decades had included SWANU, OPO, SWAPO, PLAN, DTA, MFC, MPLA, SADF and UNTAG, as well as a few incursions across the border by UNITA. That stands for the National Union for the Total Independence of Angola, which should really be NUTIA, except that sounds like a vegetarian spread.

The similarity to Northern Ireland doesn't end there: in the early nineteenth century missionaries arrived and gave all the natives guns, thus establishing a link between religion and loud noises with which everyone in Belfast was only too familiar.

However, all this was unlikely to trouble me, since I would be in the desert, where the only occupants are the bushmen of Namibia, one of the few tribes in the world who have learned to live with no permanent access to water.

In this they are like the indigenous landlocked people of Tyrone, although they make up for it by going on holiday to Rossnowlagh every year. In fact, being from Tyrone I should be entirely at home, I thought, going to the cupboard under the stairs where I was sure I had left my collapsible water bottle from the Sahara trek. And failing completely to find it.

Making a mental note to buy another one and not let it out of my sight this time, I returned to the history of Namibia, which was colonised by the Germans when they arrived in 1884. However, in 1914 they wanted the towels back for their attempt to colonise the rest of the world, so they handed Namibia over to South Africa.

In 1990, South Africa handed Namibia back to the Namibians, and in a few weeks the freshly independent nation would face its biggest challenge yet: the arrival of eighty-seven of the whitest people ever seen in the country, who were not only going to go out in the midday sun, but walk across the desert in it.

I arrived at Belfast Airport to find them well prepared with endless supplies of Tayto cheese and onion crisps, entire rucksacks filled with chocolate and, in the case of one large chap whose name tag identified him as Whitie, a stuffed dog.

And then there was me, wearing a pair of old volleyball shoes and pink ski socks, and clutching a book on Siberia. Still, if God had meant me to be organised, he would have bought me a Filofax.

Tragically, we arrived at Heathrow later that afternoon to find that everyone else in the world had decided to go to Namibia that weekend as well, and there was not a single seat to be had with extra legroom. Even checking in gave me vicarious DVT, and when I got to the seat I found that the only person who would have been comfortable in it was a legless gerbil.

I think the people who design economy-class seats should be forced to sit in them for ever, in the same way that architects who design pebbledash bungalows should be forced to live opposite them, and lawyers who extol the virtues of nightclubs and bookie's shops should be forced to live beside them.

Anyway, where was I? Ah yes, spending an entirely sleepless night on my way to Namibia.

At one stage I went for a wander and found an empty seat in front of the cinema screen, but the only way to get comfortable was to rest my feet on the bottom of the screen, and after a while the steward made me take them down. This was a bit unfair, since my feet were actually more interesting than the film. It was called *Bedazzled*, and if you ever get a chance, don't see it. The only good thing about it was the casting of Elizabeth Hurley as the devil, since she was entirely bad.

Many hours later, we landed in Windhoek. It was a Sunday morning, but there wasn't a Presbyterian anywhere in sight, except for the ones we'd brought with us.

It was February, but it was summer, and it was the rainy season, but there was no rain.

It was so confusing that the only thing to do was to buy a copy of the local newspaper, the *Windhoek Observer*. The three main stories were a flood, a plane crash and a boat launch, although not simultaneously.

On page three was an obituary for Mr Pieter Ignatius Botha. 'Mr Botha died recently,' it began, then added, by way of an afterthought, 'He was seriously ill.'

The more I read it, the more it became clear that all the stories had been written by the same person, a man who had once been introduced to the English language, but had not developed a lasting relationship with it.

Here was another paragraph: 'The daughters of the particular mother were active in recent years, and sex, in abandoned rail cattle trucks standing on a loop line, took place and according to the latest allegations, revived.'

Inside, things got even better. This was page 11:

> Before I tell you the story of Tuesday, a few words on the Marquise de Pompadour. She was indeed beautiful, twenty-seven in 1977, a rather uncommon face, little make-up and she seldom visited a hairdresser which added to her qualities of beauty rather than diminishing her attraction.
>
> She had a lovely and very firm body, exceptionally nice legs, a quiet person but fiery and principled. Her mouth was slightly too wide but that was not unduly disturbing because in her company a man, and I'm talking of a real hot-blooded one, soon became aware of the vigours in that shapely body.
>
> Her teeth were good, of high quality, and her hands were not delicate, strong and pleasing to the eye. Her breasts strained against her blouse.

Then, on the back page, in the middle of a report about how run-down the town hospital and swimming pool had become:

The hospital is dirty, grimy and everything reminds you of sex because it is one notice or poster after the other of sex.

The huge municipal swimming pool is in total disuse … at least an *Observer* reporter when taking the photograph could reflect back to a day in 1959 when he fell in love with a young teacher at the pool, so infatuated with her that he missed his lift with Mr Percy Niehaus, political party leader, to Tsumeb where Mr Niehaus was to address a rally.

The frantic reporter, after hurriedly and passionately saying goodbye to the young woman searched the streets for a car and lo and behold found Mr Johan Coetzee of Sanlam Insurance with his DKW Saxomat, a lovely car with a two-stroke engine. Mr Coetzee raced to Tsumbe with the reporter on a dirt road …

'Anything in the paper?' came a civilized voice from beside my shoulder, interrupting my reverie.

'You wouldn't believe it if I told you. Here, have a look,' I said, handing it over to him.

He turned out to be one of the two doctors on the trip, rather splendidly named Titus.

'After Andronicus or Oates?' I said.

'The family dog, I fear,' he said, opening page 24 to reveal four photographs of topless women which I had missed. I looked more closely, but none of them resembled the Marquise de Pompadour.

We climbed aboard a bus and set off for the oldest desert in the world, decamping some hours later in exactly the middle of nowhere and setting off across the blazing sands.

Two hours later, as the shadows lengthened towards the sharp violet and orange of a desert dusk, we found camp. I unrolled my sleeping bag and began the minutiae of winding down after a day in the wilderness: washing in half a mugful of water, setting out a clean shirt and socks for the morning and, most important of all, taping up toes before they had a chance to turn into blisters.

What seemed like only five minutes after I had nodded off, I was being awakened by the cheery voice of Daz the guide announcing *'Mesdames et messieurs,* wakey wakey, rise and shine, it's another beautiful day in the desert, breakfast in fifteen minutes!'

Ah, I had forgotten the joy of being woken before dawn, crawling out of a warm sleeping bag and washing in half a teaspoon of freezing water.

I pulled back the tent flap. All around, happy trekkers were emerging in the misty dark and making their way by torchlight like a procession of glow-worms to a welcome breakfast of bacon and eggs, toast and coffee.

As we shouldered our packs, dawn crept around to reveal that the mist had sprung the desert into life. Along the river bed that we had camped in, everything from acacia trees to rock lichen glowed vibrant green, and at my feet a small black basking beetle sat with its rear end in the air, the rivulets of mist slowly running down its carapace into its mouth to give it water for the day ahead.

From the cliffs all around came the sweetly strident cries of the rock dassie which, believe it or not, is a descendant of both the elephant and the guinea pig. One of them, presumably the guinea pig, must have had far too much to drink that night. Let's just hope he got to be on top.

We climbed out of the river bed on to a high stony plain filled with remarkable sights. There was a locust, looking so much like the pebbles around it that Kevin almost stood on it before it jumped.

There was a chameleon, its eyes swivelling independently at our intrusion.

'Are you looking at me?' several of us said simultaneously, then laughed.

Past it was a Left Ear Tree, whose pale green seed pods looked, funny enough, exactly like left ears. Or right ones, if you were walking the other direction.

There was even food, from the plant the bushmen call ostrich salad, which tastes like fish and chips with extra salt, but without the fish or the chips, and desert melon, which is like a lemon marinated in TCP.

Spitting it out, we strode on and down into the trapped heat of a river gorge, where no breeze ventured. All around, the heat had twisted and cracked the granite rocks into fantastical shapes by Henry Moore out of Dali – whales, frogs and once a giant Venice Carnival mask. Astonishing, and much cheaper than drugs.

Halfway through the morning we were joined by Joe, a lean South African guide who had just got back from a kayak trip to the Mozambique islands.

'One afternoon the kayak got ripped from stem to stern and started sinking. Then half a dozen grey sharks turned up for their lunch. I got it patched up, but by the time I got to the next island it was pitch dark. I got to the beach more by feel than anything else, and fell on to it in agony with cramps from my head to my toes,' he said, carefully sidestepping a small sand snake.

'Heavens,' I said, 'what did you do then?'

'Went for chicken and chips. They do a great feed at the beach hut there,' he said as we came upon the lonely graves of two German officers, Ferdinand Zarp and Robert Kirchgatter, who died on 26 and 27 June 1895, and whose dusty skeletons lay beneath our feet clothed in the tattered remains of their Imperial Army uniforms and topped by two tarnished picklehaubes.

There were no particular wars being fought that year, so they must have died, in all their colonial finery, from the most common of insects or the most humble virus, to be laid in the parched earth half a world away from the morning sweetness of mountain pine.

I left the wind whistling through their iron headstones and hurried on to catch the rest of the group, who had stopped to observe a rather large chameleon.

If you pick these up very gently, they will at first hiss at you, revealing a mouth the colour of a fresh lemon, then relax and slowly change to the colour of your palm. Which made me wonder: how on earth do chameleons find each other to mate? Or do they end up going out with rocks and branches for three years before finally going for chameleon counselling?

'She's just so passive, doctor. At first I thought she was just naturally quiet, but the funny thing is, I'm beginning to quite get used to it, a bit like Tom Hanks and the volleyball in that film *Cast Away.*'

At this moment my thoughts were distracted by the welcome sight of camp, in the shady gorge of a river bed.

We collapsed gratefully in front of our tents as Daz came trotting up, looking far too cheery.

'Here, if we climb that peak over there,' indicating with a nonchalant wave a 2,000ft mound of granite rising nearby, 'we'll get a great view of the sunset.'

Now, you'd think after a day trudging sixteen miles across the burning sands in temperatures nudging 50°C, we would have playfully garroted him then pegged him out for the ants, covered with a little honey

However, my little honey was at home in Belfast, so along with all the rest I said, 'Yeah, why not?' and climbed the mountain.

And yes, the sunset from the top was worth it.

But the cold beer at the bottom even more so.

As I was examining my toes with a torch before tucking myself in for the night, a middle-aged chap with the sort of expression which comes from being comfortably set in your ways trudged gloomily past.

'Are you all right?' I said in the spirit of St Francis of Assisi, who said that to give is to receive, although to be fair, he was speaking in the days before income tax.

'Can't seem to find a space in a tent,' muttered the chap, who turned out to be called Jonathan.

'Well, there's space in this one, although it'll be a bit cramped,' I said, flinging back the tent flap as generously as a sheikh.

Tragically, I was to discover that the reason he couldn't find anyone to share with was because he snored like the offspring of a sinusoidal horse and an asthmatic turkey.

The man in the tent next door, meanwhile, seemed to be working his way through every page of the *Kama Sutra*.

'Mmmm, ohhhhh, mmmmm, yes, oh yes, phfwoar, wow, ormph,' he went all night long, building to a crescendo around four in the morning.

It was like being trapped in a musical of *Animal Farm* written by the Marquis de Sade, and it was in a sleepless and disgruntled state that I staggered into the frozen dawn.

'Hope I wasn't snoring,' said Jonathan, emerging cheerily well rested from the tent. 'My wife says I do when I'm knackered or if I've had a few beers.'

Even worse, the previous day's trek had produced a rather painful chafing on the bit where I sit, and no amount of Sudafed cream seemed to soothe it.

I breakfasted heartily on toast and peanut butter, applied a large tub of Vaseline, and walked off into the sunrise like John Wayne.

I was with a new group this morning, led by Tony, the sort of quintessential blond and aquiline Englishman who during the war would have carefully folded his pyjamas and gone off to die nobly in a blazing Spitfire. Just ahead of us was a bunch led by JoJo, a former ballet dancer who was built like a small gazelle and who had most of the chaps in her group dreaming of dying nobly in a pair of blazing pyjamas.

'Right,' said Tony, 'before we proceed, let me remind you to drink far more water than you think you need. Your pee should look like champagne. If it looks like Smithwicks, you're in trouble.'

'What happens if it looks like champagne and tastes like Smithwicks?' came a voice from the back.

It was Kevin, who was going to come in very handy in half an hour, when we discovered the skull of a zebra, with the rest of it nowhere in sight.

'He must have been doing some speed when he hit that rock,' said Kevin.

'He was probably run down at a human crossing,' said someone else.

Five minutes later we came across the rest, half skeleton and half rug.

'Is he dead?' said Phelim.

'No, but it's the worst case of anorexia I've ever seen,' said Kevin, who had now been our resident zebra expert for, oh, five minutes.

Five hours later we stopped for lunch by an abandoned diamond mine. The sun had risen to its zenith, and with it the temperature. Kevin's thermometer rose steadily to 50°C, went off the scale, then expired with a weary pop.

'God, I could murder a nice cold pint,' said Peter, a veteran of the previous year's Sahara trek who had kept his indigo Tuareg headscarf, and was now wearing it at a jaunty angle. 'A really cold one, with those little beads of moisture on it, it's so cold.'

'Peter?' said Andy.

'What?'

'Shut up, shut up and shut up,' said Andy as we came around a rock to find a herd of zebra who were as surprised to see us as we them.

'Here, do you think zebra's white bits stay cool and their black bits heat up in this sun?' said Kevin.

'Aye, but every minute they take a step forward to equalise the balance,' said Andy.

We marched on, through the shimmering heat of the afternoon into the blessed cool of early evening, finally arriving in camp to discover to my delight that I actually had enough clean T-shirts to last me to the end of the week.

Honestly, when you're knackered at the end of a hard day in the desert, you wouldn't believe how happy it makes you to know that you don't have to wear a dirty shirt the next day.

In fact, I was so content that rather than take up Daz's kind offer of climbing another mountain to watch the sunset, I dragged a folding chair over to my tent, in which I was blissfully alone, had a beer and read my book about Siberia.

And so to dinner, a splendid feast of oryx spaghetti bolognese, followed by fruit salad and custard, washed down by a very nice South African red.

Even better, the next day was the last, and we set off with a song in our hearts and a spring in our steps, only to come face to face with a 6ft-wide *Weltwitschia mirabilis*, a plant which is unique to this part of the world and has a lifespan of about one thousand five hundred years.

The *Weltwitschia* is the Little Shop of Horrors of the desert. It is the ugliest plant in the world, although it does not realise it, since there are no mirrors in the desert. Not surprisingly, it reproduces asexually.

We set off again and ran into the next group gathered around Tony, who was holding up a small grey object about the size of a well-fed peanut.

'This,' he said, 'is an oryx dropping, and it is a Namibian tradition that on the last day of a great journey, there is a competition to see who can spit one the furthest.'

Well, we're the sort of group who'd believe anything, and after several minutes of intensive oryx-poo spitting, Kevin emerged as a clear winner with a rather impressive effort of just over 10m, which will stand him in good stead if it ever becomes an Olympic sport. We wandered on. I'm not sure what the rest were thinking, but I was thinking that if Cate ever got to hear about this, she'd never kiss me again.

In the afternoon we paused on a high rocky outcrop for another last-day tradition, in which we all sat apart and took a few minutes of silence to reflect on what the trek had meant to us, and to those less fortunate for whom we had done it.

We sat, and were still. The peace gathered around, vast and true, and from it came a honey bee, thrumming past on its way to some imagined meadow of my childhood.

How strange, I thought. Exactly the same thing had happened at the same moment on the last day of the walk across the Sahara a year ago, like a little leitmotif of contentment and completion.

We rose, and strode on into the last two hours of the day, our steps quickening as we descended into the burnished cauldron of a river gorge and saw in the distance the finishing line.

A breeze sprung up from nowhere, and it was with the wind in our hair and a grin of blessed relief on all our faces that we crossed the line, dropped our packs and sank on to the hot sand.

'Well done,' said Mark, the leader of the guides, handing me a plastic cup filled with champagne.

'Say that to Kevin,' I said, draining it in one gulp, 'he's the new world oryx-poo spitting-champion.'

'Oh no. You didn't fall for the old oryx-poo yarn, did you?' he grinned.

2001

Old Blue Eyes
To Palm Springs on the trail of Sinatra

The fifties. Ava Gardner was diving naked into Frank Sinatra's swimming pool in Palm Springs, and I was growing up in a field in Tyrone. Frank was having martinis with Carmen Miranda, and I was drinking National Health Service powdered milk. He was leaving Lauren Bacall, and I was leaving for school.

The fifties. When the American dream was pure, and Americans were perfecting the art of endless childhood which they continue to this day: the instant friendships, the artless lack of irony, the wearing of bright clothes well into senility.

The corollary of that, of course, is arrogance and selfishness, unthinking generosity, hedonism and the inability to defer a pleasure if it can be had right this minute.

Frank Sinatra was the epitome of all of that, and Palm Springs was where he perfected them. As a result, the ghost of Sinatra is everywhere in this California town. You go into a bar, and his voice is sailing through the air without a breath to disturb the arid desert air. You talk to a man in that bar, and

208

discover that he was Sinatra's dentist. You order a cocktail, and Sinatra is in the glass, in the effortless cool of late afternoon beneath the palms. You talk to a man outside, and Sinatra paid his father's medical bills. You check into a hotel, and the owner says of course Sinatra had a temper: he was short and Italian, so what did you expect?

A town of forty-five thousand souls, eight thousand of them millionaires, Palm Springs has had many lives. A thousand years ago it was the home of the Cahuilla Indians, who retreated to the nearby canyons in the heat of the summer.

In the thirties it became Hollywood's hideaway, and from the forties to the sixties everyone from Elvis to Liberace stalked the streets and gathered for cocktails in the tangerine dusk, which for many of them was not long after breakfast.

In the seventies it became a retirement town in which the average age and temperature were both about 88.

In the eighties, hordes of libidinous teenagers descended on it every spring break, making it more hip than hip replacement until Mayor Sonny Bono banned the testosterone tearaways.

In the nineties the gap left by the students was plugged by gay tourists, who stay in luxury private resorts where the rooms, naturally, start at standard queen-size.

Appropriately enough, I arrived in this perpetual Mecca of cool at the cocktail hour, falling from a lilac sky to a desert the colour of powdered brick.

I picked up my convertible at the airport and pressed a button by the seat. The hood tilted back, and the heat of the night filled my bones. I pressed another button, and the music from the radio poured into my veins like honey.

It was Sinatra, singing 'Lady [pause for effect] Luck'.

'Sinatra, who died a year ago today,' said the announcer, when the song had finished. 'All this week in the valley he loved so well, we will be making sure that his flame burns [pause for effect] forever.'

By the pool, a waitress was waiting with a gin martini. The darkness crept around, draping me with the scents of bougainvillea, jasmine and orange blossom. I could not sleep, and read a novel late into the night.

And the next morning, I had a Californian breakfast conversation.

Me: 'Hi. And what sort of mood have we on offer this morning?'

Waiter: 'Well, we got sunny, sunny, sunny or extra sunny.'

Me: 'I'll take extra sunny with coffee.'

Waiter: 'You got it. How would you like your coffee … hi-caf, low-caf, decaf, or no caf?'

Me: 'Extra caf with milk.'

Waiter: 'Absolutely. And will that be hi-fat, lo-fat, no fat, soya or goat's?'

Me: 'Cream.'

In the *Los Angeles Times* on the table in front of me, nine of the top ten in the bestseller list were self-help books. The tenth was the restaurant guide to southern California.

And then, before I went looking for the ghost of Frank Sinatra, I had an appointment to meet Morgan.

Morgan was, in fact, the Sinatra of the desert: cool, confident and brilliant, but known to mix with some nasty types. In Morgan's case, they're the critters you meet on her jeep adventure tours of the desert and mountains, which were apparently coming down with rattlesnakes, tarantulas, black widows and lawyers protecting their weekend retreats.

However, all I could see were lambs, and since this was California, we weren't allowed to stop and play with them because a sheep therapist had apparently proved that it causes lambs stress. Although not as much as mint sauce.

Morgan, however, was astonishing. Half-scientist, half-philosopher-poet, half-raconteur – I know that's a lot of halves, but there was too much in there for just one brain – she talked almost non-stop for over three hours about the wilderness, and if I ever get lost there, I want her by my side. In about a day she'll have a house built, curtains sewn, soap, aftershave, shampoo, moisturiser, complete medical kit and a five-course meal all made from cactus, and we'll be lying on a rabbit fur rug in front of a fire sipping home-made tequila.

Handy hint: a sheet of sandpaper is a useful substitute for expensive maps when visiting the desert.

If you prefer your wildernesses filed alphabetically, there's always the Living Desert: 1,200 acres which include an African village, a hospital which treats twenty thousand sick animals every year, and a daily show in which guides, owls, golden eagles, rats, porcupines and cervils do that talking, flying, swooping, scurrying, prickling and pouncing thing they do.

It is, of course, the closest you're likely to get to a rattlesnake or black widow spider and live to tell the tale, but all the logical arguments in the world about education and salvation from extinction fade, for me, with the sadness of being two inches away from the cougar who looked at me through the glass with terrible beauty and heartbreaking boredom. A bit like those TV presenters some people keep in little boxes in the corners of their living rooms.

I looked at my watch, and realised that it was the cocktail hour again, and that I had a date at Sorrentino's, Sinatra's favourite restaurant in Palm Springs. In the fifties, when the Guadalajara Boys played mariachi here, there were seat belts on the bar stools and the men bought dolls from the barman and gave them to the hooker they wanted.

This evening, Sinatra was the background music, as it would never have been in his day: anywhere he went out he insisted that his songs were never played.

There was even a Steak Sinatra on the menu, still served the way he liked it, with mushrooms and bell peppers. But since Sinatra's idea of good food was pork and beans out of a tin, I gave it a miss and had sand dabs with lemon and a glass of Chablis.

Hermann, the waiter, had served Sinatra here for three decades, not to mention every star in Hollywood and several Presidents, and Sinatra had been persistently generous to him and his children in return.

'My best customer? Mr Sinatra. He was always pleasant and helpful. My worst customer? Mr Sinatra when he didn't get exactly three coffee beans for luck in his after-dinner sambuca or a bottle of Château Lafite '56.'

Indeed. It was a very good year.

The owner, Billy Sorrentino, came over to the table and talked all evening. And talked. Everything he said was fascinating, but his voice was like a sheet of sandpaper, so that all I was left with was a map of the desert.

At the end of the night, I went to the toilet, and suddenly realised that I was probably using the same urinal that Sinatra had. But then I noticed another one, so I used that as well, just to make sure.

Sinatra, of course, was not the only celebrity to pee in Palm Springs, and several tours will take you around the weekend retreats of those with vast wealth, from the house up in the hills which Bob Hope built just for parties, seating 350 for dinner, to the row of four adjoining houses which author Sidney Sheldon bought: two to live in, one as a guest house and one as a gym.

Or the old Liz Taylor home, bought by a young couple who park their Rolls-Royces outside, one a convertible with the registration RR CONV – presumably in case they can't work out what it is by themselves.

At six in the morning I was due to meet a pilot in a hotel lobby out in the desert, and we were to go flying in his balloon, over the warming sands to the mountains where snow still lay in the curves below the peaks.

Twice before in my life I had risen at five for a balloon flight, only to find when I arrived at the take-off site that the flight had been cancelled due to high winds. I had, in fact, become an expert not-air balloonist. But this morning was as calm as a nun. I drove for an hour, with the hood down and Sinatra on the radio, to the hotel.

In the lobby there was no sign of a balloon pilot.

'Is this where I'm supposed to be?' I asked the night porter, a large man with a small way about him.

'Balloon flight's been cancelled due to high winds,' he said.

'Haven't I met you somewhere before?' I said.

Unable to get into the air. I drove back into town and spent a vicarious couple of hours in the Palm Springs Air Museum, pottering around assorted Thunderbolts, Bearcats, Corsairs and Spitfires, and noting with British disdain that Mustangs were fitted with air conditioning: 'Base, I gotta problem – the air con's busted and my shades are misting up.'

Outside the window, the midday heat was shimmering off the runway where Sinatra used to land with the rest of the Rat Pack in his private plane, then walk straight to a waiting helicopter to take them to Villa Maggio, the mountain retreat he built in 1968 and named after the Oscar-winning role in *From Here to Eternity* which relaunched his career.

A modest little log cabin with 9 bedrooms, 13 bathrooms, 2 saunas, pool, spa, tennis court, petrol station, heliport and separate guest house. This has been beautifully restored by a tax-fraud lawyer and his wife, who moved to Palm Springs from San Diego – 'We didn't like the people: you say hello and they're stuck for an answer' – bought this as a weekend home, and were now selling it for $2 million.

The house is full of the flotsam of fame: you're leaning on Al Capone's old table and a Shih Tzu comes snuffling by your ankles.

'That's Harold Robbins's old dog,' says the lawyer's wife. 'We got her when he died a year ago.'

Sinatra spent his early years in Palm Springs, though, in Twin Palms, a house down in the valley which he built in late 1947. A perfect example of mid-century modernism, it has now been immaculately restored by former landscape gardener Marc Sanders, who only discovered its famous history when he dug up some old planning permits.

In the heat of the afternoon we padded through the house, followed by Marc's miniature terrier – what is it with rich people and small dogs?

Here was the pool into which a drunken Ava Gardner dived naked in front of Sinatra's party guests.

Here was the room where Garbo stayed, arriving in midsummer in a heavy coat and scarf and emerging only to swim topless in the pool, clad just in a pair of baggy khaki men's shorts.

These icons passed before my unblinking eyes. But something was wrong! I had lost interest in the past, in history, in all that old stuff.

I was turning into a Californian, that's what it was.

I said goodbye to Marc and went for a drive in the convertible, the wind whipping in my hair and Sinatra on the radio, as he would be all week. I checked in the mirror. I was tanned. I filled up the tank, drank a bottle of low-sodium energy supplement and ate a diet loganberry yoghurt, then went to a car dealership to look at some pre-owned low-mileage Rolls-Royces. I felt better.

On the way back to the hotel, I was overtaken by two teenagers in a vintage Jaguar and a bald pensioner in a red Corvette.

That night I went out to the old Plaza Theatre to see the Fabulous Palm Springs Follies, a bunch of retired showgirls and boys between the ages of fifty-four and eighty-six who've put their dancing shoes and their singing hats back on for a last hoof through the twilight years of vaudeville.

It may sound like finding out your granny's become a kissogram, but it was, in fact, brilliant, and by the end of the evening I had fallen in love with not one, but several of the dancers.

Ah, if only I was an older man.

The next day I went to the Joshua Tree national park, 800,000 acres of desert, rocks, cacti and the strange trees given their name because the Mormons who travelled west through here in the 1850s thought they looked like the prophet showing them the way to the promised land. If they were right, Joshua was a ra-ra girl, eternally holding aloft several handfuls of pom-poms.

Late in the afternoon I drove over to Desert Memorial Park, the final resting place of Palm Springs' rich and famous, to see

Sinatra's grave. It is just a simple plaque set in the grass, bearing the inscription 'The Best is Yet to Come, Francis Albert Sinatra, 1915–1998, Beloved Husband and Father'.

His several wives, especially Nancy, would probably have something to say about the beloved husband bit, but after reading so much about him, it sent a shiver up my spine to actually stand on the grave where he finally sleeps with all the stars of Palm Springs. Much as he did in life, really.

That night I went to see *Sinatra: My Way*, the tribute show by Frankie Randall, a friend and fan of Sinatra's for thirty-eight years, in which Russ Loniello is a better Dean Martin than Dean Martin ever was, Louie Velez is a splendidly dreadful Sammy Davis Jnr and Randall … well, good he is, Sinatra he ain't, as he would admit himself.

The next morning I drove to the airport in the indigo dawn. On the radio, the Sinatra week had finished and they were playing 'Smooth Operator' by Sade.

I climbed into an aeroplane and rose, high above the palms, into the endless curve of a Sinatraless future.

1999

Parrot Dating Agency of Puerto Rico

Miriam, the rainforest guide, had one of those faces which was not particularly beautiful, but was so animated by what went on around her that she was impossible not to like.

She chattered away at the front of the bus as we left San Juan and passed through Puerto Rican countryside strangely like Tyrone in a heatwave, then climbed into the mountains of the rain forest, with the bright parp of the bus horn swallowed up in the tangled shade of bamboo, fern, poison ivy and elephants' ears behind the sandalwood trees.

There was no sign of the rain which gives the forest its name, but every year 180in of the stuff falls on these trees, compared to 55in in the lowlands, turning the mountains around us into a vast, roofless hothouse.

The first stop was the Yokshu Tower, a circular five-storey structure in faded terracotta which has a long and fascinating history. It was built twenty years ago for the tourists.

After you fight your way through the Sony handycams at the top of the tower and look down towards San Juan or up at the peaks, the forest looks utterly impenetrable, choked with flora like the work of a megalomaniac head gardener, so that you feel a mad desire to borrow a machete and plunge in, living on a diet of orange, lemon, banana, grapefruit and pepper until the job is done.

It might get a bit dull, though. You'd need to hire Miriam to lighten the days. You could live in a tree house with her, watching her face light up with tragic joy as she describes the fate of the Puerto Rican parrot, which numbered a million when Columbus discovered the island in 1493, but of which there are now only seventy-five, flitting somewhere out there in the dappled gloom.

Miriam's tinkling laugh as she described their beautiful downfall would attract them to the tree house, where at first they would peek out from behind the sandalwood trees, then shyly emerge to nuzzle beaks. We would establish the world's first dating agency for parrots, and be single-handedly responsible for their resurrection.

There. All that organised, I returned my attention to Miriam, who was leading the way down the road to a waterfall which was supposed to make you look younger.

I got about half a gallon down, but it only made my bladder feel older all the way back to the ship.

Around the waterfall, in the forest dusk, were the bright orange African tulips which the Puerto Rican children fill with water then run around squirting each other from the tiny green phallus at its base. They call it Peepee Three, in their high, dancing voices.

Unfortunately, since I'd spent so much time with Miriam in the forest running the parrot dating agency, I only had time for an hour wandering around old San Juan, its narrow cobbled streets shaded by wrought-iron balconies draped with virulent orange-red flowers.

On street corners, serious-looking men in Panama hats and unlikely tweed jackets talked business, while exotic women flitted from shadow to shadow like butterflies. There was a wonderful air of imminent danger, like a South American republic just before the cocktail hour.

Back on board the ship, Ken was busy by the pool sorting out the judges for the Best Male Legs on Board competition. There was just no stopping Ken. The night before, he'd started off the sumo wrestling with a bout against his assistant Sean, then got the karaoke underway before nipping down to the lounge to make sure the Country and Western Evening had plenty of both types of music. It was going to be difficult to wake up every morning at home without Ken's sunny voice over the intercom saying, 'Good morning everyone, and welcome to another day in rainy Belfast. This is Ken, your house director, keeping you up to date with what's happening in your fabulous home this morning. Just to remind you that breakfast is still available in your beautiful fully fitted kitchen at this time, and this morning we're offering the diet special because you did forget to buy your flakes and coffee yesterday.

'Next up is loading your fully automated washing machine with a load of sparkling cotton whites, and then it's an energetic and fulfilling day at work in the company of your friendly colleagues, with a break for a thrifty yet satisfying lunch from the self-service buffet in the sandwich shop around the corner.

'This evening your washing will be available for collection in the machine, and entertainment options tonight include a trip to the wonderful old pub across the road, with cabaret provided by the drunk at the bar, or for those of you who'd like a quieter evening by the fire, the coal shed is out the back, and there's a bottle of Spanish plonk in the wine rack. Please feel free to get it yourself. Have a wonderful day in your fabulous home, and I'll talk to you again tomorrow morning.'

Upstairs I found John and Joanne, a couple from Newcastle whom I'd met at the captain's table the night before. He was 5ft 6in tall and looked like ET with glasses, and she was not far behind me in the Whitest Person on Board stakes. I asked them if they'd enjoyed San Juan. 'It were grand,' said John. 'We did tour by taxi. Bugger tried to charge us $76 instead of $40, but I told him we were having nowt to do wi' that.'

Also at the captain's table the previous evening had been Joan and Claire, the Cardin sisters, from Louisiana.

'As in Pierre, but no relation, unfortunately,' they said. They were variously divorced and widowed, in their fifties, elegant and charming, and loved the art of a good flirt.

'Why, ladies, you're, both looking deliciously exotic this evening. And Claire! You've had your hair plaited. Quite gorgeous,' I said.

'Heavens, Mr Hill, what a beautiful shirt. Silk, isn't it?' said Claire, flashing me a smile of quixotic southern grace.

'Naturally,' I said, pretending to be upset.

It was all wonderful, harmless fun, and much more entertaining than chatting someone up at a disco.

'YOU A NURSE?'

'WHAT?'

The next morning, just before the ship left, I took a last walk around San Juan to say farewell to Puerto Rico.

As I sat on a wall in the sun, a young woman came walking down the road. She was wearing a black hat and a black cardigan over a bright tartan dress. She carried a wicker basket, and there was an elegant swing in her narrow hips as her basket finally disappeared around the corner and was replaced by a red bag bearing the words 'Isle of Man Steam Packet Company', which I had spotted several times on the ship, coming in the opposite direction.

Its bearer was, it transpired, Dave from Douglas.

We greeted each other, and I asked him after a while if this was his first cruise.

'Er, no, it's my thirteenth.'

'Heavens. What do you like about them so much?'

'Um.' He looked at me sideways, then muttered something which I didn't catch.

'Sorry, Dave, missed that.'

'Er ... romance, I said.'

'What, like women?'

He gave me a pained, nervous look.

'No, the ships. I love the *Royal Princess* best of all. I wanted to join the Navy, but my parents ...'

The sentence tailed off into nothing, and he toddled off eventually, leaving a faint whiff of regret and milky tea.

1994

Quebec

As the train hurtled east from Toronto, I held my breath for the moment when we all became Quebecois. The moment when the atmosphere in the carriage suddenly became an ambiance.

I looked out at golf courses carved out of the grassy wild, trying to spot the instant that the players started saying '*Merde!*' instead of 'Heavens – missed again.'

I studied back gardens, where men sat reading the Sunday papers by their swimming pools, trying to divine whether they were about to say 'Helen, throw me out a cold one there' or '*Hélène, puis-je avoir deux martinis sec, s'il te plaît?*'

I scanned the sky, waiting for it to darken from true blue to French blue. We stopped at Brockville, where a cream and red sign proclaimed: 'Brockville: City of the 1000 Islands – Relocate to a Quality Community'.

Brockville simmered in the sun as the train pulled out, the potential entrepreneurs in its first-class carriage mentally striking the town off the list of possible relocation sites for software plants and Cadillac franchises. From the well-clipped greens outside town, Brockville's golfers watched the train go by with mournful eyes, as if they knew.

Above our heads, the sky darkened with rain, and soon we crossed the border into Quebec and hissed into Montreal. I strapped accents to my vowels and went hunting for ambiance in the drying streets.

Although most of the English-speaking minority who once owned 70 per cent of Canada's wealth left Montreal in 1976 after the election of the separatist Parti Quebecois, signs and posters still hung everywhere in perfect Franglais – 'Grand Prix Nationale', 'Bar le Rendez-vous', 'Poulet Frit a la Kentucky' – as if the city was being run by a crazed GCSE French student.

Down in the old city by the harbour, painfully elegant people stalked the streets in search of the perfect bistro, couples sought each other in the shadows of horse-drawn calèches and moths tangoed to their deaths in the yellow light of ancient lamps. Above them all, the new moon rose over the steel-blue dome of the Bonsecours Market.

I went back to the hotel, and spent five minutes in the bathroom, muttering into the mirror, '*Pas de bidet? Je suis désolé.*' ('No bidet? I am so sorry.')

I tried sanity once, but it didn't agree with me.

The next morning, walking through the streets, I realised just what was different about the cities in Quebec to those in the rest of Canada.

Vancouver had grown up to be a playboy, and Calgary became a cowboy. Edmonton turned into an oilman, and Winnipeg a farmer. Toronto is a banker and Ottawa is a politician.

But Montreal and Quebec, the twin godfathers of them all, still sit in the comfortable armchair of the east looking down on their errant offspring with a faint and weary sneer.

As well they might. When all the rest were forest, swamp and prairie, these two cities were already old.

Montreal, for example, was first settled in 1642 by Paul de Chomedey as a mission. And even at the advanced ages of 325 and 334, the city was still fit and well enough to organise Expo 67 and the 1976 Olympics respectively.

Both left in their wake several pieces of architectural and financial flotsam which the city has had varying degrees of success in recycling.

Among the ones they don't like to talk about are the Olympic Stadium, originally called the Big O, then the Big Owe because it cost $700 million and was not finished until eleven years after the event, and now the Big Oh No because the roof is going to have to be replaced for another $50 million. After an Olympics whose debts gave Quebec's provincial motto, *Je me souviens* – I remember – a new twist, Montreal, to its credit, learned its lesson about using existing facilities for sporting events.

The Canadian Grand Prix track on Ile St-Helene, for example, is open to the public as a scenic drive all year, and in the week before the race is the site of the city's enthusiastic drivers queueing up for a slow motion preplay of the real thing.

And even sites like the futuristic Velodrome, built for the Olympic cycling events and rarely used since, have taken on a new life. Or, in the Velodrome's case, a lot of new lives, of the assorted beasts which plunge, climb, swim, burrow and snooze in its four artificially created ecosystems – a tropical forest, Canadian woods, the St Lawrence underwater, and the North and South poles. The Biodome, as it's called now, is all very impressive, and 1.25 million visitors have poured through its doors since it opened last June. But I still suspect that places like this are just designer zoos.

Maybe it does give children a chance to see lynx and otters without getting eaten or holding their breath for fifteen minutes. But when you've stood six inches from an emperor penguin before you've even grown out of short trousers, what are you going to do for the rest of your life? What's going to happen to your imagination? Or travel companies, for that matter?

I came out of the Biodome feeling a little like the catfish which was unaccountably swimming around in the piranha enclosure – full of admiration, but a little worried.

Any good citizen will tell you that although those stuffy old Calvinist Anglos may have taken all the businesses to Toronto, when the Parti Quebecois came to power, they left the *joie de vivre* in Montreal.

'In Quebec we say TGIF – Thank God It's Friday – but in Ontario they say TGIM,' a woman told me in a bar in the old part of the city down by the docks, which, with its warehouse apartments, patio cafés and trendy bistros, is where Montreal goes to play at the weekends when it's not sunbathing in the parklands and forests of Mont Royal above the city.

The old city is still where you'll find most tourists, too – wandering through the cobbled streets, or peering up in admiration at the astonishing carved interior of Notre Dame Cathedral.

Just across the Place d'Armes is the almost as beautiful interior of the Bank of Montreal, although I'll have to take the word of the guidebook on that, since I have an aversion to the inside of banks.

Just down the Rue Saint Jacques, once the rustling heart of Canadian finance, is the Molson Bank building, owned by the Scottish family who started the brewery in 1786. Theoretically, owning a bank and a brewery seems like a perfect autonomous fiscal system, since your customers take their money out of one and put it in another. Surprisingly, it didn't work, and the bank was taken over after the Second World War. But then, Montreal has always had a rather strange relationship between commerce and spiritual matters like drink and religion.

In 1962, when it became apparent that Christchurch Anglican Cathedral was subsiding, a city developer jacked it up then decided to use the space he'd created underneath by building a shopping mall. Today, that mall is part of a complex stretching for eighteen miles, and Christchurch is possibly the richest church in the world, taking thousands of dollars in weekly rental from the shops below in a comfortable alliance between God and Mammon. Paul de Chomedey, who founded

Montreal to turn the minds of the Iroquois to God rather than fur profits, would not be pleased, but he would understand. 'After all, what can you expect from Anglicans?' I thought, looking at my watch and realising that it was time to take the train to New Brunswick.

For someone who had just come from well-scrubbed Toronto, Montreal Central Station crackled with the romance of dance-hall tunes on an old radio. It was the flickering lights, the names of the Grande Ligne trains.

And above all, the voice of the French-Canadian announcer calling out destinations like Saint-Hyacinthe in a voice so breathily seductive that you wanted to rush up to the control room and ask her to marry you and move there just so you could ask her to say 'Saint- Hyacinthe' to you every night.

Sadly, while I was trying to work out whether this was entirely feasible or not, my train to New Brunswick was called and I was forced to contemplate the more mundane charms of my roomette.

My roomette was a space 5ft by 4ft into which was miraculously fitted a folding bed, an armchair, an ingenious sink which emptied of water when you folded it way, a toilet, a drinking fountain, a luggage compartment, a toilet-roll holder complete with soft toilet roll, a set of shelves, several coat hooks, two coat hangers, a pair of electrical sockets and a chrome fan.

There seemed to be only one problem. Since the room was only 5ft long, wouldn't the bed be the same?

But VIA Rail had already thought of that. When the bed folded down, the recess it came out of created an extra foot and a half.

It was astonishing. I was astonished. And what was even more astonishing was the landscape outside, all soggy woods and painfully green fields being devoured by arthritic cows.

It was just like home, except for the train, which was futuristic – stainless steel outside and restored Art Deco inside.

It was like travelling through Monaghan in a spaceship designed by Charles Rennie Mackintosh.

I folded myself into my folding bed, and settled down for the night.

1993

Rockies

By a glacier we found none other than P.Y. Wong, the intrepid Malaysian motorist, smoking a pipe. 'Tell me, where have you come from?' he said.

'The north.'

'Chilly?'

'Quite.'

'Ah, in that case I may put up the top,' he said, indicating Mrs Wong beaming plumply in the passenger seat of the 1958 MG in which they had completed the 1997 Peking to Paris rally, wrapped in innumerable layers and sporting a pair of navy wool gloves.

They were now driving to Alaska, as one does.

'Tell me,' said Mr Wong, simultaneously dousing his pipe and igniting his engine, 'but what is the purpose of your expedition?'

'Bears,' I said. 'We are looking for bears.'

Indeed, we had arrived in Vancouver some days previously and signed up for Bears and Beetles, a two-week jaunt through the Rockies in one of the new Volkswagens.

Tragically, when we turned up to collect the car, we found

that the travel company had sold all the Beetles, presumably because the bright colours and curvy shape had made the bears think they were sweets. ('Mmm, I like these; crunchy on the outside, soft in the middle.')

Instead, we got a bright red Jeep – which we christened Arf after its registration – in which we spent the next couple of days pottering around Vancouver, a city of so many nooks and crannies that it is like the rambling house of your favourite Aunt Cynthia.

Your favourite Canadian-Chinese-Punjabi-German-Italian Aunt Cynthia, that is, who also happens to be a fabulous cook, skier and sailor, and whose husband Rufus was a trapper for the Hudson Bay Company, the ancient firm whose fur and liquor warehouse still stands on Water Street.

The two of them have a back garden called Stanley Park, a thousand acres of ancient redwoods so untamed that at any minute you expect to walk around a tree and come face to coonskin with Uncle Rufus returning from a fur and liquor expedition, a bear over one shoulder and two bottles of rye clinking in his back pocket.

Here, you sit by a lake and three goslings waddle past. Then a black squirrel sits on your foot. A horse-drawn carriage clops past, and through the trees several chaps are playing cricket on a green by the sea, their West Coast accents mingling quaintly with the click of cork on willow.

If this was the United States, you would start looking behind bushes for Disney engineers, but it is Canada, and real.

The next morning, we climbed into the Jeep and set off for Vancouver Island, looking out carefully for bears.

Or beahs, as Cate would say, being a well brought up gel. Being a ragamuffin from the wilds of Tyrone, I say bearrrrrs, and if I had to justify it I would say that it must be a bearr because it says 'Grrrr', whereas a beah would be more likely to say 'Geahhhh. Now, are you fwightened?'

Whatever they were, we had seen none by the time we arrived at a lakeside bed and breakfast on Vancouver Island.

In the UK, B & Bs may sport brown Dralon sofas whose finest hour has been and gone, but in North American versions you are more likely to be offered wine, firelight, a hot tub on the patio and a rowing boat. We were offered the lot, although getting the boat into the tub was a bit of a struggle.

'Tell me, my dear,' I said as we sat surrounded by rowlocks and rubber ducks, 'am I wrong, or is it my birthday?'

'No, you are right,' she said, taking me out for an extravagantly fabulous mountaintop meal, as a result of which I was somewhat the worse for wear when we returned to the mainland the next day and drove north to Whistler on the Sea and Sky Highway.

Rarely can a road have been better named. On our left were bottomless fiords of a blue so deep it hurt our eyes. On our right, cruel mountains impaled innocent clouds, and icy waterfalls dropped hundreds of feet into the dark forest, so close that we could feel the spray on our faces through the open windows. Great hangover cure.

In a landscape so forbidding, it was easy to imagine a sasquatch pottering about, filing his nails and waiting for a passing fur and liquor trapper for supper.

By nightfall we were in Whistler, a mountain ski resort built in the quaint Hansel and Gretel Gothic Massive style. There were few skiers about this late in the season, but the streets were full of chaps wearing hooded sweatshirts and baggy combat trousers, carrying wide planks and exchanging complex handshakes.

It was, I imagine, a convention of unemployed Masonic carpenters.

The next day we drove east through the mountains and found by chance a gliding club, run by men called Rudi and Attila, who wore aviator sunglasses and studied the clouds, reading texts in them that we could not decipher.

We went soaring up the fertile valley with them, curving giddily among the peaks until we found a circular lake so emerald that it seemed like absolute green, compared to all the other greens we had ever seen.

Late that afternoon we found the lake again in Arf, then crunched on foot through the snowy forest to its edge and took off our clothes. The snow was a shock against our skin, but not as much of a shock as the temperature of the water. We got as far as our ankles before hypothermia set in.

We drove on to the ranch where we were spending the night; one of many which in the last century were the homes of remittance men, the daft younger sons of the English gentry, dispatched here with orders not to write often. Among them was Lord Martin Cecil, son of the Marquis of Exeter, who ran his ranch as the base for the Emissaries of Divine Light until his death.

And so to bed, in a rustic cabin. Wildlife count for the day: cows thirty-seven, horses six, muskrats two, Japanese tourists one. Bears nil.

All night long we slept the deepest of sleeps, in a silence interrupted only by the ranch's two pet emus talking emu business to each other, with a sound like the burping of trumpets.

In the morning we woke to find two horses parked outside, so we climbed aboard and went for a poggle through the woods as the sun burnt off the dawn mist.

Ah, the rhythmic creak of leather, the smell of damp wool, the crack of the whip.

Still, enough about my private life.

We returned the horses to the barn, where they sleep standing up so as not to crumple their pyjamas, and motored on to the most beautiful waterfall in the world, at Helmcken on the way to Jasper. Here, the Murtle River tumbles 450ft into a black abyss, separating as it does into white plumes that look like lost souls plunging to Hades. It is at once thunderous and contemplative, and we could have stayed there watching it all day, had we not had to get on with the business of killing every bug in Canada. For it seemed that no matter how often we cleaned the windscreen, within minutes it had become a bug graveyard again.

We drove on, knowing that in bug households all over the land tonight there would be empty chairs by the fire, nervous glances at tiny watches. And, down at the Bug Bar, tales of narrow escapes by more agile bugs who had caught the airflow and surfed over Arf's roof as deftly as unemployed Masons.

However, at this stage my thoughts on the life and times of bugs were distracted by Cate.

'Oh, look, a beah!' she said.

And it was. A black bear loping beside the road: such a remarkable sight that it was difficult to resist the temptation to leap out of Arf and take a closer look. Many do, and become bear lunch.

There are several ways to avoid being eaten by a bear. One is to live in Clapham. Another is to go to Canada, but stay in your car. However, if you are out for a dander in the woods and you are confronted by a large black furry thing, don't run, scream, wear deodorant, climb a tree or make love, because bears are apparently attracted by all these things, which is why you never hear of bears eating fat, smelly monks with vertigo.

What you should do, according to our guidebook, is stand there meekly and mutter to the bear in a comforting voice. The guidebook didn't say exactly what you should mutter, but something like 'Here, I hear they're doing a really good deal on honey down at the Critter Creek general store, which is THAT WAY,' might work.

Anyway, where was I? Ah yes, on the way to Jasper, where we had arrived fifty-eight years too late to witness the building at nearby Patricia Lake of the world's only ever aircraft carrier made of ice.

You see, in 1942 Allied shipping losses were so heavy that when one Geoff Pike came up with the idea, Louis Mount-batten was impressed enough to demonstrate it in Churchill's bath at 10 Downing Street. Whether Churchill was in the bath at the time is not, sadly, recorded.

Pike was ensconced at the time in a London mental hospital, but madness has never bothered governments, and Churchill sent him to Jasper with a budget of almost £37 million. Sadly, Pike's creation proved less buoyant than Mountbatten's ice cubes, and the project was finally scuppered when the pacifist Doukhobor labourers who were building it found out its true purpose and downed ice picks.

Two days later we arrived at Revelstoke, where the brochure promised us a sumptuous lodge, to find it not quite built. Still, we opened a bottle of red and spent the evening sitting on the porch of our log cabin in the grounds, looking around at the other brand new cabins and feeling somewhat like pioneers.

On the lake below, a fat beaver unzipped the dark water, and before us tawny clouds were ruptured by the jagged peaks and fell dying down the mountain towards us, spilling rain.

In the sunshine after the rain passed, a rainbow curved to the meadow a couple of hundred yards away, in which a familiar furry shape could be seen snuffling through the damp grass.

It could have been Uncle Rufus, but it wasn't.

'Beah,' I said to Cate.

'Grrr,' she smiled, raising her wine glass to her lips in the golden light of evening.

2000

Spain

2400 BC
Iberian peninsula inhabited by Beaker People, named after ceramic drinking vessels, and Urn Burial Folk, named after habit of burying folk in urns.

480 BC
Celts arrive and attempt to populate peninsula but fail, possibly because habit of cleaning teeth with urine makes getting dates impossible.

20 BC
Romans arrive, name country Hispania and bring civic pride, justice, roads, Latin and, eventually, Christianity.

5th century AD
Roman empire collapses. Visigoths take over, but find the place so well-run they change nothing.

8th century
Arabs arrive, rename country al-Andalus and bring tolerance,

allowing Jews and Christians to retain faith and Frankish kings to potter about in the north.

980

Dictator al-Mansur ruins everything with jihad against Franks which sours relations between Christians and Muslims for centuries. Or possibly forever.

1100–1492

Christians, having warmed up with the Crusades, retake country.

1492

Columbus discovers America, ignoring fact that natives, Vikings and possibly Irish had got there first. Spanish subsequently establish huge empire, kill twenty million natives and ship home mountains of gold and silver which kings such as Carlos I and Philip II spend on succession of wars.

1598

Philip dies, leaving country broke and starting long period of decline into intolerance which reaches its nadir with the Inquisition.

19th century

Colonial uprisings finally strip Spain of its empire, leaving it bankrupt and backward.

20th century

Civil war, followed by Franco.

1975

Franco dies. Brits discover Costas. Spanish wonder where it all went wrong, then sigh and open pubs with Watney's Red Barrel on tap, full English breakfast and live Premier League soccer.

Seville

The importance of the hairdryer in the history of the twentieth century is often overlooked.

If young Corporal Hitler had treated himself to a decent blowdry after bathing, for example, the other officers wouldn't have laughed at his wayward cowslick and sowed the seeds of misanthropy which led to the Second World War.

If Stalin had washed, dried and got a nice gentle perm instead of smearing his head with Crimean sump oil, he could well have ended up as a harmless folk singer in a Georgian nightclub penning ditties of unrequited Bolshevik charm.

If Isadora Duncan had been able to dry her famous locks on that September day in Nice in 1927, she wouldn't have rushed out with them wrapped in the scarf which strangled her in the wheel of a Bugatti.

And yet you won't find a single mention of a hairdryer in either Eric Hobsbawm's *The Age of Extremes* or the *History of Islamic Spain* I was reading as the plane descended towards Seville Airport.

No sooner had I landed in Seville than I was rushed straight to the Melia Hotel for a one-hour tour of the bedrooms, during which the manager pointed out not once but half a dozen times that every single one of the bathrooms had a hairdryer fixed to the wall.

Not only that, but you could choose between ten different types of pillow, he said, as we descended to basement conference rooms in which, at a conference on human reproduction, men in grey suits were sitting around tables earnestly discussing oestrogen levels and sperm counts.

Safe in the knowledge that the entire population of Seville would sleep on a satisfying pillow that night before waking the next morning, drying their hair and going forth to propagate the species, I went out to a splendid dinner of giant olives, Serrano ham and Rioja.

Lots of Rioja.

I woke early the next morning and read the entire *Rough Guide to Seville* – the city quaintly described by Byron as being famous for oranges and women – so that when I arrived at the Plaza de España after breakfast, I felt as if I'd been there before. Mind you, it was hardly surprising; when the Plaza was built in 1929, it felt as if it had been there before, too. Planned in 1914, it was scuppered by the little matter of the First World War, and only constructed for the Spanish Americas Fair in 1929, just in time to avoid being scuppered by the Wall Street Crash.

A dazzling mixture of all the architectural styles brought to Seville, it is one of several perfect symbols of this Jerusalem of Europe, where Rome, Marrakesh and Constantinople met and married while the rest of western civilization was still struggling in the darkness.

Spain was an Islamic country from 711 until 1492, when it was finally recaptured by the Christians. But they seem to have been the most relaxed of conquests and reconquests. When the Moors arrived, the Christians were allowed to keep their faith, and responded with a widespread admiration for the luxurious elegance of Arab culture. As the Christians slowly regained power, and in spite of growing tensions, Muslims were allowed the same right.

The result of this benign dialectic was that buildings were generally adapted rather than torn down by invading hordes, a process which is still happily going on. All around the Plaza de España, the 122 national pavilions built for the 1929 fair had been transformed into police stations, lecture theatres and schools. Well, except for Guatemala, which has become a public toilet.

In between the pavilions, white doves fluttered in the love trees, those ephemeral explosions of lilac-pink blossom on what is also known as the Tree of Judas, from which Iscariot is believed to have hanged himself.

The same symbol, of both love and betrayal.

For in Seville, everything is something else. Most of the city's fifty-two churches, for example, were once mosques; the university, not content with being the building which once housed the country's largest tobacco factory, also doubles as the setting for Bizet's *Carmen*, and the Alcazar, the great palace of al-Mu'tadid of the Abbadids, was simultaneously a harem of eight hundred women and a shrine where today you can still trace with your fingertips the verses of the Koran carved into the cool alabaster walls.

Al-Mu'tadid was a keen gardener, but not the sort who would phone up Radio 4 for advice on his hollyhocks, for instead of flowerpots he used the skulls of his slaughtered enemies. After he passed on to the great rose garden in the sky, the Alcazar became the setting for the wedding of Carlos V and his Portuguese bride Isabella, and in the twentieth century the occasional home of Franco, who ordered the kitchens to be expanded so that he could wander through these shady groves of marble with a full belly.

Which reminded me, it was time for lunch – ham and tomatoes at a little table outside a nearby café, where I had my shoes polished by an old man called Enrique.

'Image is everything in the twentieth century. You need a new pair of brogues,' he said, proving that in Seville, not only are the churches mosques, but the shoeshiners are philosophers. And only five minutes walk away, admiring the nutty gleam of my feet all the way through the tiny streets, I found Seville's most beautiful paradox of all.

The 300ft minaret of the Giralda, one of the most important and beautiful monuments of the Islamic world, was built between 1184 and 1196. After the city was recaptured by the Christian Ferdinand III, the city fathers at first used it as a church, then built the world's largest cathedral on to the side.

Here, within a matter of yards, many worlds meet and history becomes real. In the square where Muslims came to wash their feet and pray to Mecca, you can close your eyes and admire the Moorish art of creating these cool places of marble and tile, orange blossoms and flowing water. Outside, in the brick-and-mortar join between the Giralda and the cathedral, you can see and touch the physical line where the Islamic and Christian worlds met.

And inside, looking up at the vast, airy archways which were built between 1402 and 1506, you can follow the happy journey between the complexity of Gothic and the simplicity of Renaissance architecture.

The cathedral is the home of two important works of art, *The Vision of San Antonio* by Murillo and *The Statue of the Blind Virgin* by Martinez Montanes, so called because she is looking at the floor. Popular mythology has it that she is gazing at the trio of angels at her feet, but the truth is that she has just had her sandals polished by Enrique and is admiring them.

Everywhere, Seville recreates itself. It is still doing so today in the shape of the Isle Magica, an adventure park on the theme of Spain's sixteenth- to seventeenth-century relationship with America, built on the site of a former monastery and surrounded by pavilions from the 1992 World Expo, all designed by architects who wouldn't recognise a right angle if one walked up and introduced itself. And quite right, too – as any Irishman will tell you, the longest distance between two points is always a straight line.

Nearby, another monastery, built in 1399, became in 1839 the tile factory of English merchant Charles Pickman, and in 1986 a local government office and archaeological study centre. The old chapel is still there, for you to sit in the cool and airy shade and be at peace with yourself, or whatever you call God.

And so, having fed my soul, it was time for my stomach again, and dinner at the quaintly named Hotel Colon, where the bullfighters stay when they win at the nearby Plaza de Toros. When they lose, they stay at the local hospital, and the bulls end up in the kitchen either way, as I found when their tails ended up on my plate at dinner. Still, I'd rather eat the back than face the front, and they were delicious.

Outside the restaurant as we ate, thirty-six youths were busy struggling to lift what looked like an enormous dining table.

They were, in fact, practising carrying one of the hundreds of religious floats which are borne through the streets in the annual Easter parade, a celebration which went on even when it was banned by Franco. When the police challenged the marchers, they simply said, 'But we are communists – and this is a communist Virgin on top.' In Seville, where mosques become churches and tobacco factories become universities, even the Virgin Mary can become a communist.

And men can become horses – the next morning, driving to the countryside for lunch through fields in which small, dark farmers were out riding their squat, muscular Berber stallions, it was easy to see why when Hernán Cortés arrived in Mexico with his conquistadors in 1519, the Aztecs thought that his men and their horses were one beast.

Lunch was at Esparragal, a white and sprawling seventeenth-century farmhouse which takes in paying guests. We ate on the patio as the sun poured down on us like honey. Bulls slept in the fields around us, horses mated peremptorily in the stables behind us, and storks circled above our heads. On the white linen tablecloth was a chilled glass of the deliciously nutty aperitif manzanilla.

We broke bread, and drank wine, and gave thanks. For the bread, for the wine, for the blue sky, and for a city we would return to that evening for dancing and laughter.

A city where many differences meet and which is fascinating because it is the happy dialectic caused by the meeting of differences which creates love and art.

A city which over the centuries has received its invaders, absorbed the best of them, and in an antithesis of the maxim of St Francis that to give is to receive, now has everything to give.

I raised my glass to Seville, to life, and watched the beaded rim rise to greet the sun.

1997

Barcelona

I went out walking with a rusty nose, beneath the bananaless banana trees. All around, women with eyebrows like angry hedgehogs strode purposefully about, and painfully stylish teenagers on small motorcycles flung themselves suicidally into the traffic, popping up on the other side of the street with surprised expressions on their faces that they were still alive.

But let me explain about the rust.

I had arrived in the Hotel Ambassador and looked in the mirror to discover to my horror that there were hairs growing out of my nose.

And sure enough, when I checked my diary, I was thirty-seven.

Unfortunately, the only sharp implement I had on me was a pair of scissors which had been given to me by an ex-girlfriend, presumably with the intention that I should trim myself painfully to death, but which I tossed into the bottom of a damp toilet bag and forgot about.

Hence the rust, which was not helped at all by the drizzle.

You don't really expect drizzle in Barcelona, but then, it is a city which is never sure whether it's a southern city in northern Europe or the other way around. It's also not sure whether it's rich or poor, ugly or beautiful, serious or humorous, commercial or hedonistic. In fact, it hasn't even got a clue whether its streets should be big or small.

In the old part of the city, they're so narrow that anyone over six feet tall falling down sideways will get stuck and have to be liberated by the application to their extremities of large quantities of virgin olive oil. But in the various modern bits which have been built at the drop of any convenient excuse, like the Universal Exhibition of 1888, the sequel of 1929 and the Olympics of 1992, the boulevards are as wide as several elephants laid trunk to tail. African elephants, that is.

The most famous of those boulevards is La Ramblas, an artery of green which runs for a mile from the Placa de Catalunya to the sea. Wandering down it is a tradition so enshrined in Barcelona life that it has given the Catalan language the words *ramblejar*, which means to walk down La Ramblas, and *ramblista*, which describes a person addicted to the verb. Whoever dreamed up the cliché 'All life is here' was, undoubtedly, a *ramblista*, since the boulevard sings with life from dawn to dewy dawn.

From when the chefs of the city's top restaurants gather for the day in the nineteenth-century covered market of La Boqueria to sniff, squeeze, poke, haggle and finally choose their fresh ingredients for the day. It takes a while – there are twenty-one types of olives alone.

From that dawn to the next, when the sleepless few finally emerge from the bars and wander home, their bellies full of Rioja and the dying stars reflected in their bleary eyes as they buy the first edition of *La Vanguardia* from the all-night stalls which sell everything from flowers to caged songbirds, and choose a passing cab. This takes less time than choosing olives, since there are eleven thousand taxis in the city.

At the end of La Ramblas is a statue of Christopher Columbus, holding what looks like a large cod in his left hand and pointing vaguely out to sea with his right. He has reason to be vague. Not only did the builders get it wrong and point him in the direction of the Balearic Islands rather than America, but he's now generally reckoned to have found America about five hundred years after Bjarni Herjolfsson, a Viking who got lost on the way to visit his dad in Greenland.

Although you could spend a week's holiday in La Ramblas and never be bored, you really should get a guide and see some of the rest of the city.

A guide like Joanne. Joanne was half Swiss and half Catalan, and had an accent that would seduce you at ten paces. I could have listened to her all day, even though half the time I hadn't a clue what she was talking about. But then, that's normal for Barcelona. If you ask three different people to tell you the history of the city, you'll get four different versions.

Which brings me to the bananaless banana trees, for the first thing I asked Joanne was what the trees down La Ramblas were.

'Banana trees,' she said. 'But they have no bananas.'

I looked out of the taxi window, but it was difficult to tell whether there were any bananas or not, since it had started to rain with such ferocity that I felt as if Joanne and I were extras in *Voyage to the Bottom of the Sea*.

To say that it was coming down in bucketfuls would have fallen some distance short of addressing the issue. After ten minutes the streets were a foot deep in water, and it was with a sense of soggy surrealism after another ten minutes that I looked out of the taxi window and saw the Temple of the Sagrada Familia, or Holy Family, looming out of a gap in the clouds.

I'd seen photographs of it before, but nothing could prepare you for the magnificent irrelevance of the real thing.

The Sagrada Familia is the most famous work of the modernist architect Antoni Gaudí, whose lunatic creations sit in the middle of otherwise grey facades in Barcelona like clowns at a business meeting.

Gaudí was born in 1826 and became a genius, a recluse, a man who fell under a tram, and dead, in that order. It was three days before Barcelona realised that the 74-year-old apparent vagrant lying in the mortuary was in fact their most famous architect, which just goes to show you how ungrateful people can be.

The Japanese, by contrast, now love him so much that those who have accidentally booked their Spanish holidays in Madrid regularly take the 2 a.m. flight from there to Barcelona, spend two hours touring his buildings, and fly back at dawn.

Gaudí is now buried in the crypt of the Sagrada Familia, with which he became so obsessed that he lived there for the last six years of his life, begging for money to continue building it.

And it's not even finished. Many of the models designed by Gaudí, smashed in the Civil War, have been rebuilt from a mountain of fragments by Jordi Cusso, who admits to frequent nightmares about the complexity of piecing together the third facade and the 650ft central tower.

When, if ever, it will be finished is one of the great topics of conversation in Barcelona, along with when they'll ever get around to fixing the fountain on the mountain. For in the same way that Irishmen wax lyrical about the best pint of Guinness they ever had and Italians come over all misty eyed about their first Vespa, the good citizens of Barcelona almost hum with bliss when they talk about the fountain on the mountain.

Designed by Carlos Buigas for the 1929 World Expo, this magical dance of moving water, lights and music comes to life every Saturday and Sunday evening in the Montjuic park, high above the city smog. This is where Barcelonans come on a weekend, to touch the air and breath the sky, and drape themselves in the rainbow cloak of the fountain up the mountain.

Or came. For a couple of years ago, it went the way of all marriages between metal and water, grinding to a messy divorce in a recrimination of rusty cogs.

The man from the city council came up, had a look, and went away scratching his head. A large sum of money was mentioned. Breath was sharply intaken, and the city council started saving its pesetas.

In the meantime, all is still up the mountain at the fountain, and at the nearby Mies van der Rohe pavilion, a song to simplicity in marble and water, glass and chrome.

The architect Peter Berhens described this German contribution to the 1929 Expo as the most beautiful building of the twentieth century.

The Barcelonans, taking the view that since Berhens was both German and Mies van der Rohe's professor he would say that anyway, dismantled it and only rebuilt it in 1985. Today, like most of Mies van der Rohe's architecture, it looks fresh off the drawing board.

Still, at least you can't accuse the Spanish of chauvinism – they were going to dismantle their own pavilion as well, and it's only recently that they've got around to refitting it properly as the Museum of Catalan Art, containing an astonishing selection of frescoes from eleventh- and twelfth-century

Pyrenean churches which were being ruined by renovation, vandalism or theft until a concerted campaign from 1919 onwards to save them. Today, they are brilliantly displayed in replicas of the mountain churches from which they came.

You have to admire the Barcelonans for recycling buildings so effectively, whether it's Expo pavilions or the beautifully cloistered Pedraldes Monastery, formerly the home of the fabulously poor nuns of St Clare and now the home of seventy-two paintings and eight sculptures from the collection of the fabulously wealthy Baron Hans Heinrich Thyssen-Bornemisza de Kaszon, the only man in the world with an extendable chequebook.

There were once hundreds of Clarissa nuns here, but today there are only twenty-two. The youngest is thirty-five, and the oldest had died three days before. Upstairs, the dormitory where they slept is the home of the Thyssen Collection, the most famous of which is *The Madonna of Humility* by Fra Angelico, in which Mary's long-suffering expression can be explained by the fact that the baby Jesus has been tickling her neck with a white lily since 1433.

A little less iconoclastic than the Sagrada Familia, but quite as famous, is the work of Joan Miró, whose simple white museum stands on the Montjuic hill high above the city, near the Olympic stadium and the diving pool where the famous Olympic photographs were taken of tiny Chinese teenagers apparently about to impale themselves on the towers of the Sagrada Familia.

Most of Miró's best work is, unfortunately, on display in New York, but there's still enough in the museum, like an astonishing 50ft-high wall-hanging and Alexander Calder's fountain of liquid mercury cascading down a series of black metal curves, to make a visit worthwhile.

I bought an expensive poster to try and console myself for the fact that Joanne had somehow forgotten to ask me to marry her when she said goodbye, and got a taxi back into the city for dinner at the Four Cats, the restaurant where Picasso had his first exhibition and didn't sell a thing – rather appropriately, since its name is taken from the Catalan equivalent of one man and his dog, as in 'Nobody turned up, just four cats'.

Like all Spanish meals, it was a dizzy combination of satisfaction and fear. Fear that every time you sat back, patted your full belly and thought what a wonderful meal it had been, another course would arrive.

Beneath the huge arched windows at the end of the room, a pianist with a battered face tinkled the minor classics on a baby grand. Like all the piano players in all the restaurants in the world, he looked as if he had suffered a flat tyre on the motorway of love. Or was just about to, arriving home to find a note saying:

> Darling, I have left you for someone with a day job. I cannot bear you arriving home in the middle of the night with the air of doomed romance which comes from playing Rachmaninov all evening. The click of the door at three, the way you climb politely into bed hoping that I am awake, the way we both know I am pretending to be asleep. I am truly sorry, but this is your destiny. It is the destiny of all restaurant pianists.
>
> Love, regret
> Emily

When he left, I held the door open for him. It seemed the least I could do.

I went for a walk, and at two in the morning found myself on the seafront. On my left was the giant lobster on top of the Amerinis restaurant, on my right was the Olympic village, and behind that were rows of narrow streets in a state of crumbling, aromatic decay.

In the little squares off La Ramblas, a saxophone played, and teenagers sat at zinc-topped bars drinking Rioja from glasses beaded with ice and trying to get each other into bed.

I sat at a table outside in the balmy air, drinking beer and arguing for the next three hours with a man from Aberdeen about modernism, which was quite an achievement when you consider that neither of us knew anything about it.

At five I walked back to the hotel and went for a swim in the icy rooftop pool as forked lightning flickered across the city, investigating careless television aerials. Unelectrocuted in spite of myself, I crept into my warm bed, only to be awakened at nine by the receptionist on the telephone.

'I am sorry, but we cannot give you an extra heater in your room,' she said wistfully.

'That's all right,' I said, since I hadn't asked for one.

I got up and pulled back the curtains. The sun was shining, and all the way down La Ramblas the eyes of the caged birds watched the pigeons soaring above the bananaless banana trees until they were lost to sight.

I checked my nose for rust, and went back to sleep.

1994

Tunisia

'The last two times I was here,' said Moncef Battikh as we pulled up outside the hotel in Tunis, 'was with Ursula Andress and Sean Connery.

'She was lovely, but he was a bit of a problem. He fell in lóve with the belly dancer, and she already had two husbands.'

We unloaded our bags, donned ties and went to dinner in a little Moroccan restaurant nearby. As the resident belly dancer worked herself into such a frenzy that her navel was later found several blocks away, we tucked into a spread of, by my estimation, 610 courses. Which was, by a remarkable coincidence, exactly the year that Mohammed sat down under a tree and started writing down the Koran as God dictated it to him, occasionally interjecting as the day wore on with a tetchy, 'Slow down, slow down, for, well, Your sake, really. Now, what were those directions to Mecca again?'

Fortunately, God took his advice, the Koran was published, and unlike most first books, made a significant prophet.

Anyway, where was I? Ah yes, in the bar listening to two Tunisians telling an old joke about a Tunisian who comes across a Libyan in the desert whose Mercedes has broken down.

'Ah, my brother, a car is like a balloon. You can fix it by blowing into the exhaust,' he says.

Several hours later, as the exhausted Libyan is still blowing into the exhaust, another Tunisian comes by and receives a stream of abuse for the foolish advice of his countryman.

'Ah, my brother, he was right, and it is you who are the fool. You have forgotten to wind the windows up,' says the Tunisian.

As I said to Moncef the next morning over breakfast on the patio, I was sure I'd heard the same joke last year about a Kerryman.

'Ah, we have a lot in common with the Irish,' he said, 'We both drink like fish and adapt our religion to our needs rather than the other way around. Even our national poet, Abou Nawas, says: "Wine today, decisions tomorrow".'

At our table, sunlight danced between the glasses. Beyond, it filtered down through the plane trees which shaded the graceful French colonial boulevards, and beyond that, daisy meadows sloped down to the sea.

A butterfly rested briefly on the tablecloth, then fluttered on.

Coming from the long curse of a British winter, I felt suddenly blessed by heat and light. And then blessed again, later in the morning, by the colours at the Bardo Museum, the former royal palace which now houses the finest collection of Roman mosaics in the world.

Inside, over every wall and vaulted ceiling, are a million postcards from the edge of an empire's imagination. All of them are remarkable, from the remarkable everyday (a herd of ostriches being prepared for the hunt) to the remarkable mythical (a group of Cyclops wielding mighty hammers as they forge thunderbolts for Jupiter). Even two millennia on, you still step back from the heat of their massive endeavours.

There was a time, of course, before the blazing glory of Rome came to Africa. It was the time of Carthage, and we shall never know whether it was dark or light, because the Romans laid waste to that city so utterly, even ploughing salt into the ruins so that nothing would ever grow there again.

Today, as a result, we know little of it. We know of Dido and Aeneas, we know that its noblest citizens sacrificed their favourite children to Baal, and we know that Hannibal left it with his elephants to cross the Alps.

But all that remains of it in the Bardo Museum is a little collection of self-effacing statues in a corner room, and the site of Carthage itself, just up the coast from Tunis, is even more poignant.

The city, as you may remember, was founded by Dido, Queen of the Phoenicians, in 814 BC. According to Virgil's *Aeneid*, she came home from hard days on the building site, threw off her hard hat and jumped into bed with Aeneas, sole survivor of the Greek destruction of Troy.

This is usually taken as myth nowadays, since Troy fell five centuries before Carthage rose, although it could just have been typical builders: 'Listen, Mrs Dido, I know we said three weeks, but those architraves are a bloody nightmare.'

Of the city itself, there is nothing. In a way, because Carthage died so young, it has become the James Dean of cities, its mythical glories forged almost entirely in the crucibles of our imagination. If we imagine it at all, we imagine it walking down a wet New York street, its collar up and a cigarette clamped between its teeth, or driving its Porsche down a sunlit road, blithely unaware that the Romans are hurtling towards the junction in a truck.

'Anyway, enough culture,' said Moncef, interrupting my thoughts. 'Time for dinner.'

Dinner was so much cous cous that I looked around in vain for someone else to eat the other cous.

At midnight, just as I was looking forward to bed, Moncef announced that we were going to a wedding. We got into a taxi and drove ten miles to another hotel, in which a vast room was filled with women like Sophia Loren and men like Lee van Cleef. Everyone was drinking Fanta.

At one in the morning, the bride and groom arrived and sat on matching white thrones onstage beside the band. He looked like the cat who had got the cream, and she looked suitably virginal, for although Tunisia is the most secular and liberal of Arab states, men are still expected to sow entire fields of oats before marriage, and women to remain pure.

How this is supposed to happen simultaneously is a subject that is not discussed in polite Tunisian society, but at least it's a change from the days when the bride's mother observed the consummation; a practice whose psychological effects must have done more to reduce national population growth than any government family-planning scheme.

The next morning, my eyes prickly with sleep, we drove south to El Jem, accompanied by Moncef's sister. On all sides stretched the descendants of the olive trees planted by the Romans which had first made this country rich two thousand years ago.

We stopped once, to buy warm bread. Outside the butcher's next door hung a cow's head, looking rightly pissed off that it wasn't still attached to the rest of the cow hanging next to it.

We drove on, through fields of lavender from which rose at last the great colosseum of El Jem, only slightly smaller than the one in Rome and the single most impressive Roman monument in Africa.

Its isolation has left it almost intact, down to the tunnel where the gladiators awaited their fate, its walls lined with graffiti saying 'Maximus is a big girl's blouse' and 'Well, Decimus did say he likes a lion on Saturday mornings'.

Even today, standing in the sandy oval arena and looking up at the rows of seats, you can almost smell the fear and sweat, almost hear the roar of the mob. Better to climb to the highest point of the expensive seats, look down and thank the gods that rather than dying that day in the sand, you are going home to a glass of wine and a warm concubine.

The next morning, breakfast with the Minister for Tourism was cancelled: praise Allah, for it gave me the morning off to have bread and honey on the lawn as bees hummed and an ancient retainer trimmed the hedges.

It was like being in Kent, and that afternoon I found myself in Tunisia's Tuscany, the fertile western region of verdant hills and olive groves which cosset Dougga, the country's best-preserved Roman site.

With an almost complete amphitheatre and capital, it is all the more remarkable for its rural setting, with a couple of Algerian picnickers and a baffled goat adding to its surrealism.

'Tell me, Moncef,' I said the next morning as we drove to the airport, 'what did you do before you joined the tourist board?'

'Well, my first job was feeding the lions at Regent's Park Zoo, if you can believe it.'

I did. In fact, I checked with one of the lions. Who, funny enough, was a direct descendant of the one who had eaten Decimus at El Jem all those years ago.

2003

Upgrades

One of the great joys of travel is getting an upgrade.
There are several ways of doing this. The first is paying
for it, but since an average business-class fare across the
Atlantic is about £2,500, it would be cheaper to buy a second-
hand microlight and fly yourself over.

Furthermore, since actually paying for something is against
the strict code of journalistic ethics, I always try to use one of
the other three methods:

1. Wear a smart suit and look as if only a tragic gambling
   debt or the loss of the family rubber plantations in Malaya
   have prevented you from claiming your natural place at
   the front of the aircraft;
2. Be at least 6ft 7in tall, and drag your left leg up to the
   check-in desk as if you are in the early stages of DVT;
3. Be with the boss of the airline you are flying with.

As a result of an assiduous combination of these three
fundamental principles, I have on occasion been admitted to
the holy of holies. Of the most memorable occasions, one was
by design, and the other by chance.

The first time, I had been in Japan for several weeks, and had run out of money after, oh, forty-eight hours. Having lived on noodles from street stalls since then, I crawled up to the British Airways check-in desk at Tokyo Airport weighing less than my ticket.

'We have a request here for an upgrade for you. Would you like to move up?' said the girl behind the desk sweetly.

'Lovely,' I croaked faintly.

Less than an hour later, I was sitting in an armchair being served champagne by a man in a white jacket, and over the next twelve hours I proceeded to drink all the drink, eat all the food, listen to all the music and watch all the movies on the plane.

The second time, I was checking in at Mexico City with a group that included a fat, pompous woman from the *Daily Mail*. We had been promised a chance to try out BA's new first-class sleeper seats, but it turned out there was no space in either first or business class.

'This is preposterous!' spluttered *Daily Mail* woman. 'I am a travel writer for a national newspaper, and I always get an upgrade. I am a personal friend of Lord King, and I'll have your job, young man.'

The young man, who politely declined the offer to tell her that she could have his job anytime if it meant dealing with people like her, replied that he would be only too happy to give us seats, if there were some, but there were not.

In any case, we got on and found there was plenty of room to stretch out in economy. I was just opening a book to read when the stewardess tapped me on the shoulder.

'Here, you don't have much legroom there,' she said.

'No worries. I've got three seats here, so I've loads of room,' I said.

Two minutes later, she returned.

'Come with me,' she whispered. 'There's one seat left in business.'

I looked across to where *Daily Mail* woman was glaring the

other way, and tiptoed up to the front.

However, I had never dared to try all of these techniques at the same time until a couple of weeks ago, when I found myself in Abu Dhabi queuing for a flight to Bangkok with Ahmed Hussain Aljanahi, the marketing manager of Gulf Air.

The airline had been started in 1940 by Freddie Bosworth, a Scottish ex-RAF pilot who arrived in Bahrain with a seven-seater Anson and a dream to make a living offering sightseeing trips around the islands. Freddie, who was killed on a test flight in 1964, would hardly have recognised the vast silver beasts which made up his airline today.

'Let's see if we can get into First,' Ahmed said suddenly, interrupting my thoughts.

'But Ahmed, we've already had dinner, and it's midnight. It'd be a complete waste of time,' I wailed.

But it was too late. He had already gone off to talk to persons of influence, and fifteen minutes later I found myself being carried up the aircraft steps by carefully oiled Nubian slaves while several Balinese dancing girls wafted my fevered brow with ostrich feathers.

Upstairs, they laid me down gently in an adjustable armchair which ran the gamut of positions from Languid but Alert to Comatose but Happy.

From a bottomless fountain up the front, a Thai stewardess brought me champagne which according to the wine list was 'a sober wine, with a touch of natureal and a hint of local specific taste'.

It went on: 'In the mouth, it surprises by its liveliness. It lines the palate, frank and mature. Its moderate evolution shows its happiness with ease.'

Heavens. That was a lot to ask for, in just one glass. It was a Heidsieck Heritage, in case you ever want your palate lined frankly and maturely.

A personal chef asked me what I would like for dinner, then cooked it for me, and the rest of the night passed in a happy welter of fine wines, fine food and fine music.

Well, almost fine music: no matter what audio channel I turned to, I always seemed to end up back at the Arabic one featuring those old desert favourites 'Stop the Camel, I Want to Get Off' and 'I'd Love Her if I Knew What She Looked Like Under Her Burka'.

I finally found a classical channel, and fell asleep at three in the morning listening to strains of Grieg's *Piano Concerto*.

Thanks to a man from Bahrain, I was on an airline started by a Scot, full to the brim with wine and food from a Thai stewardess and French chef, falling asleep listening to one of the finest creations of a Norwegian composer and on my way to the exotic and mysterious Orient.

It was, to be frank and mature with you, a first-class experience.

2003

Vermont

'Have you ever been convicted,' the US immigration form asked, 'of moral turpitude, drug trafficking, espionage, sabotage or war crimes?'

'Funny you should mention it,' I wrote carefully, 'but I did strangle my granny because she sold my SS uniform to buy heroin while I was away on that Iraqi intelligence job. Mind you, I think the old bat was just annoyed because I was sleeping with my sister.'

Several months later, I emerged from jail to find Cate waiting patiently for me.

'Hello dear,' she said pleasantly, 'our motorcycle's here.'

We climbed on, zipped up our leather jackets and adjusted our shades. As we left the bike-hire depot in Boston, we had a full tank of gas, the open road and a week in Vermont in front of us.

It was a state I knew practically nothing about. I had a vague childhood memory of an autumn postcard from a distant aunt, which looked like a riot in a forest, with angry leaves of every description demanding their territorial rights on a spectrum from acid yellow to vermilion. There was also, although I may have made this bit up, a white church steeple sticking up somewhere.

It made me wonder quite what we were doing, in black leathers and on a big motorbike, booked into some of the most genteel inns in New England. Still, no point letting reality change anything. I gunned the throttle and we turned west for Vermont.

If you are unfamiliar with the state, it is the shape of Arnold Schwarzenegger's torso, with his head in Quebec and his naughty bits in Massachusetts. Thankfully, we entered at the waist, crossing the river bridge from New Hampshire and realising immediately that there was something heart-stoppingly special about Vermont.

Perhaps it was the fact that we were on a motorcycle. As Robert M. Persig pointed out in *Zen and the Art of Motorcycle Maintenance*, in a car you are completely cocooned, but on a bike everything is real: the road rushing a few inches below our feet, the cool wind on our arms, the sweetness of pine and maple in our nostrils, the flicker of sunlight through the passing trees.

No, I know what it was. It wasn't the flicker of sunlight through the trees, it was the fact that we could see the trees: in Vermont, roadside billboards are banned and chain stores frowned upon. As a result, in eight hundred miles of travelling over the next week, we were to see one mall and two McDonald's, and in every village, with its green, its two-pump gas station, its general store and its white wooden church, which I had not imagined after all, we found an America that I thought had vanished in the 1950s.

For heaven's sake, they even leave their cars running when they go to the post office in the morning. Mind you, at a quid a gallon, they can afford to.

'I asked one of them about that,' Jack Burns, an innkeeper who moved there from New Jersey, told me. 'He said, "Well, everyone knows it's my car. If it wasn't me driving it, they'd know something was wrong." '

And when Jack and his wife bought their inn in Chester two years ago and asked the lawyer for the door keys, he scratched his head. It's not that they don't have house keys in Vermont.

It's just that no one can remember where they've put them.

'The first time I went to the grocery store,' said Jack, 'there was only one woman in the queue, so I thought I'd be out of there in a minute. It took half an hour. The next time I gave up and joined in.'

People come here to slow down, and we did too: our bike could do well over a ton, but at times we found ourselves going so slowly we were in danger of falling over. Once we joined a queue of cars that had pulled over for a jaywalking duck.

All this Arcadian bliss, however, doesn't mean that you're bereft of the pleasures of urban sophistication; they may stop to let a duck cross the road, but that evening you'll find it on your plate with a very nice cranberry glaze. I polished off the little darling, who had not died in vain, and went to bed. In the night it rained, and the next morning, steam ghosted off the road in the summer sun.

That's another thing about Vermont: they have proper seasons. In winter, snow piles to the eaves. In spring, the forest bursts with iridescence; in the summer the heat hangs heavy in the glades and in autumn the trees are ablaze in a riot of colour.

But nature is only half Vermont's story. The people are the other half. Night after night we arrived at elegant inns, dusty, sweaty and with the sort of wild hair you get from a day under a helmet, only to be greeted like long-lost cousins.

And it wasn't just have-a-nice-day friendliness: arriving at an inn in Stowe, we got talking to a woman climbing into a convertible. We were still there after half an hour. Two days later, as we were leaving a shop on the other side of town, she crossed the road to say hello and to see if we were enjoying ourselves. We were, believe me.

The best thing is that all of it's entirely genuine, and not invented yesterday by a public relations company: down the road from Chester, for example, we found the extraordinary Kim Kendall, sole proprietor of an eponymous barn packed to the rafters with treasured junk. He had been there forever, and the junk for even longer.

And a few miles away from his bargain basement of retail therapy was the Vermont Country Store in Weston, selling everything from traditional canoes to tins of fiddlehead ferns. (You eat them, since you ask.)

Only in rural America could you find, sold without irony, a publication entitled *The Good Citizen's Book*, a compendium of government manuals since the 1920s, which starts 'Only by pursuing proper dental hygiene, cheerfully paying your taxes and obeying even minor laws can you ensure the prosperity of your family, community and country.' Other sections include 'The Importance of a Meat Diet' and 'Why it is Never Right to Poison your Neighbor's Dog'.

Old canoes and fiddlehead ferns notwithstanding, Vermont is most famous for the brave new world of independence, socialism and eco-capitalism. Ice cream, in other words, which is why later that day we found ourselves near Stowe having the Ben and Jerry experience.

It all began, as you may know, at a Long Island high school in 1963, when the chucklesome twosome discovered a mutual dislike of exercise and love of food. In 1977, with the help of a $5 correspondence course in How to Make Ice Cream, they started a corner shop that is now a $235-million international business. There are seven hundred staff in the Stowe factory alone, most of them fighting to work in the tasting section. 'Not much turnover in that team, but a lot of growth,' said Phil the guide.

Forthcoming flavours, and you read it here first, include the Full Vermonty – presumably you strip off and rub it all over – while outside is a little graveyard for the flavours that didn't make the grade, like Fred and Ginger, Tennessee Mud, Oh Pear! and Sugar Plum.

Tragically, the merry duo have sold the business to another little family business run by a Mr and Mrs Unilever, but their spirit lives on in the expanding waistlines of the nation at large.

Talking of which, it was time for lunch. We found it at Pickwick's in Stowe, an English pub run by a former Royal Navy man Chris Francis and his wife, Lyn.

'We came out here for a holiday and fell in love with it. The people are genuine, caring and endlessly helpful. They've got zero crime, good steaks, four seasons and beautiful surroundings,' he said over fish and chips on the porch.

'And the food's better too,' said Cate, tucking into a ploughman's lunch. 'It's not fluffed up, blow-dried and pre-digested like most other places in the States.'

Indeed, something was happening to me. I was being seduced by Vermont. I wanted to live here and bring up little Vermonsters who would live on free-range chicken and ice cream, hike in the summer, ski in the winter, let old old ladies cross the street and grow up to be the world's first caring lawyers.

To celebrate my decision I had a beer in a nearby sports bar, in which several fat blokes were watching large black millionaires put a ball through a hoop.

When that finished, the news came on, read by Marselis Parsons and Sera Congi, whose parents had obviously picked their names from a Scrabble set.

That night we found ourselves at The Inn at Mountain View Farm, originally a gentleman's farm built by Elmer A. Darling to supply the Fifth Avenue Hotel in New York, which was founded by his grandfather Ebenezer in 1859. When young Elmer graduated from college, according to the clipping on the wall from the *St Johnsbury Republican* of 2 May 1906, he was employed to do all the marketing for the hotel.

Heavens, I thought, how very prescient to have a head of marketing in 1906. But then I read on.

Elmer's job, in fact, was to go to the market at four every morning and buy fresh food for the hotel.

How very Vermont, I thought, to have a head of marketing who gets up at dawn and goes to buy carrots rather than dressing up in a suit and selling everyone a hill of beans.

2002

Western Australia

I had bought the floppy hat, and almost killed myself drinking the dozen bottles of wine for the corks to hang from it. And, although I believe a criminal record is no longer necessary, I had brought with me a copy of Rolf Harris's 'Stairway to Heaven' just to be on the safe side.

It was, as you may have guessed, my first visit to Australia. I arrived in Perth, bought a pair of sunglasses and walked out of the shop straight into a downpour.

As a result, my first impression of the city was that it was dark and wet. It also seemed to be filled with people strangling cockatoos then running away. However, when I took the sunglasses off, this turned out to be the rather strange sound of Perth pedestrian crossings: a muffled squawk followed by a receding pitter-patter.

Perth was part British colonial and part Oriental, both high-rise and low-key, like Vancouver on valium. The glittering steel and glass towers of the city centre are the legacy of the eighties economic boom, fuelled by men like Alan Bond and Kerry Stokes, whose mansions line the lapping shores of the Swan River to the south-west of the city.

The river flows into the Indian Ocean at the sleepy little town of Fremantle, which in 1987 woke up, rubbed its eyes and realised with a mixture of excitement and panic that the Aga Khan and thousands of sailing aficionados were arriving in town for Australia's defence of the Americas Cup.

'Great time, mate. Non-stop bonking,' said one Fremantle taxi driver about that summer. In Australia, taxi drivers do exactly what they say on the tin, and then some. Within five minutes of getting into a cab, you will know their opinion on everything from women – 'I knew this Pom Sheila once ...' – to Aborigines – 'I'm not a racist, but ...' – to sport – 'Aussie Rules, that's the stuff, mate. Soccer's for pansies. Except quokka soccer on Rotto, and that's been banned.'

Rotto, or Rottnest Island, is where Perth escapes for the weekend. A miniature version of Australia, it has little hills, little beaches, little lakes and trees, and a little church, pub, library, cinema, police station and restaurant, all frozen in the amber of the fifties. It even has little kangaroos called quokkas which the local lads used to celebrate the end of the high school year by playing football with. Hence quokka soccer.

Looking at quokkas, it is hard to believe how anyone would want to harm them. As I cycled around the island, one hopped out in front of me. I got off the bike, bent down and stroked the soft fur behind its ears. It looked up at me with glossy, innocent eyes, and wet itself.

In the taxi from the Fremantle ferry terminal back to Perth, the taxi driver had an opinion on Rottnest Island too.

'Nothing to do there but drink. Bloody perfect, mate.'

Not that all Australians are beer-swilling boors: most cringe at the thought that Sir Les Patterson or Paul Hogan are their countrymen. But even when liberals are recalling a particularly fine Shiraz or a bloody marvellous night at the opera, their opinions are always presented as an instantly open book.

In Australia, a spade is always a spade. No wonder they have such a distrust of Japan, where every truth is hidden beneath a thousand layers of ritual.

'They're taking over everything, mate. Bloody organised bunch, though,' said the taxi driver on the way to the airport for the flight north to Paraburdoo.

I climbed into the plane and rose into the uncanny light, then fell at last through white clouds and a vermilion sunset to the black earth. And woke the next morning to the red heart of western Australia.

At a hearty breakfast of toast and Vegemite – the indigenous yeast extract which tastes of salted tar with a hint of anchovies – I met my guides for the day. Richard was an ex-accountant from British Columbia. Tim was a former sheep shearer from just up the road, and their vehicle of choice was an Oka, which looked like a civilian troop carrier.

'Is this in case we get attacked by rabid crocodiles?' I said.

'No, it's so we can get more beer in,' said Richard.

The Karajini area, where we were heading, is big mining country. Long ago, before the Queen Mother was born, unimaginable pressures crushed the earth here into the diamonds and gold, opals and sapphires which, along with pearls from the coast, are borne south to Perth then out into the turning world, where the necks and wrists of gracious society await them.

But it is iron ore which has made this land so rich and so red, and it is hauled from it in vast quantities. The trains carrying the ore south on the world's largest private railway are up to 4 miles long, hauling 540 cars and weighing 57,000 tonnes each. Oh, and the workers laying the track drank 400 gallons of beer for every mile laid.

From the coast the iron ore goes to Japan, where it is turned into Toyota Land Cruisers, which are shipped back to Australia, where they eventually rust back, with a wonderful circularity, to exactly the same colour as iron ore.

Anyway, where was I? Ah yes, driving through the outback with Richard and Tim. This used to be big sheep as well as mining country, but today wool is a fifth of the price it used to be.

'Synthetics. Everyone's buying them,' said Tim, and laughed. 'What we need is a good war. In a cold place.'

Out here the land is vast, and apart from the rich red earth, the colours are tiny even after rain: purple and yellow flowers, or little flames of periwinkle blue dancing in the breeze. We climbed deeper into the gorge, swimming through icy pools then inching along nervous ledges. If I had fallen I would have died, but I dared not ask if this was all a bit dangerous, or I would have been pointed out forever as the whinging Pom who was afraid of a little death.

Late that afternoon, we finally climbed back into the sunlight, and Richard reached into the Oka and handed me a tinny from the Esky. Or a beer from the coolbox, for those of you who are hard of Strine.

'Here, this beer's warm,' I said.

'No, it's ice cold. You're just colder than it is,' he said.

I liked it so much that I had several more that night at the only pub in Tom Price, a mining town so basic that Richard's tour of it had taken 28 seconds. Beside the pool table and jukebox, an entire wall was filled with greyhound racing schedules.

'Looks like the whole country's gone to the dogs,' I said to a bearded man who was trying to find the bar so he could lean on it.

'Yeah, we like a good gamble, we do,' he said blearily.

'No, I mean the country's gone to the dogs,' I said, tilting my head meaningfully towards the wall.

He looked at the wall, then at me, with amiable bafflement.

'Fancy a pint, mate?' he said. He was, it later transpired, the local JP.

This is not to say that Australians have no sense of humour. It's just that, like Americans, when they emigrated to the New World, they left irony behind as unnecessary baggage.

I staggered home from the pub and went to bed. The next day I went snorkelling off Ningaloo Reef with Eddie Izydorski, a man who had perfected the didgeridoo player's art of circular breathing so that he could talk all day without pausing. Fortunately, he was so interesting I could listen to him all day as well. Looking for whale sharks, which in theory only eat small fish and are perfectly safe to swim with, we headed out past the reef and over the edge of the continental shelf.

Down below, careless crabs out for a Sunday stroll plummeted into deep space with expressions of baffled regret, and all around us, the swell was like a turquoise rollercoaster. Overhead, a spotter plane radioed down. Eddie listened.

'Shark! Eighteen-footer!' he shouted suddenly. 'Get in the water!'

Now, I have had some breathtaking experiences in my life: Cate's apple crumble and my last bank statement spring to mind.

But plunging into the water and seeing a shark ten feet away coming straight for me was right up there. I did what anyone would have done in the circumstances: discovered that you can't swear into a snorkel, and turned right.

The memory of the shark was still with me the next day as Richard dropped me at the little local airport, a song of aluminium curves and primary colours soaring from the silent desert. The staff numbered two, and on the wall was a sign saying 'Fish may not be carried on as hand baggage'.

Half an hour later, the plane carried less than a dozen passengers as it rose above a region which is still the great undiscovered secret of Australian tourism.

So go there. But don't tell a soul.

2002

Wiener Kreis

In the twenties and thirties, Austria was the home of the Wiener Kreis, a group of logical positivists who, having nothing else to do in the long winter evenings, invented the verifiability principle which stated that things were only meaningful if you could prove they existed.

They suffered a serious blow when the Nazis arrived in 1938, since although you can't prove a stormtrooper exists, having one on your doorstep is still deeply meaningful. However, they suffered an even more serious blow when they realised that they couldn't even prove that the verifiability principle itself existed.

At this point the heads of several members exploded, and most of the rest went to America to become taxi drivers, leaving only Ludwig Wittgenstein, who spent the rest of his life analysing language before realising that he couldn't really use language to analyse itself.

Faced with such a national predilection for imploding paradoxes, you can see why Julie Andrews thought it was far simpler to fling on a habit and skip down a mountain singing 'The Hills are Alive'.

And yet, within an hour of arriving in the country I hadn't seen her once. Nor had I seen anyone slapping their lederhosen, playing the alpenhorn in an oompah band or wearing one of those little felt yodelling hats with a feather up the side.

Even worse, in spite of the fact that it was midsummer's day, it was pouring with rain.

Still, since I couldn't prove it, there was no point analysing it, so I got on a bus to Söll, the village where in 1945 the Germans surrendered to the Yanks at a round table in the Postwirt restaurant, then ordered pudding.

I found a nice little hotel and had a beer. It was so good I had several more, gazing out of the window at the twilight and the mist embracing each other around the mountains. After a while the waitress seemed to be bringing more beers than she was taking away glasses, and at first I thought this was due to the effect named after the Salzburg scientist Christian Johann Doppler, who discovered that the frequency of a note changes as it approaches then leaves an observer.

But then I realised it was because Austrian beer was stronger than I had thought, and had reduced me to that absurdly happy state known as illogical positivism. Since by now I was incapable of proving the existence of anything, or analysing it using language, I went to bed, and dreamt of marmots.

The regional mascot of the Tirol, these look like gerbils on steroids, and last year became an endangered species because summer tourists fed them so much chocolate that by the time winter came, half of them were too fat to get back into their burrows and froze to death.

The rain was still hurtling down when I woke the next morning, so I took a bus to a spa in Holzkirchen and spent the morning lying in a large wooden bath full of hot, oily water, while across a screen on the wall flickered time-lapse clouds and falling leaves.

As content as a stuffed marmot, I strolled through the village and found a steam train just about to leave for the journey down the mountain and along the lake to Jenbach. During the war, this little train bad been used to transport parts to the Messerschmitt factories in the bomb-proof caves up the mountain.

I climbed aboard and we set off behind a tiny locomotive which seemed like a distillation of the day as it huffed and puffed its way through the dripping undergrowth, the clouds of steam issuing from its funnel mingling imperceptibly with those already resident in the treetops. In the afternoon, the rain stopped enough to take a cable car up to the rather appropriate spot of Hexenwasser, or Witches' Water, a series of ponds and waterfalls which in the sixteenth century was the site of the home of two sisters. When bad weather ruined the crops in the valley below once too often, the farmers came to the inevitable conclusion that the sisters were witches, stormed up the mountain and burnt them at the stake. This is known as illogical negativism.

These days, Hexenwasser is a children's playground of wood, water and stone overlooked by a restaurant. I ordered a bowl of cheesy noodles and sat at a table outside, waiting for Anita to take me barefoot forest walking.

Anita, when she arrived right on time, was the sort of hearty outdoor type who looked as if she was happiest splashing around naked in mountain tarns, and, indeed, five minutes later we had whipped off our shoes and socks and were off into the woods, tramping across grass, mud, pine cones, fir branches and river beds while singing selected hits from *The Sound of Music*.

Honestly, you wouldn't believe how difficult it is yodelling 'My Favourite Things'.

It was all delightfully squelchy and organic, like being a couple of giant hobbits, and we emerged blinking into the sunlight to find Alex standing in a mountain glade. Alex was an instructor in Nordic walking, a sort of permanent lunging which looks like cross-country skiing for people who've forgotten their skis: hardly surprising, since it was dreamed up by Finnish skiers who wanted to practise in the summer.

It feels as silly as it sounds, but after an hour of lunging heartily across mountain pastures, sending cows stampeding in a symphony of bovine campanology, I felt as if I had gone three rounds with a demented marmot. Inspired, I went back to the hotel and invented the sport of Nordic drinking. Here are the instructions. Place pint on bar. Stand well back. Lunge towards pint, sip and hold position. Return to start. Repeat with other leg and arm.

Advanced Nordic drinkers can set up two pints and use continuous alternate lunging, although do be careful not to break your nose on the bar by lunging forward with both legs at the same time.

Tragically, the next morning I discovered that Nordic

drinking gave me the same hangover as normal drinking. What I needed was some gentle activity, like edelweiss arranging, to ease me gently into the day, I thought as I emerged from breakfast to find Anita standing in the lobby. 'Ah, good morning,' she said in a hearty fashion which suggested that she had spent the night sleeping deeply in a moon-dappled meadow, covered in a warm blanket of organic hay. 'Are you ready to go paragliding?'

Half an hour later, I found myself in a field 4,000ft above the valley, being strapped into a harness by a grizzled veteran called Reiner, then sprinting down the grass and rising gently into the air.

It was the most dream-like of experiences, drifting high over cow pastures and pine forests, and for a man suspended several thousand feet above the earth by only a few lengths of nylon, I felt illogically positive.

Which, as any member of the Wiener Kreis would tell you, is a great feeling, even if they can't prove it.

2004

Wolves

In an ideal world, a chap would prepare for an expedition such as this by sitting in front of the fire in his study with a smoking jacket and pipe, reading *My Life with Wolves* by Freddie Fortescue-ffrench.

However, there were two problems. Freddie did not exist, and I had employed to renovate our house a team of builders who, unfortunately, did.

As a result, the study resembled a building site, possibly because it was, and I spent the evening before leaving in it, covered in plaster dust and looking out with wistful irony at the wooded hill where the last wolf in Ireland was allegedly killed early in the eighteenth century.

The next morning, I rose at dawn, put on a fur hat and left for Sweden, my sole knowledge of wolves, gleaned from boyhood books on Canada, that they stood on stark peaks howling at the moon, weighed as much as a man, hunted in packs of fifty and ate trappers called Black Jacques and Sven the Swede for lunch and sometimes afternoon tea as well.

None of which, it transpired, was true. Wolves, for example, have rarely attacked humans, and humans have just as rarely returned the favour. Demonised as symbols of the devil and the dark by everyone from Descartes to Little Red Riding Hood, European wolves were driven to the edge of extinction. In Sweden in the fifties, there were six left.

Today there are about a hundred, but sightings are rare. Which is why I needed a man like Anders Stahl: wildlife painter, ex-soldier, Arctic ranger, fireman, guide and wolf tracker. He was standing on the platform at Leksand as I stepped off the early train north from Stockholm into flurries of snow. We climbed into his Toyota, called at the grocers to pick up provisions – unaccountably, I bought three bananas – and set off for the wilderness. It was not too far away, since Leksand is exactly between nowhere and nowhere else.

After an hour we abandoned the car, shouldered our

rucksacks and took to the forest on foot. Wearing borrowed Dutch paratrooper's trousers, a Russian fur hat and Anders's old Swedish army winter smock, I looked like a reject from a NATO charity shop as we set of on the trail of a pack once led by a great wolf who had died three years before.

Since then his partner had led the pack alone, but had now found a new mate, presumably after an ad in the lonely hearts section of *Wildlife Weekly* saying 'Partner wanted for friendship and possible romance. Must have own fur coat and like long walks, cold nights out and raw elk. Non-smoker preferred. Must be a wolf.'

There were, it had to be said, plenty of elk to eat: the population numbers a quarter of a million, and ninety thousand are culled every year by jolly Swedish hunters. The older, wiser elk, who know something is up, escape by donning sunglasses, leaning against a tree and saying 'Me? No, I'm not an elk. He is, though.'

At least I think that's what Anders said. I was busy trying to keep up with him through a landscape of silver birch and lakes so cold that the air above them dared not move in case it cracked. There was no sound except the crunch of our feet in the snow and the occasional muffled thwack as I walked into a tree.

Suddenly, Anders held up his hand and looked down at a row of tracks in the snow. But they were too tiny to be the mighty pawprints we were looking for.

'Fox,' said Anders. That's the way men talk when they're outdoors.

'Or a wolf wearing stilettos?' I suggested.

'In this weather?' he said, and proceeded.

Then, 100 yards later, the real thing, each one 6 inches long and 5 across. There was, I have to say, something spookily primeval about looking at tracks in the snow and saying 'Wolves were here.'

We moved on, up hill and down dale of increasingly deep drifts. After another hour, the snow was, oh, about up to our necks. Ahead of me, Anders stopped, unshouldered his rucksack and produced two aluminium and leather tennis rackets.

'I think,' he said with Nordic stolidity, 'it is time for snowshoes.'

He was right. The going went from impossible to almost impossible. I looked up to thank him when I realised he had vanished. I hunted around in vain for five minutes, vaguely aware of the stupidity of not being able to find prints the size of tennis rackets, then spotted a large pile of elk poo. And another.

Finally, by following the droppings, I found Anders standing in a clearing with the elk responsible. It hadn't run away as he walked up to it, probably because half of it was missing. As someone from the Sainsbury's school of Buddhism, who loves animals but refuses to see any connection between them and the contents of the meat shelves, it was both troubling and humbling to be confronted with the fact that I was so obviously wrong.

Nearby was a smattering of wolf droppings, black with blood. 'Smell it,' said Anders. I did. I wish I hadn't.

'Right,' he said, 'have you ever used cross-country skis?'

After a mile we came across fresh wolf tracks. Darkness fell in a silent storm of lilac, but we plunged on regardless, keeping our track by the North Star. Oh, and by following the path. After a while, though, even that ran out, and after another hour of colliding with trees and stepping into icy streams all exactly an inch higher than the tops of my boots, I saw to my complete astonishment that Anders had found the log cabin which was to be our billet for the night.

He produced an axe from his bottomless rucksack, and I set to chopping firewood while he rustled up sausage and pasta. Then we had some howling to do.

Anders stepped on to the porch, cleared his throat, and produced a sound that was not quite of this earth. The hairs on the back of my neck stood briskly to attention.

'Anders,' I said, 'how do you do that?'

'Practice.'

But from the forest there was no reply. The pack were all down at the wolf bar, telling tall elk tales. We curled up in our sleeping bags, and slept the exhausted sleep of men who have been out not finding wolves all day.

2002

Xavier Furtwangler's School of Getting to the Point

This was a newspaper column about a conversation with Joris Minne, brother of Paddy, the world-famous Franco-Belgian motorcycle mechanic, on the subject of sponsorship for riding two Royal Enfields from Delhi to Belfast.

It later became part of the original manuscript of Way to Go, *but was cast aside by the editor for missing the point, even though I pointed out that missing the point was the whole point.*

After crying for a few days, I swore I would get it published somewhere, somehow, some sunny day, and here it is. If you see the publishers, for heaven's sake don't tell them.

Heavens, schmeavens, and buckets of pink socks with little yellow bobbly bits on, but I've been overwhelmed by a deluge of criticism over the fact that the account of my conversation with M. Minne the Slightly Elder, which I published in my column in the *News Letter* last week, ended without getting to the point.

Colleagues have stopped me in the office and poured warm chocolate over me, friends have phoned me up in a state of bafflement and one elderly reader is suing me for hastening her decline into terminal bewilderment, in spite of me pointing out to her that you don't need to be elderly to be terminally bewildered, since I've been that way since I was born.

The problem is, I told them all, that they had fallen into the trap of assuming that all dramatic constructions have to conform to Aristotle's definition of having a beginning, a middle and an end, and that because they had this expectation, they were, naturally, disappointed.

It would have been much better, I said to them, if they had adopted the principle of Buddha when he said that when you expect nothing, then everything is a gift. In that way they would have appreciated last week's column for exactly what it was – an exercise in the stillness of perfection.

But it was no use: they were all members of Continuity Zen, who believe that if you don't find perfection just the way you want it, you insist that someone changes it immediately, or else you'll be round with a bunch of indolent youths armed with a wet lettuce.

Finally, a decision was reached – I would have to sign up immediately for a course at Herr Doktor Xavier Furtwangler's School of Getting to the Point, high in the Austrian Alps.

A whip-round was organised for my travel expenses, reaching the princely sum of £1.27, 5 Spanish pesetas, an old teabag and a piece of fluff of dubious origin, and I was off, wobbling my way towards the Belfast docks on the company unicycle, which the editor had been kind enough to lend me. Mind you, he could have put a tyre on it, but I suppose I shouldn't be ungrateful.

Anyhow, after several weeks of cycling, during which time the solitary wheel had collapsed – reducing me to pogoing along the verges while huge transcontinental lorries thundered past, covering me either in a miasma of fine dust or a sprinkling of fresh rain, depending on the weather – I arrived outside the town hall of the little Austrian burgh of Feldkirch, where I had arranged to meet Gretchen, Dr Furtwangler's assistant.

As I dismounted from the unicycle – not a difficult task, since by now there was nothing left but a saddle – a large, black, very old Hispano Suiza limousine swept into the cobbled square and drew to a halt beside me.

A tinted rear window slid down to reveal Gretchen, even at first sight a charming girl with hair like sunlight which had fallen to earth and been woven by the trolls who live beneath the mountains, eyes the colour of rainwashed meadows in spring, and skin which spoke silent volumes of a life far from the cares of the grey city which I had left many weeks before.

'Mr Hill, I presume,' she said in a delicately ironic voice which was the most beautiful thing I had heard since I dreamed one night that I had arrived at Verdi's funeral at the very moment that the thousands of people who had turned up to pay their last respects began spontaneously to sing the song of the Hebrew slaves from his opera, *Nabucco*. Gretchen pressed a hidden lever, the door of the limousine swung open, and I found myself sitting beside her clutching the saddle of the office unicycle as we left the village and began to climb into the mountains.

I closed my eyes and drank in all the sensations that the interior of the vehicle offered me: the occasional touch of the freshly laundered cotton of Gretchen's blouse against my arm as we rounded corners, the dark and nutty aroma of leather seats which have been worn and cared for over many decades, the staccato play of light on my eyelids as we drove past a stand of firs. I even imagined I could smell the walnut of the dashboard, an aroma quaintly reminiscent of manzanilla, the fine aperitif which the Andalucians are fond of drinking before lunch.

At last we rounded a final bend and I opened my eyes to behold the remarkable sight of an entirely white building so close to the top of the mountain that its spires seemed to be only just short of reaching heaven, and yet so close to the edge that the building looked to be at risk of plunging in its entirety to the other place.

And yet I knew this to be an illusion, for this was none other than the famous Feldkirch Sanatorium, built so that the tens of thousands who suffered from the tuberculosis which was endemic between the great world wars could escape from a life of blood-spotted sheets and unendurable inactivity to recover in its pristine air.

The limousine ground to a halt in front of a side door, and Gretchen gently took my hand and led me into a spartan room in which the furnishings, though few, were evidently of the highest quality.

And there, behind a massive desk, sat the great man himself, his grey eyes unblinking behind a pair of polished steel-rimmed spectacles.

'Ah, Mr Hill,' he said in perfect English as Gretchen closed the door behind us. 'And what can we do for you?'

'Dr Furtwangler, it seems impossible,' I replied. 'For two weeks now I have been trying to say in my newspaper column that Nambarrie the tea company have sponsored my attempt to ride back from Delhi on two Royal Enfield Bullets with Patrick Minne, the world-famous Franco-Belgian motorcycle mechanic, and have been completely unable to get to the point.'

Dr Furtwangler smiled, in a stern yet kindly fashion.

'Mr Hill, you have cured yourself,' he said. 'Gretchen, fetch us three glasses and a bottle of the 1957 Gevrey-Chambertin.'

'Ah, the wine of which Victor Hugo said, "I cannot remember the town, and the name of the girl escapes me, but the wine was Chambertin"?'

'Precisely. And while Gretchen is fetching the wine, can I offer you a cup of tea?'

'Nambarrie?'

'Naturally,' said Dr Furtwangler, as a merry tinkle heralded the return of Gretchen.

1998

Yachting

There are many ropes on a boat, but none of them are called ropes.

Some of them, for example, are halyards. They are the ones that make the sails go up.

Lazy jacks occasionally lift a hand in spite of themselves to help when the sails are coming down.

Sheets, on the other hand, make the sails go in and out, and painters are the ones you hold when you are standing on shore to stop the boat drifting off in the general direction of America.

Unless you decide to go off to the pub and tie them to a bollard, a tree or a passing pensioner, in which case they become warps.

Except when they are stopping the boat drifting forwards or backwards, in which case they are springs. Or if they are attached to a dinghy, in which case they are painters.

Lazy jacks are not to be confused with lazy lines, which are ropes lying in the water that you tie the bow of the boat to when you moor, holding it in delicately tender opposition to the gently swaying warps on the stern.

There. I hope that's all clear. Now, if you'll excuse me, I'm going to lie down in a darkened room for a while.

Except there are no rooms on a yacht. They are called cabins, the kitchen is called a galley and the bathroom is called a head.

I looked at my watch.

'What's six o'clock on a boat?' I said to Paul, who was busy tying a double-clove overhead slipdonglehitch to a cleat.

'About four bells.'

'And what's a gin and tonic called?'

'A gin and tonic.'

'Thank God for that. I think I'll have one.'

Ah, that was better, and just in time for our briefing by Simon, the flotilla skipper for our week in Croatia.

Simon, who was a lawyer until he realised there was more to life than getting rich by pushing paper around a desk, was one of those impossibly healthy, blue-eyed young Englishmen who had been doing outdoorsy things for so long that, although he knew he must have a suit and a pair of shoes somewhere, he couldn't quite remember where just at this minute.

He briefed us for a good three-quarters of an hour on the workings of the boat, and the only word I understood completely was fridge.

I was becoming aware of two things: that Cate and I were glad that Paul and Sharon, both experienced sailors, were with us.

And that boats were designed by midgets who never went to bed, probably because they were up all night designing the perfect windlass. If I had designed a boat costing £130,000, for example, I would have included big, spacious, airy bedrooms with the sun streaming through French windows and dancing playfully on the pure white Hungarian goose-down duvets, filled with fluff picked from the virgin breasts of ten-day-old Kecskemét goslings.

Not a slightly widened coffin whose already claustrophobic ceiling had been further lowered by the addition of several bumps, corners and edges all perfectly placed to fracture heads, elbows, toes and any other innocently passing extremity.

Oh well, there was nothing else for it than to make supper.

As the sun went down in a blaze of glory across the bay and a fat yellow moon rose over the mountain, we ate pasta and sausage, drank wine with indecipherable labels, and felt deliciously, exotically abroad.

We put everything away for the night and, after several hours, Cate and I had managed to laboriously fold ourselves into bed for the night. I plumped up my pillow and, with a deep sigh, prepared to sink into a deep and dreamless sleep.

Then realised that I had to go to the toilet.

I sighed, even more deeply, and began the whole process in reverse.

The next morning, there was Simon again, bright-eyed and bushy-tailed, with the sailing briefing for the day. He talked for half an hour this time, and I understood the words island and beer.

So I went and bought some beer, and we set off for the island, motoring out to sea then switching off the engine and hauling up the sails using various halyards, sheets, gizmos and bonglesprockets.

Tragically, no one had told the Croatian weather that it was supposed to be late summer, and as we left the shelter of the mainland it was to a hefty swell and dark clouds. Still, apart from the giant waves, torrential rain, sub-zero temperatures and the fact that Cate fractured her spine on the edge of the oven and Sharon threw up over the side, it was a splendid day, and it was in a state of only mild hypothermia that I was prised from the helm at teatime.

We had docked in a little wooded cove lined with ancient red-tiled houses, a mist-shrouded church in which several locals were praying for sunshine, and a solitary restaurant which must have been, oh, a good ten yards away. It was too small a place to have been blessed by the presence of guide-book writers, and was none the worse for that.

We sipped beer at the back of the boat as rain dripped slowly off the awning. It was like childhood holidays in Rossnowlagh in

Donegal, when we sat for two months every year listening to the rain on the caravan roof, playing Spot the Earwig and Guess What's for Supper (clue: it was always Fray Bentos steak-and-kidney pie; the one with the crust a quarter of a micron thick).

Still, one of the pleasures of adulthood is that you can always have another beer, so I had another beer.

After that, I looked at the dank, dripping forests rising all around, and felt as if I was in the South American jungle and was, rather than a little boy growing up in Tyrone who went to Donegal for his holidays, the son of the Swedish ambassador to Bolivia, a country to which, as Martin Stephenson has pointed out in a song which deserves to be better known, you cannot catch a boat.

A son who would grow up to be, not a diplomat like his father, but an SAS airline pilot who married a stewardess from Uppsala and realised, almost too late in life, that he was a better writer than a pilot, subsequently penning a short but beautiful novel which made grown men sigh with vicarious happiness for the insight it gave them into a more noble and heroic life, and which made grown women cry for the insight it gave them into what they had previously dismissed as the closed or, at best, indifferent hearts of men.

'What are you thinking, love?' came the voice of Cate, interrupting my reverie.

'Several things at once, dear, which cannot be good for me,' I said, and went off to get another beer.

The next morning, things looked up. The sun came out, and we slid painlessly through the little islands, stopping at little coves which were completely deserted except for other yachts that were using the same *Guide to Croatia's Deserted Coves* as we were.

We swam, and sunbathed, and thought, and paddled, keeping a careful lookout for the agonising spines of sea urchins. These are easy enough to spot, since they are usually lined up on the seabed singing hits from *Oliver*.

In the afternoon, as the boat plunged through heavy swells, I spent several happy hours keeping the handrail on the horizon by moving my head up and down. You wouldn't believe how entertaining this is. You can do the same thing on trains with an imaginary radio-controlled plane, making it dip and swoop over passing houses, hedgerows and cows, who will never know how close they came to being rammed by an aeroplane that wasn't there.

In the balmy evening, we docked beside a little restaurant, under a sign announcing that night's special – lobsters at £50 a kilo.

Fifty quid? I knew fish were scarce in the Adriatic, but fifty quid? I went over to the lobster tank, to see if they were Gucci lobsters or something. There they were, scuttling about waving their antennae, and every so often turning around to exclaim, 'Here, where's Jim gone? And how come we're so expensive, if there are so many of us? And has anyone seen Larry?'

Faced with guilt and penury, I had the squid.

At midnight, the rain came again, and then the lightning, leaving the freshly washed night smelling of iodine and singed photons.

The next day turned out lovely, thanks for asking. Well, apart from the lashing rain and 40mph gusts which signalled the arrival of the bora, the big wind that normally arrives in October, but which had obviously got fed up sitting in the wind waiting-room chatting up mistrals, siroccos and meltemis, and decided to bugger off and create havoc a month early.

But apart from that, and the fact that one of the gusts blew away Paul's favourite shorts, and a large bee, seeking shelter from the storm, crawled up my own shorts and stung me on the bum, all was well.

We found ourselves a haven in a little harbour and, pausing briefly to foul the propeller with a mooring line as a finale to a short but disastrous day, finally tied up for the night. As the torrential rain, impossibly, became even more torrential, and was joined in the heavenly cacophony by lightning and thunder, we battened down the hatches, changed into what dry clothes we had, and opened a bottle of 1998 Fonseca.

It was not their finest year, but any port in a storm, I always say. And besides, there was someone worse off than we were: Simon the flotilla skipper, who according to the radio, was out there in the howling gale under one of the boats, trying to unblock the toilet.

All in all, the scene beneath the frazzled sky and the turbulent waves must have been much calmer, as several dolphins took turns trying on Paul's shorts, saying, 'Here, Cynthia, does my bum look big in this?', then collapsing into fits of hysterical laughter in the way that only dolphins, of all the creatures in the otherwise humourless sea, do.

However, the Croatian weather is as fickle as Zsa Zsa Gabor, and by evening the sky had transformed itself into a palette of slate grey, rose and duck-egg blue that could have been painted by Turner after a bottle of Maraska gin.

It was a harbinger of the day to come, which dawned as still as a canvas. We hoisted all the sails we had, and set off into the blue at a rate so languid that several sea snails hurtled past us with looks of unaccustomed mockery.

Still, at least we now knew what we were doing enough so that when Paul called out 'Sheet-in the main' or 'Unlock the jib halyard', we no longer looked around with the expressions of rabbits caught in headlights.

And, since Simon now trusted us not to get lost or sink the boat, we were set free from the flotilla for a couple of days to potter across the high seas, practising tacking, gybing and reaching, whatever they were, for several happy hours before berthing in the harbour of the striking medieval town of Korcula with such professional aplomb that three local fisherman paused from repairing their nets and leaped up bearing placards saying '5.9', '5.8', '5.9'.

Tragically, the gloomy harbourmaster then came over and told us rather snottily that we couldn't park there, and must either go around the corner to be battered into oblivion by the onshore wind, or moor in the sophisticated marina, which would cost us £30, not including lobster.

Naturally, we cut his throat with a breadknife, machine-gunned all the inhabitants except the three fishermen, and burnt to the ground the lovely old town which had stood since the fifteenth century, given rise to some of the most exquisite synergies of Gothic and Renaissance architecture in the Balkans and been the birthplace of Marco Polo, author of the world's first great travel book and founder of a very fetching range of Swedish leisurewear.

Oh, all right, only joking. We just sailed around the corner and, after wrapping the dinghy rope around the propeller in a playful riposte to our earlier hubris, anchored in a little bay where we swam, drank, cooked pasta and fell asleep at last under the gently rocking stars.

2003

Z

Zebedee

Zebedee was the husband of Salome, the uncle of Jesus and the father of James the apostle, who arrived in northern Spain in the year AD 44. Unfortunately, the apostle did not enjoy his visit, since he had just been beheaded by Herod. His body, the legend goes, was taken by two disciples from Jerusalem to Jaffa, where a stone boat without crew or sails carried them to the Spanish coast in seven days at a speed barely equalled by the cocaine smugglers who arrive on that same coast today in black speedboats from Colombia.

The body was then rather carelessly lost for seven hundred and fifty years until a shepherd called Pelayo saw a star in a vision and dug up the saint's bones in a field. The local bishop, Theodomir, immediately pronounced the bones authentic and Santiago de Compostela, which means St James of the Field of the Star, became the destination for a pilgrimage which would soon overtake the great routes to Jerusalem and Rome.

James, inspired by a fame in death he had never known in life, promptly started popping up all over the place to help the Spanish in their holy war against the Arabs. At the battle of Clavijo in 844 alone, his ghost personally dispatched sixty thousand unfortunates, and over the next seven centuries he was spotted helping out at forty battles, even lending a hand with the massacre of American Indians in the New World – all of which, since he was originally a fisherman, must rank as the most successful late career change ever.

Today, thousands of pilgrims every year still make their way from all over Europe to Santiago de Compostela, knowing that by doing so they halve the time they will spend in Purgatory.

This year, since St James' Day falls on a Sunday, a pilgrimage to Santiago means that on the Monopoly board of Catholicism, 1999 is a 'Go straight to heaven, do not enter purgatory' year. In terms of salvation, it's like getting all your hotels on Mayfair, which means that the city is expecting up to half a million faithful to make the long trek this year by foot, by bicycle, by horse or by bright yellow sports car.

Ah yes. This is, I should say, the traditional lazy Protestant's method. It is, in fact, a very new tradition, but that's because I've only just thought of it.

Even worse, before I picked up the car in Dover, I had spent the night dancing at a jazz club in the crypt of a church in Camberwell. It could only be a matter of time before God got me in the back of the neck with a well-aimed thunderbolt.

I had, in fairness, tried to get a couple of proper Catholics to come with me, partly in mitigation and partly in the hope that God, whose eyesight can't be what it was when he was a younger god, would hit them instead.

But fate had taken a hand, and it was alone that I sat on the boat to Calais, realising with a sinking feeling that my entire preparation for the trip had consisted of reading a book on rural Japan and a copy of *Biggles Hits the Trail* (the one with the giant Tibetan caterpillars, if you remember). Still, at least I had brought with me *A Journey to the West*, the diary of a seventeenth-century Italian pilgrim called Domenico Laffi.

That evening I drove through the ancient gates of the village of Montreuil-sur-mer, which has not actually been *sur mer* since its harbour silted up five centuries ago, but before that was a major stopping point for pilgrims from northern Europe. As a result it was once coming down with churches, although many were destroyed in the sixteenth century when the village was sacked rather unluckily by the English and the Spanish in quick succession, and one became a pub, another a brewery and a third a garage, in that order.

I hurried past, sure that if God caught me near any more examples of religious buildings turned secular he wouldn't miss and hit the wall, never mind his dodgy eyesight, and found myself in the relative sanctuary of the pilgrims' hospital chapel.

Above the altar in a tiny glass phial was a piece of the true cross, one of only, oh, fifteen trillion which exist in the world, and dotted around the walls were scallop shells, the traditional symbol of the Santiago pilgrim, beautifully carved by members of the Companions of St Jacques, a bunch of tradesman who did the pilgrimage as a sort of medieval NVQ during which they picked up new skills and styles in cathedrals en route.

Well, that was quite enough culture for one day, and it was well nigh dinnertime, so the next thing I knew I was sitting in the dining room of the hotel tucking into snails and frogs' legs.

To be honest, I can't think what came over me: any time I order snails I imagine them trying to escape across the kitchen floor at 0.00001mph while a crazed sous-chef pursues them with a meat cleaver, and with frogs' legs I always think of that cartoon where the man is just about to tuck in when the kitchen doors swing open and a sad little convoy of frogs in wheelchairs emerges.

I can only think that I was attempting to plunge into French life at the deep end, a suspicion confirmed when I proceeded to a bar near the pavée St Firmin – where Victor Hugo set much of Les Misérables – got remarkably drunk on marc, the stuff they distil from the skins of grapes, and had a lengthy conversation about postmodernism with Claire, an architect from Paris.

This was a remarkable conversation for two reasons: first,

my French is so bad that even I don't know what I'm saying; and second, I don't even know what postmodernism is in English.

Tragically, at this point Claire's boyfriend arrived and took her home, so I was unable to pursue the matter any further in either language.

However, they say that the sin is in the thought, and the next day I paid the price for sliding off the pilgrim's path by driving the long road south to Poitiers listening to French radio, which was a choice between pop music so inane that the government had to pass a law forcing stations to play it, monumentally dreary chamber music and heavy metal so dire that not even a Norwegian Hell's Angel would give it the time of day.

Thankfully, halfway through the afternoon the classical channel presenter died of depression and was replaced by a woman whose tastes veered between Wagner and Debussy, so that for the rest of the day I alternated between tearing along Teutonically and waltzing lyrically down the centre of the road.

Still, at least the car, an Ibiza Cupra Sport lent to me by Seat, turned out to be entirely splendid: whenever you pressed the thing on the floor, it overtook everything else on the road, while a very satisfying noise came out of the back. Not only that, but a readout on the dashboard told me how long I had been driving, how many miles I had done, my average mph, mpg, engine oil temperature and outside temperature.

I imagine if I had known the right buttons to press it would have told me the time of high tide in Shanghai, the capital of Outer Mongolia and the last time I changed my underwear.

Those of you who like Wagner, meanwhile, should be aware that he reduces your average fuel consumption by 34.7 per cent. Indeed, he was entirely to blame for the fact that I overshot the Loire Valley and ended up in Poitiers, whose most surreal attraction must be Futuroscope, the theme park where for about fouteen quid you can engage in a series of experiences such as Le Tapis Magique, in which you fly to Mexico on the back of a giant butterfly.

Tragically, by the time I got there it was closed, so my alternatives were to drive the four hundred miles north to Amsterdam, where for about a fiver I could have a similar experience in a coffee shop, or drive the seven miles south to Poitiers, where for about the same price I had a pizza in an Irish pub while watching the Australian skydiving championships on television.

On the wall in front of me as I watched Brad plummet to victory was a graffito saying 'An Irishman is never drunk, so long as he has a blade of grass to cling to'.

Next morning, I had my first every power breakfast: a meeting with Mme Sarazin and Martine Brissoneau from the tourist board, who presented me with fifteen thousand brochures and a list of the five million essential sites I had to see on the road south before I stopped in Blaye that night.

As a result, here is the potted guide to the pilgrim's route between Poitiers and Blaye:

Poitiers

Home of the world's longest job interview, in which for three weeks Joan of Arc had her ideology and virginity extensively verified by the local bishops and matrons respectively. Also home of France's weirdest church, Notre Dame de la Grande, the western facade of which is covered in a riot of carvings detailing the early life of Jesus. In one scene he lies snoozing in his crib, being admired by a baffled sheep and a daft pig, and in another he sits in his bath with a bemused expression while being admired by a couple of dodgy-looking handmaidens.

Poitiers is also home to the university where Descartes wandered around gloomily pondering whether he existed or not. He eventually proved he did, then went to Sweden and died of pneumonia, after which he didn't.

Lusignan

Village built by a fairy called Melusine, who married a mortal called Raymond on condition he never saw her on Saturday, when she did all her building. When he did, she turned into a dragon. Motto: if your wife goes out on Saturdays with a magic wand and a hod, give her the benefit of the doubt.

Melle

Without the help of Melusine, the locals went mad in the eleventh and twelfth centuries and built three churches. The best of these is St Hilaire, where below the simple nave a local woman had placed a little display of sand, rocks and wild flowers in memory of her dead son. Christian church, atheist pilgrim, Zen moment.

Aulnay

Romanesque church, facade of which depicts diminutive breed of Poiton donkey, resembling shaved teddy bear, and eternal battle between wise and foolish virgins. Question: if they were so foolish, how come they were still virgins? Discuss. Write on one side of the paper, but both sides of the virgins.

St-Jean-d'Angély

Twinned with New Iberia, USA. Home of twin-towered abbey on hill which must have been an astonishing sight to pilgrims. Also home of museum containing first caterpillar car to cross Sahara and souvenirs of classic Citroëns, the cars of which weary mechanics say, 'Ah, if God had meant life to be simple, he would never have invented hydropneumatic suspension.'

Sainte

Eleventh-century abbey run by nuns; stunning remains of 20,000-seat Roman amphitheatre; rare double-decker church, St Eutrope, in which monks worshipped above and pilgrims below, in the same way that pilgrims were asked to use side entrances of churches rather than front. Theological reason: they were unclean. Practical reason: they were unclean.

Pons, a brief history

Built Middle Ages, destroyed by English, rebuilt by French, regained by English, regained by French, besieged, all dead, destroyed except tower. Now wet, closed except tower. Sole contents of tower is a tourist office. Other features: pleasant hotel with view of winding river; winding river with view of pleasant hotel.

Pons, a briefer history

Best visited before 1178.

Phew, late that night I arrived in Blaye, which is notable for having a citadel bigger than itself, and spurned my hotel to dine in a café which in England would have been naff, but in France was quaint.

What a splendid creation, though, is the French provincial waitress, and, indeed, waiter: they give you enough time after they deliver the menu and wine list to allow for suitable dithering, they ignore all your choices and suggest much better ones, they leave you plenty of time between courses to digest their choice, they don't ruin your meal by constantly asking if you're enjoying it and, best of all, they don't tell you that their name is Crystal and they're really an actress.

As a result, I went to bed entirely content. Tragically, the next morning I walked up to the citadel to find inside an entire town much nicer than Blaye. Even more tragically, although last night I had completely failed to find a mention of Blaye in my guidebook, this morning an entire page had magically reinserted itself which would have told me this. Hindsight is, in retrospect, the most exact science there is.

Still, it was fine to walk through the beetling arch to the citadel walls and wander around its grassy slopes and little houses amid a welter of birdsong. And to sit on a stone bench at the highest place and imagine what joy a pilgrim must have felt, hundreds of years ago, to sit on this very spot looking down at the Gironde estuary on one side and the pilgrims' hostel on the other, knowing that he was now over halfway on the greatest journey of his life.

I made it back to the car just as the rain started, and drove south to the rhythm of the wipers, with little to amuse myself except playing with the car's computer – I think it shows you've got to a certain age when you're more interested in the mpg than the mph.

By dusk I was in St-Jean-Pied-de-Port at the foot of the Pyrenees, which is where Domenico Laffi comes in, for although I had come from the north and he from his native Italy, St-Jean was where all the pilgrims met before they struggled across the mountains and on to Spain.

It was a shame that Domenico had been dead for three centuries, for I would have enjoyed a good natter with him. Curious and erudite, he found the joy of travelling in practically everything, and even when he didn't, was funny about it:

> We came upon a peasant in the company of a miller, who were having a meal. After we had pleaded with them for a long time, they gave us a little bread and cheese (which must have been made in the age of Romulus and Remus) and a little wine which, from being near the water, had become its sworn companion.

I read his journal for a while, then used my Swiss Army knife to cut a length of hair which had been hanging in my eyes all day. By not charging myself for this, I saved £15, which I spent on supper in a bar in which everyone, including the staff, was sixteen trying to act forty. Just wait until they try to do it the other way around. Still, if I thought I was sad, the man at the next table was wearing wellingtons and reading Paul Theroux.

In the morning I walked out of town on the main road and came back by the pilgrims' path, through the gate below the citadel and down the cobbled street past the half-timbered houses, one a pilgrims' hostel.

At the end of the street, the Pyrenees were shrouded in snow. Domenico would have wrapped his cloak about him and set off. I got into the car and switched on the heater.

At Roncesvalles, high above the snow line, the retreating Roland, hero of the medieval *Chanson de Roland*, sounded his horn in vain for reinforcements until it cracked, then was massacred with all his knights by the Basques.

I gave the car horn a little toot of empathy, but the only effect it had was to send a griffon vulture wheeling into the frozen sky and bring a hum of resonance from the bell of the little chapel of Ibañeta, where Domenico and his fellow pilgrims had taken refuge tor the night.

And then, suddenly, I was in Spain. I had lunch in Pamplona, where every year bulls from all over Spain turn up to run with the people, and set off for Hondarribbia, in whose central square stands a splendid palace turned luxury hotel, which was started in the tenth century by Sancho the Strong, who was 7ft 4in, continued in the fourteenth by Carlos V, who was much smaller, and stayed in during the twentieth by me, who was somewhere in between.

Pausing for a moment to free several locals who had become trapped in the hotel's revolving door by putting all their Basques in one exit, I checked in, then went for a potter down Calle Mayor – the street up which Steve McQueen wandered at the start of *Papillon* – then strolled around the block, or whatever they have in medieval towns, by which time I was soaked.

It was no use. It was never going to stop raining. I retired to the hotel bar, sank into a deep sofa with the sort of gin and tonic they only make in Spain – one gallon gin, one gallon tonic, one whole lemon, one iceberg – and read about Domenico Laffi getting soaked instead.

Then I went out to a little restaurant in the old quarter and ordered a meal in Spanish so bad that both the waiter and I were surprised when the food arrived. At the next table but one, a Dutch family slapped vowels around each other.

And when I went out, it was still raining.

As it was in the morning when I threw back the curtains. In fact, the more I thought about it, I could not remember a time when it had not been raining. I got into the car, turned on the wipers and drove west to Guernica. Since I only knew it through the eponymous painting by Picasso, I half expected it to be full of three-legged women with eyes on top of their heads, but it was normal to the point of dullness. That Picasso. What a lad.

Question: if Picasso painted a fish caught off Sellafield, would it look normal? Discuss.

It was probably as a result of making fun of Picasso that two hours later I got completely lost in Santander, with hailstones bouncing off the windscreen. Still, they made a nice change from the rain, and it could have been worse: I'd originally planned to do the trip on a motorbike.

After a while the hailstones turned into rain again, and the rain got worse. I wound up the windows and floated west past Bilbao, where the Guggenheim Museum sat glittering on the rusting scrapheap of Spain's industrial past, while around the city the glass and steel subway shelters of Norman Foster picked up its light and gave it back, like architectural apostles paying homage to the only art museum in the world more artistic than its contents.

At length I found myself in Santillana del Mar. Even Jean-Paul Sartre, the second gloomiest writer in the world after Paul Theroux, described Santillana as the most beautiful village in Spain, and it is. It is the sort of place where you imagine absurdly happy families live. The sort who hug their cows.

Absurdly happy, I wandered around in the rain looking for a cow to hug, but finding none, bought an absurdly happy flowerpot instead. Above the village in a hill are the famous Altamira caves, covered with a series of paintings which made it the Sistine Chapel of 12,000 BC. They were discovered one hundred years ago by a little girl called Maria with the immortal words, 'Look, Papa – cows!' Tragically, she went on to marry a banker.

I floated on, to Comillas, home of a monolithic Jesuit seminary high on a hill, which sent forth from its thousands of bare cells those stormtroopers of Christ to wreak havoc among the untouched souls of the world.

Around its walls hang paintings of hundreds of former inmates, and only one of them is smiling. Step forward Sr Dr Segundo Garcia Mendes, 1929–31. The rest of them put the fear of God in me. If those were the good guys, I hope I never meet a bad one.

I got back into the car and floated on through the Picos de Europa mountains. Darkness fell, the rain fell, my spirits fell, the moon rose, I found on the radio an old bossa-nova channel, my spirits rose.

I turned the heater up and drifted west in a Latin American micro-climate, while far above the reflection of the almost full moon tinkled off the snowy peaks with a sound that men cannot hear.

Finally, many hours into the night, I was washed up on the steps of the Hotel de la Reconquista, a former seventeenth-century children's hospital and pilgrims' hostel in Oviedo.

They tied up the car to stop it drifting away, led me to a suite the size of a planet and poured me a very cold gin and tonic and a very hot bath. I poured the first into myself, poured myself into the second, and felt very much better.

Several miles south and three centuries earlier, Domenico was having a similar end to his day:

> At the end of it we came to a hospice, which for its size seemed like a city in itself. I don't think there is another like it in Spain. They give much charity to pilgrims and treat them very well as regards eating and sleeping.

The next morning, it was still raining. It was raining all along the Calle de la Magdalena, where the pilgrims used to trek up the street past the old fish market – presumably the fish were always fresh, since they could swim up the street – past the erotic magazine shop and up to the cathedral, where the front door contains a carving of Eulalia, patron saint of Oviedo, tossing a pitcher of water over the city.

You wouldn't think she needed to bother, but when

Domenico passed through here in 1670, the area was in drought and he was knee-deep in locusts, which the locals ran around whacking with wooden bats.

Well, Eulalia, I've got news for you: you've succeeded too well. Get back here with a miraculous mop, you over-achiever you.

Pilgrims, of course, entered by the side door into a little chapel, which was blown up by disgruntled miners in 1934, and then into the cathedral itself, where today I could see the bishop of Oviedo showing a papal nuncio a statue of St Anthony with a rather fetching small pig.

Beyond was the mind-boggling baroque altarpiece detailing the life of Christ, and the even more mind-boggling baroque sidepieces. What on earth can baroque architects have been thinking of?

'Hey, Luigi. I've just had a great idea – let's make everything as vulgar and overblown as possible, and see if we can fool people into liking it!'

They were, I suppose, the Gianni Versaces of the seventeenth and eighteenth centuries.

But onwards, through the green and rain-washed mountains, their peaks wreathed in mist and their valleys filled with indus-trious farmers, burbling rivers, little fat trains pottering to and fro, and me in my bright yellow motorcar.

It was all impossibly idyllic, and even the rain was of an unusually soft quality: the sort that makes you feel gentle all the way through to your soul, like some sort of existential fabric conditioner, so that you feel you could sidle innocently up to a farmer's daughter, make harmlessly illicit suggestions in a spirit of universal love and harmony, and not get a boot in the bollocks.

Absurdly happy again – at this rate they'd be melting me down to turn me into Prozac – I had lunch of an apple and a pear by the harbour of the beautiful little fishing village of Cudillero – and set out on the last leg to Santiago de Compostela.

Remarkably, during the afternoon the rain finally stopped,

and it was in dazzling sunshine that I finally crested the mountain called Montjoie after the pilgrims' cry when they climbed it and finally saw their destination.

Here I was, 1,286 miles and 6 days from Calais (at an average speed of 39mph and average fuel consumption of 37.6mpg, since you ask). And here beside me, on this very spot three centuries earlier, Domenico had crested this rise and looked down on this same city.

Strangely, on his last stage he, too, had been drenched by the rain and then dried by the sun. And when he finally saw the twin towers of the cathedral from this mountain, he wrote:

> On seeing the city we fell to our knees and, with tears of great joy falling from our eyes, we began to sing the *Te Deum*. But we had sung no more than two or three verses when we found ourselves unable to utter the words because of the copious tears which streamed from our eyes, so intense were our feelings. Our hearts were full and our unceasing tears made us give up singing, until finally, having unburdened ourselves and spent our tears, we resumed singing the *Te Deum*. Singing as we walked, we carried on down ... and came to the gate of the town.

I went down myself, and took a bed for the night in one of the most beautiful hotels in the world, the Hostal de Los Reyes Catolicos, built in 1592 as a hospital for the pilgrims, many of whom had set out to Santiago for their last journey on earth after being told they were dying.

I had lunch in the former mortuary, now the hotel restaurant, and set out to buy a scallop shell, the traditional pilgrims' symbol. But everyone was at Mass, so I filled the car up at a Shell station instead and joined the queues waiting at the cathedral door under the joyous facade, in the centre of which a smiling St James welcomes his faithful as they kneel and press their fingers into the worn indentations below his feet and make their wish.

Communion was just ending, and eight men in burgundy

robes were preparing the *botafumeiro*, the world's largest incense burner, 58kg of brass and smoke which they hauled back and forth until it was sailing up to the rafters then whistling inches above the heads of the congregations.

It was such pure theatre that when it ended you had to put your hands in your pockets to stop yourself applauding and holding up a scorecard of perfect 6s.

Then I ticked off the pilgrim's final duties – tapping my head three times at the feet of Master Mateo, viewing the casket containing the bones of James the Apostle and hugging his statue, and then finally standing on the shell engraved in the centre of the square outside.

And that night, the ghost of Domenico Laffi and I went out and found a little tapas bar and got very drunk. The rain had started again, unfolding upon the bar roof with a sound as if someone was wrapping cellophane from a gift. Sometime after three we staggered back through the winding, hilly streets. The rain had stopped, and above our heads people were opening the arched windows of the eighteenth-century galleries on the top floor, flooding the damp air with laughter and light, music and the delicate spin of Rioja.

Above that, a full moon edged through straits edged with gargoyles, then sailed into the wide open sea of the cathedral square. I arrived just behind it, feeling as if my soul had just been scrubbed clean. For a fake pilgrim, it was an appropriately secular, but surprisingly real epiphany.

I turned to speak to Domenico, but he had gone, like the ghost of imagined memory.

1999

Acknowledgements

Thanks to Geoff Martin, the former editor of the *News Letter*, and to Nigel Wareing, his successor, for their permission to reprint here several of the stories that originally appeared in the *News Letter*.

Thanks also to Michael Kerr and Richard Madden of the *Daily Telegraph*, and to the late Jeremy Atiyah of the *Independent on Sunday*, who also commissioned several of the pieces.